Personality:
Theories and Processes

HARPERCOLLINS COLLEGE OUTLINE

Personality: Theories and Processes

Alan O. Ross, Ph.D.
State University of New York at Stony Brook

HarperPerennial
A Division of HarperCollinsPublishers

To Ilse

An American BookWorks Corporation Production

Project Manager: Judith A. V. Harlan
Editor: Thomas H. Quinn

Library of Congress Catalog Card Number: 91-58274
ISBN: 0-06-467115-1

92 93 94 95 96 ABW/RRD 10 9 8 7 6 5 4 3 2 1

Contents

Preface

The major personality textbooks contain between 500 and 600 pages. This outline, though longer than that word suggests, takes up fewer pages. What was left out? I wanted to make this book more than a cryptic list of disconnected statements so that it would be useful not only for students seeking a condensed version of their textbook, but also for a person interested in an overview of personality psychology; someone who can do without the many details contained in standard textbooks. To accomplish this I condensed the details of specific studies and omitted charts and graphs, tables and figures, case histories and biographies, photographs and cartoons, as well as the material in "boxes" that accounts for many of the pages in the textbooks currently in use.

To decide what to include in this outline I examined the contents of the ten most frequently used textbooks on personality and listed the topics they cover. I found that many of the topics on my list were presented in all of these texts while others appeared in only one or two of them. After eliminating some esoteric or idiosyncratic subjects and combining others that dealt with related material, I was able to reduce the list to fifteen topics. All of these are covered in the ten chapters that comprise this work.

In preparing this book I was primarily guided by the organization and content of three excellent texts: Feshback and Weiner (1991), Liebert and Spiegler (1987), and Phares (1991). The notes I had used in preparing my own personality text (Ross, 1987) were of great help.

Each of the chapters in this book ends with a list of *Selected Readings*. These are included for the benefit of those who wish to delve further into the material that precedes this list. The readings expand on some of the topics covered and are not essential to their understanding.

The section headed *References* presents the bibliographic details of books and articles that were identified in the chapters by the author's name and the year in which the publication appeared, as in the above "Phares (1991)." Dates, such as "(1842–1911)," are shown after the names of historical figures to indicate when they were born and when they died.

The Glossary serves two purposes. One is that of defining terms with which the reader might not be familiar. The other is that of a self-test. By covering the right column, which gives the definitions, leaving only the terms in the left column exposed, one can test whether one knows the meanings of these terms. Inasmuch as all of these terms do appear in the book, this tests one's knowledge of the material it covers.

I should like to acknowledge the assistance of Judy Harlan and Tom Quinn, whose comments on my manuscript I greatly appreciated. As she has for many decades, Ilse Wallis Ross, my spouse, was unstinting in providing me with moral support. The concluding paragraph of chapter 10 tells all about that.

Alan O. Ross

How to Study

FROM TEXTBOOKS

Before you begin to use a textbook, become familiar with its organization. Read the preface, look at the table of contents, and at the way the chapters are laid out. In most textbooks each chapter opens with an introduction and ends with a summary. Many carry a glossary at the end, and some contain suggested readings and a set of self-test questions. Once you know the special features of your textbook, resolve to make use of them.

Before you start reading an assigned chapter, read the introduction to that chapter and ask yourself how the topics relate to you and your experiences. There is nothing in the psychology of personality that does not have something to do with *you*. Next, skim through the chapter, look at each heading, and read a bit here and there without trying to understand or to learn it. That comes later. Now read the summary. Little of it will make sense to you at this point, but it will give you an idea of the important parts of the chapter. Now you are ready to study it.

Take your time! Studying from a textbook is not like reading a newspaper or a novel. Read slowly and think about what you are reading. Keep asking yourself, "What does that mean?" "Could I explain this point to somebody else?" Before each new major heading put the book aside and try to summarize the main points you have read by writing them down *in your own words*. If you can't do that, you have not understood the material. Go back and read the section again until you do understand it. Remember, the purpose of studying material such as this is understanding, not memorizing.

When you come to the next major heading in the chapter, see whether you can figure out what topics are likely to be covered under it. Can you see the logical relationship between the preceding material and what is to follow? When you are finished with a chapter, read the summary once more. Now it should make sense to you. If any part of it is not clear to you, return to that point in the chapter and go over it again.

Many students believe that underlining or highlighting important points helps them to study. That is fine, provided you highlight only the important points. A way to check that is to compare what you highlighted with the material in the chapter summary. There should be nothing in the summary that you did not highlight, although you will have highlighted material that is not in the summary. Highlight sparingly. Too much highlighting can interfere with learning.

When you feel that you have mastered a chapter, close the book and write an outline of the material in that chapter or make a list of the important points. Some people find it helpful to dictate this material into a tape recorder and to listen to it then and to retain it for later review.

It is a good idea to designate for your studying a particular time of day and a specific place and to use these consistently. Set yourself a reasonable goal for a session of studying and promise to reward yourself with something you really like doing once you can honestly say that you have met that goal.

Once you have finished studying a chapter, put it aside and turn to homework from other courses. Read the chapter at least once more during the week in which it was assigned. Distributing your studies in this fashion is much better than massing it all in one marathon sitting. The same is true when studying for a test. The only thing an "all-nighter" will do for you is make you tired.

FROM LECTURES

Attend lectures regularly because later lectures will refer to earlier ones and the instructor assumes that you were present. If possible, try to sit in the same seat or in the same general area in the classroom. Be prepared for the lecture by having read at least once the material assigned for that week. Lectures rarely duplicate the reading, but they often refer to what you are expected to have read.

Taking useful notes is a skill. Here are some hints. The lecturer follows an outline and, just as in a textbook, there are headings and subheadings. Although these are not usually announced, they soon become apparent from what is said. Listen before you write! Make notes only after you have comprehended a point or an idea. If you start taking notes before you have understood what is being said, you will never understand it and your notes will make little sense.

Make notes sparingly! You cannot possibly write down everything that is said, and if you tried you could not understand what you heard. Write only enough to jog your memory later or to record specific facts or numbers that you might otherwise not remember. Notes are most useful if they are used as a skeleton that is to be fleshed out later when you can sit down by yourself or in a study group to reconstruct the lecture. At that time you should be able to organize the notes with headings and subheadings, sentences and paragraphs. By organizing your notes in that fashion you are reviewing the material from the lecture. At the same time, you are making your notes into a useful resource for the time when you have to study for an exam.

Part I:
The Study of Personality

1

Personality: An Overview

Personality is an abstraction and different scholars have offered somewhat different definitions of it, but most seem to agree that personality is the combination of a person's actions, thoughts, emotions, and motivations. Individual personalities are unique, but the personalities of different individuals also share certain aspects. The study of personality can therefore focus on how people differ or on what they have in common.

A person's personality remains relatively constant, but both maturation and experience can cause it to change. An important question has to do with the role heredity and environment play in the development of personality. This question is difficult to investigate because neither of these variables can be manipulated for the purpose of an experiment. Because identical twins have the same heredity, they are often used in studies of this question.

There are a number of issues that concern students of personality. These concern how abstract concepts should be defined, how people are to be classified in terms of their personalities, how behavior is determined, and whether our choice among different options is free or constrained.

THE DEFINITION OF PERSONALITY

Personality is an abstract concept. Scientists refer to such a concept as a *construct*. A construct is not a concrete object, such as a table, that one can point to when asked to define the word *table*. The fact that personality is a construct makes definition difficult.

Different psychologists have defined personality in different ways. Thus Gordon W. Allport (1937), whom many view as the founder of modern personality studies, called personality "the dynamic organization within the individual of those psychophysical systems that determine his or her characteristic behavior and thought." J. P. Guilford (1959), another well-known student of personality, defined it as "a person's unique pattern of traits" (p. 5), while Raymond Cattell (1950) called it "that which permits a prediction of what a person will do in a given situation" (p. 2). Given this state of affairs it is no wonder that Hall and Lindsey (1978) in their comprehensive textbook on personality theories were led to conclude that there is no substantive definition of personality that can be applied with any generality.

All of us use the word *personality* in our everyday language. We say things like "I don't like Mike's personality" and take it for granted that the person to whom we are talking knows what we mean. What do we mean? What we have in mind in talking about Mike's personality is probably a mixture of things. Among these may be his arrogance, his prejudices, his frequent mood swings, and his materialistic values. What we mean by personality thus seems to be the combination of a person's actions, thoughts, emotions, and motivations as these are revealed in his or her interactions with us and other people. That is probably also what writers like Allport, Guilford, and Cattell meant when they defined personality, and that is how we will be using the word from now on.

THE NATURE OF PERSONALITY

There are several seemingly contradictory features in our conceptualization of personality. One of these is that no two people are thought to have exactly the same personality—that individuals are unique—but at the same time people are seen as having certain aspects of personality in common. Another such apparent contradiction is that an individual's personality is said to be both stable and malleable. Yet a third such seeming incongruity may be seen in the formulation that personality is formed by both hereditary and environmental influences. As we discuss each of these apparent contradictions in turn we shall discover that it is entirely feasible for an individual's personality to have both unique and shared features, that these can be both stable over time and yet subject to change, and that both heredity and environment played a role in forming that personality.

Uniqueness and Commonalities

UNIQUENESS

Conceiving personality as the combination of a person's actions, thoughts, emotions, and motivations has several implications. One of these is that each of these components of personality may be different for different people. Another is that for different individuals these components may be combined in different ways so that they form different patterns. Indeed, people differ in how they behave, in how and what they think, in how they feel and react, and in what they need and want. Moreover, some people's behavior is predominantly controlled by their thoughts, while others act primarily on the basis of their emotions. Some feel very strongly about their need for fine clothing, while others give very little thought to what they wear. All of these differences result in what is an important principle in the study of personality, *the principle of individuality.*

COMMONALITIES

What are some of the ways in which humans are alike in terms of their personalities? There is, of course, the fact that each of us has a personality; that each of us acts, thinks, feels, and has needs which, together, constitute our personality. Moreover, all of us have had a great many experiences in the past that influence the way we now act, think, feel, and are motivated.

In addition, it turns out that the way we act, think, feel, and are motivated can be classified. Thus, some of our actions can be classified as sociable, or aggressive, or helpful. Thoughts can be classified as creative, conventional, or prejudiced. Feelings may be cheerful, depressed, or bored and we can be motivated by needs for approval, power, or achievement.

Two Kinds of Research. The fact that no two people have exactly the same personality, that every individual is unique, represents a challenge for those who seek to engage in the scientific study of personality. Some psychologists—they often call themselves *personologists*—maintain that the only way to do research on personality is by conducting intensive studies of single individuals. This is known as the *case study* or *idiographic* method of research. It usually involves observing and testing the same person in different situations or over a lengthy period of time to see how he or she reacts, changes, or remains the same.

There are other psychologists who maintain that while there are individual differences there are enough personality aspects that humans have in common so that it is possible to conduct meaningful research on groups of people. That is called the *nomothetic* approach. Studies based on this approach focus on such questions as how feelings (emotions) influence action (behavior) or how needs (motivation) influence thinking (cognition). There are other studies that investigate how sociability develops, what elicits aggressive behavior, or under what circumstances people will help a stranger in distress. Research is also conducted on the role of prejudice in meeting other people and on the effect of alcohol on the need for power.

Stability and Malleability

STABILITY

It would make little sense to speak of personality if a person's behavior, cognitions, emotions, and motivations were not the same or very similar over a relatively long period of time and from place to place. Indeed, as everyone can readily observe, people generally do remain the same from one time to the next. The boy we knew as Jolly John in elementary school is still "his cheerful self" at the twentieth class reunion. The girl who always worried about her grades in high school still agonizes over them in college.

The stability of personality characteristics that can be observed over time can also be seen across situations. The fellow student who is competitive in class also exhibits competitiveness on the tennis court. The woman who is always ready to help her neighbors is also likely to be among the volunteers who go from door to door collecting money for a charity.

MALLEABILITY

But people do change, both over time and across situations. Changes over time we tend to attribute to maturation; changes across situations we are likely to call adaptability. As Jolly John gets older he is likely to express his cheerfulness in somewhat more sedate fashion; instead of playing practical jokes he may have graduated to verbal humor. It is of course also possible that a series of tragic experiences has subdued this ebullient fellow.

Changes across situations attest to the fact that most people's personalities are flexible enough to respond to the different demands of different situations. Happy Harry, who always smiles, would be deemed to have something wrong with him if he also smiled at his mother's funeral, and Jumpy Janet, who is constantly in motion, might be expected to sit still in the dentist's chair. Members of our society have certain expectations about what is appropriate behavior in a given situation. One is quiet during a lecture, but cheers loudly at a ball game; one smiles at a wedding, but is solemn at a funeral; one tries to defeat one's opponent on the tennis court, but assists that same person in changing a tire. Behavior that is inappropriate for any of these situations is deemed impolite if not abnormal.

Heredity and Environment

We have said that humans share many characteristics, yet individuals are unique. Moreover, individuals remain the same over long periods of time, yet change from situation to situation. We turn now to a third pair of concepts—heredity and environment—that also appear contradictory, but when one asks which of them applies to personality the answer again is "both." There is no aspect of personality that is solely due to the influences of either our genes or our environment. An *interaction* of genetic and environmental influences underlies all of our actions, thoughts, feelings, and needs.

What do we mean by "interaction"? As used here, interaction is what we have in mind when we explain our discomfort on a hot summer day by saying, "It's not the heat, it's the humidity." In saying that we recognize that neither high temperature alone nor a lot of moisture alone would make us feel so miserable, but that the problem stems from the combination, the interaction of the two.

HEREDITY

Research on genetic (hereditary) influences on personality is difficult. There are several reasons for this. One we have already discussed. It is that there is no general agreement on how personality should be defined. As a result there is no agreement on how personality should be measured, and research requires objective methods of measurement. Another source of difficulty is that it is ethically impossible to conduct experiments that call for the manipulation of genetic variables. To study the genetics of nonhuman animals one can use artificial insemination or selective breeding. Not so with humans. Here an investigator of genetics must seek out the so-called experiment of nature that occurred in the case of twins.

Twin Studies. There are two kinds of twins. Monozygotic (identical) twins develop from the same egg that was fertilized by one sperm. Their genetic makeup is therefore identical and they are always of the same sex. Dizygotic (nonidentical) twins develop from two eggs that were separately fertilized by two sperm. Such twins are genetically no more alike than two ordinary siblings who were born a year or more apart. Dizygotic twins may both be girls or they may both be boys or one may be a girl and the other a boy. Because of this it is inexact to refer to them as fraternal twins because "fraternal" refers to brothers.

In traditional twin research, groups of monozygotic twins are compared with groups of same-sex dizygotic twins on whatever characteristic is of interest to the investigator. If the monozygotic twin pairs are more similar to each other than are the dizygotic twin pairs, one can conclude that genetic factors played an important role in the development of that characteristic. That conclusion, however, is valid only if the twins in each pair were exposed to exactly the same environmental influences, and that is rarely, if ever, the case. Because environmental influences are not and cannot be controlled in this type of twin study, investigators in the genetics of human behavior (*behavior genetics*) have turned to a research method—the co-twin method—in which the twins' environment is presumably controlled.

The Co-Twin Method. For a variety of reasons, many twins, both monozygotic and dizygotic, are separated and reared apart. For monozygotic twins that means that their heredity is identical but their environments are different. When the personalities of these twins are later compared, any differences can be ascribed to the environment and any similarities to heredity. As it turns out, such twins' personalities are often strikingly similar.

The co-twin method, however, is also not free of problems. One of these is that it is sometimes difficult to determine whether twins are actually monozygotic. Another problem stems from the fact that there may be a bias in which twins are raised separately; a poor, unmarried mother, for example, is less likely to keep both of her twins than is a married woman who lives under more comfortable circumstances. Further problems have to do with differences in the ages at which twins are separated; some are separated at birth, others after they have lived together for some time. Moreover, there is the issue of with whom and where the twins were placed upon separation. Some may have been reared on different continents, others by sisters who lived next door to each other.

All of these methodological problems make research on human behavior genetics a difficult and challenging area. They also provide the basis for arguments by those who, for ideological or political reasons, do not wish to give credence to the possibility that aspects of human behavior, capacity, aptitude, and propensity are influenced by genetic factors. Nevertheless, the accumulated research supports the hypothesis that hereditary factors contribute to activity level, altruism, aggressiveness, anxiety, alcoholism, criminality, extraversion, intelligence-test scores, and sociability, as well as to such psychiatric conditions as affective disorders, manic-depressive psychosis, and schizophrenia.

As pointed out earlier, no aspect of personality is due solely to the influence of inherited genes. To this must be added that no single gene is ever the sole basis of the complex patterns we subsume under the term *personality*. These patterns are so-called *polygenic* characteristics—characteristics that depend on the contributions of many different genes.

ENVIRONMENT

Just as we attributed the effect of heredity on personality to the workings of genes, we can ascribe the influence of the environment to the result of learning. One can speak of an environmental influence only when it can be demonstrated that a person's actions, thoughts, feelings, or needs have changed after exposure to an identifiable condition. Such changes we call learning. The environmental conditions under which learning takes place can be divided into those in the physical world and those in the social world.

The Physical World. The physical world consists of *the natural environment* which includes climate, geography, food sources, and availability of water. Each of these influences the personalities of the people who are exposed to it. People who live in hot climates tend to move more slowly and be more impulsive than people in moderate and cold climates. In climates with seasonal changes in temperature one finds more violent crimes during the heat of summer than in winter. People who live in rugged mountains tend to be less friendly to strangers than people who live on the plains. Similarly, those who obtain their food by hunting large animals have different attitudes toward risk-taking than those whose livelihood is based on agriculture. A perennial scarcity of water teaches people to be frugal, whereas a limitless supply invites extravagance. In each of these examples we are referring to groups of people who, sharing a common natural environment, tend to develop similar personality patterns. In evolutionary terms, the natural environment selects personality patterns that are appropriate for the prevailing conditions.

In addition to the natural environment our physical world also contains *the constructed environment*, which, instead of being formed by the forces of nature, is the work of humans. The constructed environment also affects aspects of personality. It has been demonstrated that high population density elicits aggressive behavior, that seating arrangements and size of work space affect the formation of friendships, and that the number of people who are employed in a particular setting is related to the amount of work each will perform.

The Social World. A great deal of the learning that influences personality takes place not in the concrete physical space of the natural and constructed environments, but in the abstract environment that is created by the way other people behave. We speak here of culture and of social class, of child-rearing patterns, family structure, educational practices, and employment patterns. Each of these has been shown to affect the personalities of the people who experience their impact.

The attitude members of a given culture have toward old age will affect the self-esteem of the elderly. Social class membership influences manner of speech, style of dress, choice of recreational activities, attitudes toward property, and goals in life. What people experienced as children—parental disciplinary practices, feeding patterns, show of emotions, demands, and expectations—is often reflected in their adult personality. Related to this is the family structure. The number of siblings, the presence or absence of an extended family, the availability of mother and father have all been shown to play a role in children's personality development. Outside of the family personality is influenced by such aspects of the social world as the school one attends and for how long, the job one holds and where, and whether one is regularly employed or unemployed.

INDIVIDUAL DIFFERENCES

At this point it is well to recall that even identical conditions in the physical or social environment will have different effects on different people. This, of course, is—in part—the result of the interaction of hereditary and environmental influences. Take, for example, the effect of hot weather on people who are living in very crowded conditions. It is known that this raises the rate of violent crimes, but not everyone becomes violent under these circumstances. Why? A part of the answer is that some people are by nature—that is, genetically—more sensitive to heat than others, so that a hot environment will affect them more readily than those who are more heat tolerant. For them the interaction of heredity and environment results in a violent outburst. But that is only a part of the story, for that person was not born yesterday. He or she will have had many years of exposure to all sorts of environmental influences which may have affected the genetically based tendency to respond violently to high temperatures. The individual differences in people's reactions to heat under crowded conditions are thus a result of a highly complex interaction of heredity and environment. By the time an individual's violent act takes place, it is impossible to establish the relative contribution of each of these factors, but if one wanted to find a way to reduce such violence, the crowded condition and not the heredity is the place to look.

Heritability

To what extent a particular human characteristic is based on genetic factors, its *heritability*, is usually investigated by nomothetic twin studies or similar comparisons of differently related people, such as siblings and half siblings or adopted children and their biological and adoptive parents. Several statistical techniques are available for estimating the relative contribution made to the characteristic by genetic and environmental factors. Because the resulting quantitative *heritability ratios* are easily misunderstood and misinterpreted, several points bear mention.

GENOTYPE AND PHENOTYPE

The genetic makeup of an individual is known as the *genotype*. This is the actual combination of genes he or she has inherited. The location of the genes that carry certain rare diseases has now been established, but we are probably a long way from identifying the genes that contribute to such complex aspects of personality as sociability or aggressiveness. At this point we are limited to observing and measuring the *phenotype*, the behavior of the individual who displays the characteristic we wish to study. That behavior, however, will always be a combination of the person's genotype and the environmental influences to which she or he has been exposed. The accuracy of the heritability ratio therefore depends on the precision and relevance of the test used to measure an ill-defined characteristic, such as sociability, on how the participants for the study were chosen, whom they represented, how well they cooperated, and many similar factors.

THE HERITABILITY ESTIMATE IS A GROUP STATISTIC

Although the measure used to quantify a personality characteristic is typically applied to one individual at a time, the statistic used to evaluate the results always calls for data based on a group of people. This is the case because to calculate the heritability ratio (usually symbolized by H) one must know the variability among the individuals in the group tested. If behavior geneticists who have studied sociability were to report an H of .60 it would only mean that in the population they studied 60 percent of the variability among individuals can be attributed to genetic factors. It does not mean that 60 percent of the sociability of a specific individual is due to genetic factors!

GENES WORK INDIRECTLY

When one says that such personality characteristics as sociability are based, in part, on genetic factors it does not mean that there is a gene or even a combination of genes that are directly responsible for producing that characteristic. Genes are stretches of DNA that are encoded to control the assembly and regulation of proteins, the building blocks of the brain and all other parts of the body. These proteins, however, must interact with other proteins, with the nervous system, and with such environmental factors as nutrition, before they can ultimately, indirectly, and through complex paths influence a person's behavior in a certain direction.

THE IMPORTANCE OF ENVIRONMENT

If one part of a personality characteristic is based on genetic factors, it follows that the other part must be based on contributions of the environment. As far as human behavior is concerned, genes can do nothing alone; their manifestation always depends on interaction with the environment. Because the genes with which one is born are fixed and immutable, people are sometimes troubled by discoveries of hereditary factors in human behavior because they mistakenly believe this to mean that the behavior cannot be changed. Although it is true that our genotype is fixed, our phenotype is malleable because the environment with which the genes interact can be changed in innumerable ways. Thus, if we wish to change such human behavior as violence, we must focus our efforts on the environment. Moreover, because we cannot establish the exact nature of people's genotype we ought never assume that their heredity sets limits to what they could accomplish under improved environmental conditions.

ISSUES IN THE STUDY OF PERSONALITY

Constructs

Personality, as we said earlier, is a construct. To be more exact, it is a *composite construct* because it consists of the other constructs which we identified as actions, cognitions, emotions, and motivations. Psychologists employ constructs such as these to help them describe, investigate, and eventually understand the phenomena they wish to study.

Although we don't recognize them as such, we all use constructs in our everyday language. Take the word *room*, for example. You know what a room is, but try telling it to a foreigner who does not speak English. To what would you point to explain what you mean by *room?* Is a kitchen a room? Or why is a garage not a room? What about a walk-in closet? When you come right down to it, the word *room* is as much an abstraction as the words *personality* and *emotion.* Like them, *room* has to be defined if the word is to be used to communicate clearly and unambiguously. If you'd try to define *room* you would quickly discover that you have to make some arbitrary decision. A room is an enclosed space. Does it have to be inside a house to be a room? Must it have a window? Does it need four walls that go to the ceiling, or can partitions make a room? All of these decisions are your own, and others who answered these questions differently would disagree with your definition.

OPERATIONAL DEFINITIONS

The arbitrariness that is required to define constructs could pose considerable difficulty for scientists because if everyone employed his or her own definition, communication would be impossible. To get around this problem, scientists typically use *operational definitions*; that is, they define their constructs by the operation they use—by what they do—to measure them. Time could be defined by the chronograph, temperature by the thermometer, and electric current by the voltmeter.

In psychology intelligence tests are used to measure intelligence and these can serve as an operational definition of intelligence. But unlike voltmeters, thermometers, and chronographs that use universally agreed-upon units and norms, there are several different intelligence tests and different definitions of intelligence. When it comes to personality the situation is even more perplexing. There are various tests of personality, each based on a different theory of personality. Moreover, there are many ways of measuring such personality constructs as attitude, aggression, altruism, anxiety, or ambition. Among the consequences of this situation is not only that there is no agreement on how to define these constructs, but also that the results of research studies that use these different measures often lead to different conclusions.

This state of affairs would be discouraging if one failed to realize that the scientific study of personality began only around 1940. We can therefore expect that many of today's ambiguities and disagreements will be reduced and resolved as the research efforts in this challenging field continue.

Classification

One of the tasks that must be accomplished early in the development of any science is the classification of its subject matter. The study of personality is no exception. The readily made observation that there are individual differences in personality quickly leads to the question of how many different kinds of personality there are and to a desire to label them.

CHARACTER

One of the first to attempt a classification was the Greek philosopher Theophrastus (372–287 B.C.), who wrote a book entitled *Characters*. This contained descriptions of various "characters" or personalities, mostly of the unpleasant sort, like the flatterer, the penurious, the dissembler, the mean, the tactless, the garrulous, and the avaricious. These character sketches were grossly exaggerated descriptions of extreme cases which left no room for the possibility that people might show milder expressions of these characteristics or manifest combinations of them.

TEMPERAMENT

The Greek physician Galen (A.D. 131–201) elaborated on a system of classification that had originally been proposed by Hippocrates (460?–377? B.C.), the "father of medicine." According to Hippocrates the body contains four basic fluids or humors: yellow bile, black bile, phlegm, and blood. An excess of any of these could affect people's temperament: yellow bile making them choleric (irritable), black bile melancholic (depressed), phlegm phlegmatic (listless), and blood sanguine (confident). Depending on the degree to which a bodily fluid was in excess, a person could show more or less of the temperament associated with that fluid.

A more recent approach to classification that ties temperament to bodily characteristics is the system of *somatotypes* developed by William Sheldon (Sheldon and Stevens, 1942). In this system a person's body build is classified ("somatotyped") on the basis of the relative contribution of three components: *endomorphy, mesomorphy*, and *ectomorphy*. Endomorphy stands for a highly developed visceral structure, resulting in a soft, round appearance. Mesomorphy is based on a predominance of the musculature so that mesomorphs have a solid, rectangular body giving them an "athletic" look. In ectomorphy the body is delicate and fragile, often tall and thin.

To establish a person's somatotype the contribution of each of the three components is rated on a scale from 1 (minimum) to 7 (maximum). The somatotype can thus be expressed in a code of three numerals. For example,

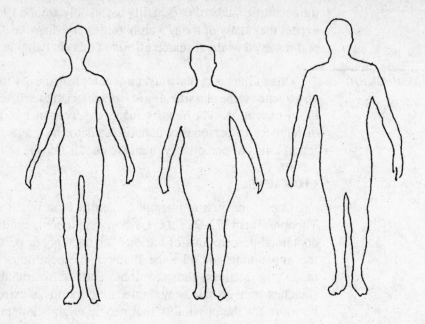

Fig. 1.1 Sheldon's Somatotypes

From left to right: Ectomorphy, Endomorphy, and Mesomorphy

7–1–1 would describe a person who is extremely high in endomorphy and extremely low in mesomorphy and ectomorphy. It is noteworthy that Sheldon's system is not limited to the three basic categories, but that, by considering their interactions, it provides for a wide variety of body types.

Of interest to the student of personality is that Sheldon went beyond developing this highly reliable system of classifying body types. He also proposed that each body type is associated with a specific temperament for which he coined the terms *viscerotonia, somatotonia,* and *cerebrotonia.* Viscerotonia, which was said to be associated with endomorphy, is characterized by a general love of comfort, sociability, food, and affection. Somatotonia, the temperament of the mesomorph, is an active, assertive, vigorous, adventurous, and risk-taking approach to life. Cerebrotonia, which is associated with ectomorphy, stands for withdrawn, fearful, restrained, and self-conscious characteristics.

Sheldon developed a rating scale, analogous to the one used for somatotyping, with which a people's temperament can be assessed and classified on the basis of their social behavior. Unfortunately it is difficult if not impossible to verify Sheldon's claim that body types are associated with specific temperaments. To do so, those rating the body type would have to have no knowledge of the temperament, and those rating the temperament no knowledge of the body type. Although it is possible to do somatotyping from photographs, thus keeping the judges ignorant of the subjects' social behavior, one cannot judge people's social behavior without interacting with them, thus seeing what they look like. Our cultural stereotypes of the jolly fat man, the muscular athlete, and the lean philosopher might easily bias the ratings of temperament.

One further point deserves mention. Sheldon asserted that the association between body type and temperament that he believed to have found demonstrates that both have a biological base which originated during the earliest stages of the individual's embryonic development. That conclusion does not necessarily follow. Even if the association could be definitively established, it would be equally feasible that a person acquires certain forms of social behavior that suit his or her biologically determined body type. Aggressive, risk-taking behavior, for example, is more likely to lead to success for a child with a strong, muscular body than for one who is frail and thin. The frail and thin one, on the other hand, might early recognize that solitary pursuits are more rewarding than attempts to compete with athletic classmates. Meanwhile, the soft and round child who is likely to be left out of the peers' strenuous games may discover that attention and approval are forthcoming when one plays the class clown.

TYPES

The approaches to the classifications mentioned thus far began with observations of individual differences in body build and attempts to relate these to individual differences in personality. Another approach is to observe the personalities of different individuals and to attempt to classify these according to their *type* without reference to physical characteristics. Both C. G. Jung (1923) and H. J. Eysenck (1953) employed that approach.

Jung spoke of two general attitudes or orientations that people assume: *introversion* and *extraversion*.* Those with an introverted orientation tend to be withdrawn and reserved, interested more in ideas than in interaction with others. An extraverted orientation, on the other hand, manifests itself in outgoing, sociable behavior, the person's interest being more in the outer world than in his or her own ideas. We shall have more to say about introversion and extraversion when we discuss Jung's contributions to personality theory.

Eysenck, whose work will also be discussed in a later chapter, views introversion and extraversion not as an either/or dichotomy, as did Jung, but as a *dimension of personality*. Extraversion is one pole of that dimension and introversion lies at the opposite pole. A specific individual's personality

---

* Jung's spelling of the term *extraversion* is followed by most writers in the field of personality.

type may thus be located at either pole or at any point between them. This allows for a wide range of individual differences.

TRAITS

In discussing the classification of personality, whether by character, temperament, or type, we invariably define these categories by describing how people behave. These descriptions use such adjectives as avaricious, irritable, adventurous, sociable, or withdrawn. The categories are collections or clusters of such adjectives, adjectives that one refers to as *traits*. Traits are characteristic ways in which a person behaves. There are many different ways in which people can behave and each person behaves in many different ways. If one wanted to categorize people by their traits one would have to list all of the traits a person exhibits. That would result in a long list and many of the adjectives on it would probably be similar, such as friendly, outgoing, active, optimistic, impulsive, talkative, and lively. Why not summarize them by simply saying, "This person is an extravert"? That, in fact, is what the various systems of classification we discussed have done—offer categories that group and summarize similar traits.

Determinants of Behavior

TRAITS OR SITUATIONS?

One of the issues in the study of personality has to do with whether the way a person behaves is due to his or her particular combination of traits or to the situation in which he or she happens to be at the moment. Which is more important, traits or situations; what is inside the person or what is on the outside?

We met similar questions before. Which determines personality— heredity or environment? What characterizes human personality—stability or malleability? There the answer turned out to be "both," and that is also the answer to the trait-or-situation question. Traits and situations interact to produce a person's behavior. In highly structured situations where a specific kind of behavior is prescribed—as at a service in a house of worship, for example—most people will behave the same way, regardless of their individual traits. In less structured situations, such as a picnic at the beach, people's behavior will differ, depending largely on the type of people they are—that is, on their traits.

Studies of the relative contribution to behavior by traits and situations are complicated by the fact that whereas a person's traits can be identified by his or her answers to a standardized personality test, we lack standardized methods for describing situations. What, exactly, is the situation referred to above as "a picnic at the beach"? Moreover, the nature of a situation, as far as its impact on a person's behavior is concerned, depends on how that person perceives that situation. Different people bring different experiences, expectations, and attitudes into a situation so that one and the same situation will represent different things to different people. An experimenter might set up a laboratory task that she sees as a test of creativity. The first subject may view this situation as an opportunity to display his intelligence, whereas the second perceives it as a trap to find out how gullible he is. If the two respond to the task in different ways is this due to the situation, to their traits, to both, or to neither?

CHOICE OR DETERMINISM?

The question whether behavior is controlled by internal (trait) or external (situation) factors is closely related to another issue that often arises in discussions of human personality. It is whether our actions are freely chosen or determined for us by factors over which we have no control. Almost all people, when faced with this question, intuitively settle for free choice. We know that we chose college A over college B. But the question is whether that choice was free in the sense that we could just as easily have chosen college B over college A.

This issue is sometimes referred to as the question of free will, but free will is a theological problem that has to do with evil, sin, and personal responsibility. It need not concern us here, nor should we confuse determinism with predestination, which is the notion that everything that happens was decided at our birth or long before. What we are dealing with here is the apparent incompatibility of our sense that we have freedom of choice and the basic assumption of contemporary Western science that there is a lawful relationship between cause and effect; that causes determine effects. As far as human behavior is concerned, it follows from this assumption that if all the influences that act on a person at any given moment were known it would be possible to predict accurately how that person would act. This is what is meant by determinism and it cannot be reconciled with freedom of choice because freedom of choice would make such prediction impossible.

It is of course highly unlikely and probably impossible for anyone ever to know all the influences that act on a person at any given moment. That limits predictions about human behavior to statements of probabilities (not unlike weather forecasts), but it does not open the door for the notion of free choice. We are the product of the interaction of our heredity and our environment, neither of which we chose. The decisions we make today are determined by events that happened in the past, plus the present situation which we perceive in terms of our past experiences. It is only when one construes human behavior in this fashion that human behavior can be studied with the methods of science.

Where does this leave my strong sense that I have freedom of choice? The answer lies in looking at what I mean by "I." If "I" am the sum of my heredity and my past experiences, then it is indeed I who is making a choice at this moment, and not some power beyond my control.

*P*ersonality is an abstract concept that encompasses a person's actions, cognitions, emotions, and motivations. There are both individual differences and commonalities in people's personality which can thus be studied by either the idiographic or nomothetic approach.

Personality is both stable and malleable and it results from an interaction of genetic and environmental factors. The relative contribution of each of these has been investigated in twin studies, but these are not without their methodological difficulties.

A number of issues arise in the study of personality. One of these is how to define the abstract concepts with which personality research must deal. Operational definitions are helpful, but they do not assure universal agreement among investigators. Over the years many scholars have dealt with the question how to classify different kinds of personalities. Among the concepts used for this purpose have been character, temperament, types, and traits.

The answer to the question whether traits or situations are dominant in determining behavior is that they interact. Neither can function alone. Related to this question is the puzzle whether all of our actions are determined or whether we can freely choose among alternatives. The answer to this may well lie in what we mean by "we."

Selected Readings

Mayr, E. 1982. *The Growth of Biological Thought: Diversity, Evolution, and Inheritance.* Cambridge, MA: Harvard University Press.

Pervin, L. A. 1984. *Current Controversies and Issues in Personality.* New York: Wiley.

Plomin, R., J. C. DeFries, and G. E. McClearn. 1990. *Behavioral Genetics: A Primer.* 2nd ed. New York: Freeman.

Rubinstein, J., and B. Slife. 1988. *Taking Sides: Clashing Views on Controversial Psychological Issues.* 5th ed. Guilford, CT: Dushkin.

2

Personality: Theory, Research, and Assessment

All science begins with observations. Observations usually lead to a theory. A theory serves two functions. It organizes what has been observed and guides investigators to further observations. Two kinds of thought processes connect theory and observations: inductive processes and deductive processes. Theory construction can be approached in several ways. Among these are the use of models, the inductive, and the functional approach. Almost all of us have our own implicit theory of personality, but only through controlled research can we establish with confidence how various aspects of personality are related.

There are many methods for conducting research, and investigators select the method most appropriate for the topic they wish to study. Because ethical considerations restrict the kinds of experiments that may be conducted with humans, some of the methods are limited in what they can discover about cause and effect.

Many techniques are available for the assessment of personality, but to be useful all must demonstrate both reliability and validity. Some assessment techniques are objective. Their results are expressed in scores that are interpreted by referring to norms. Other techniques are projective. Their interpretation depends a lot on the judgment of the examiner.

Whether psychologists conduct research or carry out assessments, the fact that they are dealing with human beings demands that they adhere to ethical principles that govern these activities.

THE NATURE OF THEORIES

Two Functions

A scientific theory has two functions, an *ordering function* and a *guiding function*. In its ordering function, the theory organizes, relates, and integrates discrete phenomena that have been observed. In its guiding function, the theory predicts new relationships among phenomena and suggests new observations that should be made to confirm them. Observed phenomena are often called *data* (this is a plural noun, the singular is *datum*), and the predictions are usually phrased as *hypotheses* (singular: *hypothesis*).

OBSERVATIONS

The observation of phenomena may take several forms. They may be *casual observations*, as those made when one unexpectedly comes upon an intriguing phenomenon, or *controlled observations*, where one sets out to look for or create the phenomenon or to see its relationship to other phenomena. An experiment is a form of controlled observation where the investigator systematically varies a condition to see what effect this has on the phenomenon of interest. We shall have more to say about these observations later in this chapter.

Two Processes

In the pursuit of science, observations sometimes precede the formation of a theory. A scientist or group of scientists may have gathered many specific data over a number of years before someone develops a general set of assumptions about their relationship—a theory. This is known as the *inductive process* of theory development. There are also occasions when a theory precedes the gathering of observations, often because the technique for making the suggested observations is not yet available. This is known as the *deductive process*. Once the observations suggested by the theory have been made, the theory may be modified so that further predictions lead to new observations.

Theory Construction

Philosophers of science who concern themselves with such matters have identified several approaches to theory construction. We need to concern ourselves with only three of these: the use of models and the inductive and functional approaches.

MODELS

When a theorist proposes that personality is like a steam engine in which pressures build up so that the engine would explode if they are not released, that theorist is using the steam engine as a model. Inasmuch as that model suggests a variety of observations for the study of personality, this is an example of the *deductive approach* to science. Models can be useful when they serve the guiding function of science; they work less well for the ordering function. There are aspects to human personality, such as thoughts, for which there is no analogous part in the steam engine.

Though they have their use, models must be employed with care. Theorists at times become so attached to their model that they fail to adjust it when new data do not fit the model. As with other theories, a model should be modified or discarded when the facts demand this.

THE INDUCTIVE APPROACH

Whereas some scientists prefer to use models to guide their gathering of data, there are others who gather data without relying on theory. Those who use this *inductive approach* often believe that the data speak for themselves. They seek to establish cause-and-effect relationships and consider these as the essence of science. That is not to say that these investigators have no guide for what phenomena to observe. It simply means that this guide is not spelled out in a formal theory. The investigator's own or other's research results often suggest the next place where relationships among phenomena are to be explored. No serious scientist goes around observing nature's phenomena at random.

THE FUNCTIONAL APPROACH

Although it is useful to differentiate between the inductive and the deductive processes and to think of a theory as having a guiding function and an ordering function, it is also important to realize that in the actual conduct of research and theory construction data influence theory, theory guides data gathering, and gathered data, in turn, serve to modify theory. This is known as the *functional approach* and it is followed by most contemporary investigators in the field of personality. They thus assign equal value to theory and data.

Evaluation of Theory

One cannot ask whether a theory is correct because the theory itself cannot be tested. What can and should be tested are the questions (the hypotheses) that are raised by a useful theory, and such questions are more likely to be raised by a theory that is simple rather than complex. There thus are two questions one should ask in evaluating a theory: Is it useful? Is it simple?

When we ask whether a theory is useful, whether it has *utility*, we want to know whether it serves well the two functions of a theory: the ordering function and the guiding function. A theory is useful if it generates questions that can be answered by the methods of science and if it manages to organize and integrate the diverse facts these methods have uncovered. To possess utility in this fashion also requires that the theory is explicitly and unambiguously stated so that its meaning can be communicated.

When we ask whether a theory is simple we want to know whether it bases its predictions and explanations on the fewest assumptions. The more assumptions a theory requires, the more difficult it is to test the hypotheses that flow from it. The simplicity or *parsimony* of a theory also makes it easy to modify it in the light of new data that do not support an assumption. Theories that cannot be readily modified usually lack both utility and parsimony and should be discarded.

IMPLICIT PERSONALITY THEORY

Theories, and theories about personality in particular, are not the exclusive province of psychologists. It is likely that all of us have some notions about what people are like and why they behave the way they do. Occasionally we express these notions as when we say that fat people are fun to be with or that we don't trust people who smile all the time. More often we tend to keep these ideas to ourselves. They may, in fact, not be sufficiently thought out and organized to be put into words. This is why such a collection of notions is called an *implicit personality theory*.

Sometimes implicit personality theories consist of no more than a collection of prejudiced cultural stereotypes which have little basis in reality. In that case such notions can be damaging because they may cause social discord. At other times implicit personality theories can reflect the recognition of some psychological reality. That talkative, active people tend to be sociable is an example of such a theory. If, acting on that notion, one invites such people to a party the outcome can be positive because the party is likely to be a success.

An implicit personality theory can affect not only how we perceive and treat others; it can also affect our own behavior and the perception we have of ourselves. A woman whose implicit personality theory tells her that shy people find it difficult to talk to strangers may conclude that she is shy after a few experiences in which she had trouble talking to strangers. Once having classified herself as shy, she is likely to predict that she won't have a good time at a large party and therefore turns down an invitation to one.

If we apply the criterion of utility to implicit theories of personality, we can readily see that they are not theories at all and would more appropriately be called hunches, notions, suspicions, or prejudices. The point on which these ideas differ most from scientific theories is that they do not generate hypotheses that can be tested by research. To this we turn next.

RESEARCH

It is possible to think at great length about a theory, to speculate about it, discuss it, or argue about it, but none of these can settle the issues the theory raises. That can be done only by the *empirical method*—by looking at facts, by making observations. There are a number of ways of making such observations, some are more rigorous than others, but all are more productive than argument or name calling or appeal to authority ("Freud said so, therefore it must be true").

Casual Observation

Using unsystematic and unplanned observations is probably how any science gets its start. It is likely that the early classifications of characters and temperaments began that way. Even today an unexpected, serendipitous observation may arouse someone's curiosity and lead to a more formal, planned, and systematic study such as a naturalistic observation.

Naturalistic Observation

Here the observer is guided by a question to which he or she wants to find an answer. Observations thus made are usually recorded so that they can be reviewed at a later time or by someone else. The record can take the form of codes, notes, drawings, photographs, tape recordings, movies, or videotapes. Many studies conducted by anthropologists, such as those of Margaret Mead (1949), are based on naturalistic observations. They are also known as *field studies*.

Naturalistic observations may give the impression that one is seeing people as they really are, but that is an illusion. There is, first of all, the problem that the presence of an outside observer may lead the observed not to display their typical behavior. Second, the observer's expectations or biases may distort the observations; and, third, whatever is observed can only be a fraction of what goes on elsewhere and at other times.

Case Studies

As in naturalistic observations the focus of *case studies* is on the behavior of individuals in their natural environment. The difference is that in case studies the observations cover a relatively long period of time, sometimes many years, and are typically made by the person who is the object of the study. That individual usually keeps a record of his or her behavior and later delivers these *self-reports* to the investigator. In addition to gathering these records, the investigator may interview the subject or ask him or her to take psychological tests or respond to questionnaires.

The case-study method is used extensively in personality investigations, particularly in clinical settings, but it has many of the disadvantages of naturalistic observations, particularly the potential for distortions.

Controlled Observations

To cope with some of the drawbacks of naturalistic observation and case studies, investigators have turned to observations that are made in the field, but under controlled, prearranged conditions. This usually calls for a *confederate*, a person who works with the investigator and is instructed to behave in a specified way. An example of a study that uses controlled observations might be one where a confederate pretends to be blind so that the investigator (who typically remains hidden) can observe what kind of help various people are likely to provide.

This approach is less likely than the other methods mentioned thus far to be influenced by chance events over which the investigator has little or no control. The observations are also less likely to be biased, and because they take place under standard conditions, they lend themselves to comparisons with similar studies done elsewhere and with other people. This enhances the *generalizability* of the results. This means that the findings are likely also to apply to other situations and persons.

The Correlational Approach

Any of the research methods mentioned thus far may lead to the observation that two or more phenomena appear to be related because they have a tendency to occur together. Such a co-relationship can be investigated by the *correlational approach* and its associated statistic, the *correlation coefficient*, which is a number that expresses the degree of the relationship.

MEASURES

To use the correlational approach one must have the results of at least two sets of measurements. These may be two different measures taken on the same people (for example, a personality test and an intelligence test), the same measure taken on the same people at two different times (an intelligence test given at age five and again at age ten), or the same measure taken on two different groups of people (an intelligence test given to mothers and to their children).

VARIABLES

All measures vary along a dimension, from a simple "yes" or "no" to scores ranging from 1 to 150. That is why the phenomena that the measures quantify are called *variables*. When two variables are related in such a way that as one changes, the other also changes, we say that the variables are correlated. If the change in both measures is in the same direction (the higher the mother's test score, the higher her child's test score), the correlation is said to be *positive*. If the change is in the opposite direction (the higher the mother's test score, the lower the child's test score), the correlation is called *negative*.

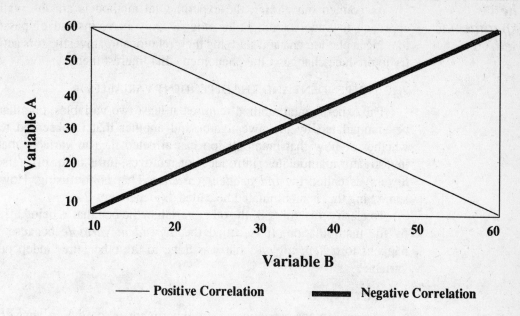

Positive—As A increases, B increases
Negative—As A increases, B decreases

Fig. 2.1 Two perfect correlations (r = 1.0)

THE CORRELATION COEFFICIENT

The statistic that expresses the degree to which two variables are related is the *correlation coefficient*, symbolized by *r*. This is followed by a plus or a minus sign and a number, *r* = +.79, for example. The plus sign indicates that the correlation is positive, the minus sign that it is negative. The correlation coefficient (*r*) can range from +1.00, a perfect positive correlation, through 0.00, reflecting the absence of correlation, to –1.00, a perfect negative correlation. "Perfect" here means that for every unit of change in one variable, there is a comparable unit of change in the other. One hardly ever finds perfect correlations between measures of human attributes, where a coefficient as high as *r* = +.85 is relatively rare. The diagram in Fig. 2.1 depicts a perfect positive and a perfect negative correlation.

CORRELATION AND CAUSALITY

It is easy, but *wrong*, to assume that when two variables are correlated, one has caused the other. There may or may not be a causal relationship, but a correlation coefficient, whatever its magnitude, can neither confirm nor refute it. The only permissible conclusion to be drawn from this statistic is that there is a relationship. To investigate causes of phenomena one must employ the experimental method.

The Experimental Method

As pointed out earlier, the experimental method is an observational approach to understanding phenomena. Only here, instead of passively looking at phenomena and studying their relationship, investigators actively try to produce change in the phenomena that interest them.

THE INDEPENDENT AND THE DEPENDENT VARIABLES

The experimental method requires at least two variables, one that can be manipulated by the investigator and another that is observed to see whether or how that manipulation has affected it. The variable that the investigator manipulates (introduces or removes, turns on or off, raises or lowers) is called the *independent variable*. That is confusing. How can something that is manipulated be called "independent"?

To clarify this, think of the other variable, the one that is being affected by the manipulation. It is called the *dependent variable* because what happens to it *depends on* what was done to the other, the "independent" variable.

THE EXPERIMENT

The reason for carrying out an experiment is to find an answer to a question. That question is framed in the form of an assertion that the experiment is designed to test. The assertion is the *experimental hypothesis*. An example might be, "Candlelight increases romantic fantasies." Here, candlelight is the independent variable, and romantic fantasies the dependent variable. To conduct the experiment an investigator would select a group of people, a *sample*, to serve as research participants ("subjects"). The sample is meant to represent the larger group, the *population*, from which it was drawn so that the results of the study will have relevance to more than the relatively few people who participated.

Romantic fantasies might be measured by having people make up a story to go with a picture that shows a couple sitting next to each other on a sofa. To manipulate candlelight, the independent variable, the investigator might divide the sample into two smaller groups. One, the *experimental group*, would be asked to make up their stories by the light of a candle, whereas the other, the *control group*, is asked to do the same thing under fluorescent light.

Note that it is important to make sure that the two groups in this experiment differ only in the kind of light by which they make up their stories. The experiment would be *confounded* if, in addition, one group sat on soft chairs, the other on hard chairs. The kind of chair is just one of many variables, such as the time of day or the age and gender of the subjects, that the investigator must keep constant—*control*—to obtain meaningful results.

Once the experiment is completed, the romantic content of the stories would have to be evaluated. This could be done by trained judges who assign a score to each story. Such judges must be *blind*—that is, must not know to which group the individual who made up the story belonged. The average (*mean*) scores of the two groups are then compared by a statistical technique to see whether they differ. If they do, a statistical test is used to estimate the probability that this difference could have arisen by chance. When that probability is low (less than 5 in 100) the result is viewed as *statistically significant*. That, however, refers only to the likelihood of the result having been due to chance. It says nothing about the importance, social relevance, or practical meaning of the result!

ASSESSMENT

The stories told by the subjects in the above imaginary experiment are an example of the methods psychologists employ to assess, evaluate, and measure personality and its various aspects and components. The methods used to assess personality differ in the extent to which the person who is being evaluated knows that this is the case. With some assessment methods the purpose is quite obvious, with others it is disguised, and with some the person is unaware that he or she is being evaluated. We shall examine a few of each of these methods, but first we must review two requirements that all forms of assessment must satisfy: They must be reliable and they must be valid.

Reliability and Validity

Every instrument that is designed to measure something, be it time, length, weight, intelligence, or an aspect of personality, must be trustworthy. That is to say the information the instrument provides must at all times be true or correct. A scale is useless unless it shows your correct weight every time you step on it. The same is true of a psychological test; it must consistently provide correct information. The consistency is called *reliability*, the correctness *validity*.

RELIABILITY

There are a number of ways for checking the reliability of a test. Those of greatest concern in the case of a personality test are *test-retest reliability* and *interjudge reliability*. Test-retest reliability asks whether the test results are the same when the test is administered to the same person on two or more occasions. Interjudge reliability asks whether two or more trained persons who score and analyze the test arrive at the same conclusion.

VALIDITY

A test may be highly reliable, but it would be useless if it did not also possess validity; if it did not measure what it is supposed to measure. A test of personality should measure personality and not intelligence, and vice versa. Again there are a number of ways for checking this. One of these ways is *content validity*. It asks whether the items on the test appear to tap the characteristic in which we are interested. Because personality is so difficult to define so that judges may disagree on what a given item is tapping, content validity is rarely used to answer the question whether a test is valid.

Criterion validity is more useful for evaluating personality tests. Here the question is whether the test correctly identifies people who possess a given attribute or characteristic which serves as a criterion. That criterion may be something that is currently available, in which case we speak of *concurrent validity*, or something that lies in the future. In that case, we speak of *predictive validity*.

An example of concurrent validity might be when it is found that a test of sociability correctly identifies children whose teachers report that they have many friends. An example of predictive validity might be when the same test, administered to a group of preschool children, correctly identifies those who have many friends when they are in second grade.

For personality tests that were developed in the context of a particular personality theory it is important to ask whether the test has *construct validity*—that is, whether it is logically related to the constructs employed by the theory. Because most personality theories make use of many interrelated constructs, numerous studies may be required to establish the construct validity of a theory-based test.

RELIABILITY OR VALIDITY: WHICH IS MORE IMPORTANT?

If we think of reliability as the consistency with which the test answers the questions put to it and of validity as the truthfulness of these answers, the question of which is more important is easily answered: We need both. A valid test must also be reliable; if it is not valid it does not matter whether it is reliable. In other words, we can trust a test only when we know that it consistently tells the truth. If the test lies it does not matter whether it lies all or only some of the time because we can never trust it. With that in mind, let us look at some assessment methods.

Self-Report Methods

Individuals whose personality is being assessed by a self-report method are well aware of what is happening because they are asked to answer a series of questions that have to do with what kind of people they are.

THE CALIFORNIA PSYCHOLOGICAL INVENTORY (CPI)

This instrument has the form of a True or False test. It is made up of statements such as, "I enjoy telling jokes." Like other such *self-report inventories* it is called an *objective personality test* because its scoring and interpretation do not involve the examiner's subjective judgment. In that way it is like the familiar true-false and multiple-choice exam.

Although the items on such a self-report inventory seem pretty straightforward, the person who takes the test is not told how the test is scored and analyzed. This is important because otherwise some people might try to distort the picture they are giving of themselves. To check on that tendency the CPI contains items designed to reveal attempts to portray either an exaggeratedly positive or negative personality.

The CPI is an *empirically based, criterion-keyed test*. This means that the scoring norms are based on research in which the test had been given to groups of people whose personality characteristics were already known. One of these groups might have been composed of individuals who had been identified as highly aggressive. When a Jim Jones now takes this test and answers it in a manner that is similar to the way that the aggressive *criterion group* answered it, the examiner can conclude that Jim Jones has aggressive tendencies.

The California Psychological Inventory has been shown to have high test-retest reliability (with an *r* around +.90). It also has good predictive validity, for research has demonstrated that it predicts participation in extracurricular activities, cheating on exams, leadership, conformity, employability, adjustment, and physiological reaction to stress (Megargee, 1972).

THE MINNESOTA MULTIPHASIC PERSONALITY INVENTORY (MMPI)

The MMPI is probably the most widely used and best known of the objective tests of personality. Like the CPI, it is empirically based, criterion-keyed, and uses straightforward statements such as "I lack self-confidence." People who are given this test are asked to indicate for each such statement whether they consider it true or false, or whether they cannot say. The test contains items from which the examiner can determine whether the person who took it attempted to make a good impression or was trying to fake mental illness.

It is important to realize that answers to individual items tell the examiner very little. People who take this test often wonder what their answer to a statement such as "I enjoy reading the newspaper" could possibly indicate about their personality. By itself, this question means little, because the interpretation of the MMPI does not depend on the content of specific items but on the *pattern* of a person's responses. This pattern is usually shown in the form of a graph, a *personality profile*, which is interpreted in terms of its similarity to the profiles obtained by the various criterion groups who were used in the development of the test (Graham, 1990).

THE SIXTEEN PERSONALITY–FACTOR QUESTIONNAIRE (16 P–F)

The 16 P–F is an example of an objective personality test that was developed by using the statistical technique known as *factor analysis*. This technique enables an investigator to identify interrelationships among a large number of correlated items.

Factor Analysis. In the case of the 16 P–F, Cattell (1957) took a list of approximately 170 adjectives descriptive of human behavior and asked college students to use these adjectives in describing their friends. As one might expect, some of these adjectives tended to be used together a lot of the time. Someone for whom "cheerful" was descriptive, for example, was also likely to be considered "outgoing," "friendly," "talkative," and "sociable." The same person, on the other hand, would probably not have been characterized as "quiet," "careful," "reserved," and "sober," whereas these adjectives might well have been used for someone else. In other words, there were adjectives that were highly correlated with each other, but not with different adjectives which, in turn, were themselves intercorrelated. It is these intercorrelated *clusters* or *factors* that a factor analysis is designed to identify.

Factor analysis enabled Cattell to reduce his list of adjectives to sixteen dimensions or factors. These he labeled *source traits* and they form the basis of his personality questionnaire.

THE INTERVIEW

If one wants to know something about people's personality, the thing to do is to ask them about it. Objective tests are designed to do just that, but in an impersonal and somewhat indirect manner because the responses take the form of checkmarks on a printed sheet. A more direct method of asking people questions about their personality is to talk to them in a face-to-face interview.

There are two kinds of interview: unstructured and structured.

In an *unstructured interview* the examiner talks in a more or less freewheeling manner with the person whose personality is to be explored. Questions may range from the open-ended "Tell me about yourself" to a specific "How do you feel about going to large parties where there are lots of people you don't know?"

The answers to these questions may then lead to other questions on related or different topics so that the interview proceeds in a very flexible manner.

Compared to an objective paper-and-pencil test this approach to assessment has certain advantages. It makes it possible to pursue unexpected and unusual topics that might not be touched upon by the questions of a standardized test. In addition, the interview enables the examiner to observe the interviewed person's behavior and his or her reactions to the various questions and topics. These observations later contribute to the conclusion that can be drawn from the interview. These advantages, however, are accompanied by a major disadvantage. It is that the interviewer's own personality, biases, expectations, and interests may influence the focus and outcome of the interview, as well as color the reactions of the person being interviewed. This raises serious questions about the reliability and validity of such an interview as an assessment instrument.

The *structured interview* was developed to deal with these disadvantages. Here, instead of roaming over a wide terrain of topics, guided only by his or her own interviewing skills and interests, the examiner is expected to cover a series of previously determined topics and to ask questions in a fixed order. This approach reduces the examiner's influence on the interview, but sacrifices the flexibility and spontaneity that is the hallmark of the unstructured interview. At the same time, there will be far more uniformity from interview to interview and among different interviewers so that reliability is likely to be enhanced. Moreover, the validity of the structured interview may also be better than that of the unstructured version because the influence of the interviewer's biases and preconceptions is greatly reduced.

Projective Methods

The purpose of self-report measures and interviews is usually quite obvious when even unsophisticated people encounter them. The purpose of projective methods of personality assessment is somewhat disguised, and one has to have a certain level of sophistication to recognize them for what they are. Here, instead of answering questions in an interview or on a questionnaire, the person being examined carries out an assigned task that seems to have little to do with what kind of person one is. Another difference between objective and projective methods is how the results are interpreted. With objective tests the answers are scored and the scores compared with published norms so that their interpretation calls for little or no judgment by the examiner. Not so with projective methods, where responses are encoded, rather than scored, and interpreted in a manner that entails a good deal of subjective judgment on the part of the examiner.

Projective methods derive their name from the assumption that when people are asked to make sense of an unstructured, ambiguous stimulus (such as a vague picture or an incomplete sentence), they tend to fall back on their imagination, feelings, desires, and attitudes and reveal these by "projecting" them onto the stimulus.

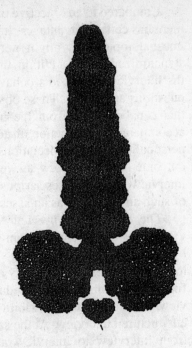

Fig. 2.2 An inkblot like those used in the Rorschach test

THE RORSCHACH INKBLOTS

This well-known and widely used assessment device consists of ten inkblots such as the one depicted in Fig. 2.2. The subject is shown these one at a time and asked what they look like or bring to mind. Having been assured that there are no right or wrong answers, the subject is given no further instructions and the examiner answers any questions in a noncommittal manner. During this *performance* portion of the test administration the examiner records the subject's responses. After all ten inkblots have been gone through, these responses are reviewed in what is known as the *inquiry*, during which the examiner seeks to ascertain what aspects of each stimulus (shape, color, shading, and so forth) had led to the subject's various associations.

The examiner later encodes each response to facilitate interpretation. Responses that made use of the entire blot, for example, are coded *W* (for whole). If only a major part of the blot was used, the response is coded *D* (for large detail). These codes and their relationships (whole versus detail, for example) are considered the *scores* of the Rorschach. Unlike the interpretation of scores on objective tests, the interpretation of the inkblot test is quite subjective and depends greatly on the examiner's theoretical view of personality. This subjectivity has made it difficult to establish the validity of this projective method, and some skeptics have asked whether it does not tell as much about the personality of the examiner as about that of the person being examined.

THE THEMATIC APPERCEPTION TEST (TAT)

Another well-known projective method is the Thematic Apperception Test, or TAT. It consists of thirty cards (Fig. 2.3). One of these cards is blank and the rest show a vaguely drawn picture. The person to whom this test is administered is shown these pictures one at a time and asked to make up a story about it that includes what led up to the scene depicted, what is happening now, what the characters are thinking and feeling, and what the outcome is going to be.

The TAT is similar to the Rorschach in that the subject must draw on ("project") his or her own fantasies, needs, memories, and emotions to concoct a response, but it differs from the inkblot test in that the pictures show actual scenes, such as a young boy looking at a violin. The pictures are designed to elicit *themes* that reflect the individual's *needs,* such as achievement, dependency, power, aggression, and sex. The name of the test is derived from these themes and the word *apperception,* which the dictionary defines as "the process of understanding something that is perceived in terms of previous experience."

Unlike the Rorschach, where all ten cards are always shown in a prescribed order, examiners rarely use all of the thirty TAT cards and present these in no particular order. Interpretation of the responses to the TAT is even more subjective than the analysis of those to the inkblot test. Here the examiner scrutinizes the stories to locate in each the central figure or hero and to identify the motives and environmental forces he or she has to reconcile and whether and how well this is accomplished. All of this requires the examiner to draw a lot of inferences and these greatly depend on her or his training, experience, and theoretical sophistication. Given all of these variables the validity of the TAT is difficult to establish, but when individual cards are used to assess achievement motivation, for example, this instrument permits one to conduct rigorous, well-controlled research.

Observational Methods

Thus far we have discussed methods of personality assessment in which the person being evaluated is an active, though not always well-informed, participant. There remain three methods in which the person in question does not know that she or he is under scrutiny: *frequency counts, peer nominations,* and *ratings.*

Fig. 2.3 One of the cards used in the Thematic Apperception Test (TAT)

FREQUENCY COUNTS

This is a more systematic version of the naturalistic observations discussed earlier in this chapter. Here a trained observer is placed in the setting, such as a classroom or workplace, where the person to be observed can regularly be found. Instead of watching and recording everything the subject is doing, however, the observer is instructed to focus on specific *target behavior*, such as talking to another child or smoking a cigarette. These instances are counted, usually so that their frequency can again be checked after some intervention such as therapy has taken place.

PEER NOMINATIONS

This method is often used in personality research on people who spend much of their time in the company of others who thus know them well. All members of such a group are asked to *nominate* those in the group who have a characteristic that is of interest to an investigator. All children in a classroom, for example, might be asked to write down the answers to such questions as "Who fights a lot?" or "Who has the most friends?" By inspecting all answers to these question, the investigator can identify the child who was most frequently nominated as fighting a lot or as the most popular. It is possible to score these nominations by dividing the number of nominations a child received in a given category by the number of children in the classroom.

RATINGS

This method also uses the judgment of the subject's acquaintances to assess his or her personality. Here the investigator asks a friend, teacher, or supervisor of the subject to indicate on a list of personality characteristics which of them the subject manifests and to what degree. Such a *rating scale* is similar to the self-report questionnaires discussed earlier, except that someone other than the person in question is asked to respond to it.

There are several sources of potential bias in ratings of this nature that can threaten the validity of the results. One of these is the so-called *halo effect*. It comes about when people who are doing the rating permit their general impression of the subject to influence their judgment of specific characteristics. For instance, someone who is seen as a friendly person may also be given a high rating for honesty even though the rater has little basis for that judgment. With ratings, as with all other methods of personality assessment, investigators must take great care to make sure that the information they gather is valid as well as reliable.

ETHICAL CONSIDERATIONS

*A Human
Relationship*

Both personality research and personality assessment involve psychologists in a relationship with another human being. It is a sensitive relationship because the psychologist and the person with whom the research or assessment is to be conducted do not have equal status. They are in a *power relationship* where the psychologist is the person in charge who tells the other person what to do. The unequal status of the two individuals is reflected in the fact that one of them is usually called the "subject." Because this expression evokes the image of monarch and subject, "participant" is now the preferred term, but "subject" continues to slip in, as it did in some parts of this chapter.

Whenever one person has, or is perceived to have, power over another—be that in the relationship between physician and patient, lawyer and client, teacher and student, or psychologist and research participant—ethical issues emerge, calling for careful consideration of the rights, interests, and welfare of the subordinate individual. With this in mind professional organizations, such as the American Psychological Association (1990), have adopted ethical principles to guide the conduct of their members. Here is the gist of some of the principles that apply to conducting psychological research and assessment.

AN IMPORTANT GENERAL PRINCIPLE

In their professional relationships with research participants, clients, students, those under supervision, or employees, psychologists must refrain from sexual or other exploitation.

PRINCIPLES GOVERNING RESEARCH

The investigator must inform a potential participant of all aspects of the study that might reasonably be expected to influence his or her willingness to participate.

The participant has the right to refuse taking part in the study and to withdraw from it at any time without fear of adverse consequences.

After careful consideration of the need to not fully reveal all aspects of a study beforehand, the nature of and reason for such deception must be explained to each participant at the earliest possible moment.

Upon conclusion of a study or as soon thereafter as possible, all participants must be informed of its outcome and given an opportunity to ask questions about any aspect of it.

The investigator must protect the confidentiality of all information obtained about participants in the course of a study, unless an exception to this was agreed upon in advance.

PRINCIPLES GOVERNING ASSESSMENT

The person on whom an assessment is to be conducted ("the client") has the right to a full explanation of the nature and purpose of the techniques, and this explanation must be offered in terms that the client can understand.

The client has the right to know the results of the assessment, the interpretations made, and the basis for the conclusions and recommendations, if any.

When reporting the results of an assessment, the psychologist must indicate any reservations that exist about the validity or reliability of the methods used.

The psychologist must guard the confidentiality of assessment results and protect them against misuse.

A theory has two functions, an organizing function and a guiding function. Observations that have been made are organized by the theory and further observations are guided by it. Both inductive and deductive processes can connect observation to theory. Theory construction can make use of models or it can proceed by the inductive approach. The functional approach is characterized by a free interchange between theory and data. It is used most frequently. Theories are evaluated not by whether they are true, but whether they are useful and parsimonious.

Research can take several forms. We spoke of case studies, casual, naturalistic, and controlled observations before discussing the correlational approach that evaluates the relationship of two or more variables. The correlation coefficient expresses the degree of that relationship, but it cannot establish their causal connection; that can only be done with the experimental approach in which the independent variable is manipulated to observe its effect on the dependent variable.

In the assessment of personality, psychologists employ various techniques. To be useful each of these must have demonstrated reliability and validity. Validity addresses the question whether the measuring instrument measures what it is meant to measure. This question can be answered by one of several methods. Among these are content, criteria, and construct validity.

The major categories of assessment techniques are self-report methods, which include criterion-keyed tests and interviews, projective techniques such as the Rorschach inkblot test, and such observational methods as frequency counts, peer nominations, and ratings.

The roles of either research investigator or assessment examiner place the psychologist in a relationship of unequal power. This raises important ethical considerations in which the rights, interests, and welfare of the participant must be of prime concern.

In this and the previous chapter we have reviewed the definition and nature of personality, the influences that form it, and the ways of classifying it. We examined how theories are formed, how research on personality is conducted, and how personality can be assessed. With this we turn to an examination of the major theories of personality that have been advanced in the course of the twentieth century. We shall do so mindful of the criteria of utility and parsimony by which all theories must be evaluated.

Selected Readings

Frick, W. B. 1984. *Personality Theories: An Experiential Workbook*. New York: Teachers College Press.

Hendrick, C., and M. S. Clark (eds.). 1990. *Research Methods in Personality and Social Psychology*. Newbury Park, CA: Sage.

Lanyon, R. I., and L. D. Goodstein. 1982. *Personality Assessment*. 2nd ed. New York: Wiley.

Rosenthal, R., and R. L. Rosnow. 1991. *Essentials of Behavioral Research: Methods and Data Analysis*. 2nd ed. New York: McGraw-Hill.

Part II:
Personality Theory

3

Psychoanalytic Theory

*S*igmund Freud's psychoanalytic theory is a comprehensive contribution that covers every aspect of personality from its development to the treatment of its disorders.

The theory construes a child's development as passing through stages in each of which the focus is on a different part of the body. After a period during which the child is in rivalry with the parent of the same sex, much of the individual's future personality has been determined.

Personality is viewed as made up of three levels of consciousness and as divided into three parts—id, ego, and superego—each of which has a different set of functions. Ego is charged with the management of the system. It can resort to various mechanisms to defend against anxiety which signals threatening imbalances among the three components of personality and the outside world.

Psychological disorders can develop when ego is unable to carry out its many responsibilities. Freud treated such disorders by psychoanalysis. This treatment consists of the patient's talking freely about whatever comes to mind so that the therapist can help by bringing troublesome unconscious conflicts to conscious awareness.

Psychoanalytic theory has strengths and weaknesses. Some of the weaknesses stem from the fact that almost a hundred years have passed since Freud began proposing his theory.

SIGMUND FREUD'S PIONEERING CONTRIBUTION

A Comprehensive Theory

We begin our review of the major conceptualizations of personality with a look at the work of Sigmund Freud (1856–1939), whose *psychoanalytic theory* remains the most comprehensive formulation of personality ever proposed. Freud's theory encompasses the development, the structure, and the operation of personality in both the normal and the abnormal individual. We shall have occasion to take a critical look at his work, but there is no denying the magnitude of Freud's achievement. His contributions changed our view of human nature and with it Western culture itself. Novels, plays, movies, educational systems, interpretations of history, biographies, methods of advertising, the way we talk to and about one another, and how we raise our children, to say nothing of the treatment of psychological disorders, for better or worse all bear the imprint of the extraordinary mind of Sigmund Freud. Together with Copernicus, Darwin, Marx, and Einstein, Freud revolutionized our thinking about the world and about ourselves.

Psychoanalysis

Freud had been trained as a physician who specialized in neurology. The context in which he created his theory was his medical practice, where he saw men and women who came to him with problems that were then called "nervous disorders." While working with these patients Freud gradually developed *psychoanalysis*, which he used both as a method of treatment and as a technique for studying personality.

THE BASIC CONCEPTS

Instincts, Homeostasis, and Hedonism

Freud's background in medicine is evident in that he recognized the human as a biological organism possessed of basic needs that sustain life and perpetuate the species. These needs, often referred to as *instincts*, are a source of tension that must be reduced because we are so constructed that we seek a stable state or optimal balance, called *homeostasis*. Tension upsets this balance, creating an unpleasant state that we seek to terminate because another basic aspect of human nature, *hedonism*, makes us seek pleasure and avoid pain.

Libido

A HYDRODYNAMIC MODEL

Freud was impressed by the physics and physiology of his day. Much of his theorizing suggests that his model was based on hydrodynamics, the science of fluids. Thus, Freud asserted that all activity, whether physical or psychological, whether working toward a goal or merely thinking about it, requires energy. He viewed the human as a closed system that has a fixed and limited amount of energy available so that energy spent on one task is not available for another. The notion of energy flowing within a closed system led to the characterization of Freud's formulation as a *psychodynamic theory*.

THE IMPORTANCE OF SEX

The psychological energy needed for thinking, fantasizing, or dreaming Freud called *libido*, a Latin word meaning "desire" or "lust." This reflects the emphasis he placed on the sex instinct. Though Freud recognized the existence of other bodily needs, he considered sex preeminent. That emphasis probably stems from the observations he made in his clinical practice where most of his patients had problems that seemed rooted in one or another form of sexual difficulty.

Psychosexual Development

THE EROGENOUS ZONES

Freud located the source of libido, or the sex instinct, in the skin and particularly in the mucous membranes. Mucous membranes line the openings of the body that communicate with the external environment. They are highly sensitive and their stimulation can produce pleasurable sensations. Freud referred to them as *erogenous zones*.

Erogenous zones play an important role in Freud's conceptualization of the development and channeling of sexual impulses. He saw *psychosexual development* as passing through four stages, each characterized by its focus on the stimulation of a different erogenous zone.

STAGES OF DEVELOPMENT

The *oral stage* takes place during the first year of life when, during the feeding episodes, the principal focus of the interaction between infant and mother is on the mouth. During the next two years, the *anal stage*, this focus shifts as the mother seeks to bring the child's elimination under control through toilet training, and the child, presumably, obtains pleasure from the excretion and retention of feces. Around the beginning of the fourth year the focus shifts again. Now the primary source of erotic (sexual) pleasure is the excitation and stimulation of the genitals, and this period is known as the *phallic stage*. This is followed by a *latency period* during which sexual interests are thought to be subdued, to emerge again with puberty when the individual enters the *genital stage* with its adult sexual interests and pleasures.

THE OEDIPUS AND ELECTRA CONFLICTS

The transition from the phallic stage to the latency period is marked by a period of stress that is referred to as the *Oedipus conflict*, in the case of boys; and the *Electra conflict*, in the case of girls.

Freud asserted that during the phallic stage all children form a biologically determined erotic attachment to the parent of the opposite sex and fantasize about the exclusive possession of that parent. In these fantasies the same-sex parent is seen as a hated rival whom the child wishes to destroy. This wish arouses anxiety, however, for if it were to be discovered, that parent might hurt the child in self-defense or retribution. That fear of punishment comes to focus on the genitals and takes the form of *castration anxiety*, an anxiety about being castrated or otherwise hurt by the same-sex parent.

Identification. Like all anxiety, castration anxiety is unpleasant and leads to attempts at reducing it. Here these attempts take the form of curbing (repressing) the sexual desires for the opposite-sex parent and identifying with the same-sex parent. This step resolves the conflict. In the process of identifying with the same-sex parent the child *internalizes* and thus adopts that parent's behavior pattern and value system, including the gender-appropriate sex role pattern.

The resolution of the Oedipus or Electra conflict is crucial to the individual's sexual adjustment in the adult years. Failure to bring this conflict to satisfactory resolution results in problems that are sometimes referred to as an *Oedipus complex*. This complex is characterized by excessive dependence on and an inability to separate from the opposite-sex parent, sex-role confusion, and limited ability to relate in a mature fashion to members of the opposite sex. Freud thought that *homosexuality* had its origin in a failure to resolve satisfactorily the Oedipus or Electra conflict, but there is no reliable evidence to support this notion.

Fixation

Just as failure to resolve these conflicts appropriately can lead to problems in adulthood, so can difficulties in the oral and anal stages leave their mark on the adult's personality.

If, during the oral stage, the child was overindulged, a *fixation* may occur that, in adulthood, manifests itself in the passivity, dependency, and optimism of the *oral character* who obtains pleasure from such mouth-centered activities as drinking, eating, and smoking. Should the oral stage have been marked by deprivation, however, the adult may turn out to be pessimistic, suspicious, sarcastic, and contentious.

Fixation at the anal stage is the result of overly strict, punitive, and early toilet training. The *anal character* who emerges from such childhood experiences is typically an obstinate, precise, overly neat, miserly person. On the other hand, if toilet training was overly permissive and late, the adult's behavior may be marked by excessive generosity, messiness, vagueness, and malleability.

Levels of Consciousness

Mental life, according to Freud, takes place at three levels: the conscious, the preconscious, and the unconscious. The *conscious level* represents the sensations, perceptions, thoughts, feelings, and memories of which we are aware at any given moment. What we are aware of, however, was to Freud only a small part of what goes on in the human mind. Some of it is located at the *preconscious level*. This takes the form of thoughts and memories that, though not immediately available, can be reached with a bit of effort. Someone's name that one has "on the tip of the tongue" is an example of preconscious material. All the rest of mental life takes place at the *unconscious level*. Of it we are totally unaware. At this deep, ordinarily inaccessible level are stored the urges and drives of our instincts as well as unpleasant memories and events we experienced before we had words with which to label them.

UNCONSCIOUS MOTIVATION

Freud maintained that a major part of what we do, think, and feel is motivated by needs that originate at the unconscious level where instincts and needs actively seek expression and satisfaction. Behavior thus determined is said to be the result of *unconscious motivation*. Freud also asserted that unconscious motivation is the source of humor, dreams, slips of the tongue, accidents, and forgetting; that nothing we do happens by chance, that everything has a cause. This notion is known as *psychological determinism*.

THE STRUCTURE OF PERSONALITY

Id, Ego, and Superego

Freud conceived of personality as composed of three interrelated and interacting systems or structures that cut across the three levels of consciousness we just discussed. To each of these structures—*id, ego,* and *superego*—he assigned specific psychological functions and methods of operation. This makes it easy to *anthropomorphize* these structures and to think of them as three little people inside our head who carry out missions, have responsibilities, and send messages to one another. At no time did Freud conceive of the three in this way, but his colorful, metaphorical way of writing often

Character Type	Sub-type	Child-rearing Style	Traits
Oral	Oral-passive	Indulgent	Optimistic Gullible Dependent Manipulative
	Oral-aggressive	Restrictive	Pessimistic Suspicious Quarrelsome
Anal	Anal-retentive	Indulgent	Stingy Stubborn Punctual Precise Orderly
	Anal-aggressive	Restrictive	Cruel Destructive Hostile Disorderly
Phallic	Phallic-dominant	Indulgent	Vain Proud Domineering Ambitious Virile
	Phallic-submissive	Restrictive	Meek Submissive Modest Timid Feminine

Table 3.1 Freud's character types, their sub-types, origins, and traits

sounds as if he did. When we adopt some of Freud's language that follows, we must remember that the three components of personality are no more than useful theoretical structures. They have no actual existence in a specific location in the brain or body, nor did Freud ever suggest that they did. This conceptualization is depicted in Fig. 3.1.

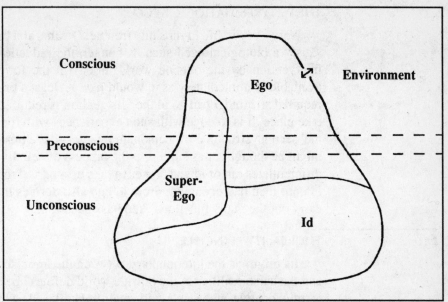

Fig. 3.1   Schematic depiction of Freud's conceptualization of personality

Id

ALL OF ID IS UNCONSCIOUS

Freud conceived of id as the part of personality with which the human is born. In that original structure he located the biologically based instincts. It is out of id that the other two structures will eventually evolve. Id serves as the reservoir of all psychological and libidinal energy and is thus the source of all motivation. It is entirely unconscious, which is to say that we have no *direct* access to or awareness of the existence or the nature of our instincts. Only when ego arrives on the scene and is able, when not otherwise engaged, to serve as an agent of id will we be conscious of our bodily needs.

THE PLEASURE PRINCIPLE

Operating at the unconscious level, id is the primitive, uncontrolled, and uninhibited part of personality that seeks immediate gratification of all impulses and instantaneous release of any tension. It operates by what Freud called the *pleasure principle* and uses the *primary process* in pursuit of this principle. The primary process expresses itself in fantasy, dreams, and hallucinations—illogical, unorganized, immature mental images that usually revolve around the gratification of primitive impulses and tend to emerge in *dreams*.

THE DIFFERENTIATION OF EGO

Very early in life id runs into trouble. Dreams and hallucinations cannot satisfy a biological need such as hunger, the reduction of which requires intervention by the outside world. Food (in the form of milk) is never available as immediately as id would like. At least a brief wait, like the one required so mother can go to the refrigerator, is required before feeding can take place. It is to cope with such experiences with the world's reality that the second structure of personality—*ego*—develops. This development might be thought of as similar to the process of cell division (mitosis). Ego differentiates out of id and comes to take up a part of the imaginary "space" id until then had occupied. From id ego also derives the energy it needs to carry out the many functions Freud assigned to it.

Ego

THE REALITY PRINCIPLE

Its origin as the intermediary between the impulses and demands of id and the harsh realities of the outside world defines one of the ego's tasks. It is an executive who deals with reality. Unlike id, which operates on the pleasure principle, ego operates on the *reality principle*. It must find out what id wants and reconcile that with what reality makes possible. That usually means that impulses must be restrained, gratifications postponed, and fantasies controlled. In carrying out its organizing and controlling functions ego uses the *secondary process*. This entails cognitive functions such as perception, memory, reality testing, time orientation, attention, learning, control of motor activity, maintaining an image of oneself (the self-image), and distinguishing between reality and unreality.

A PART OF EGO IS CONSCIOUS

Its responsibility for dealing with reality requires that at least a part of ego operate at the conscious level and that is indeed the case. Unlike id, all of which operates at the unconscious level, ego functions at the conscious, the preconscious, and the unconscious level. At the conscious level are all the cognitive functions of which we are readily aware. Some marginal functions, such as the well-learned motor responses used in riding a bicycle, and the sense of time, take place at the preconscious level. Ego material at the unconscious level consists of ideas and memories that are too painful or disturbing to think about and experiences encountered before the individual had the words with which to label them.

THE FORMATION OF SUPEREGO

Thus far we have described ego as entirely pragmatic. It finds out what can be done and does it, concerned only with serving id by maximizing pleasure and minimizing pain in true hedonistic fashion, without judging whether the action is good or evil, right or wrong. By itself, ego has no values and it follows society's rules only to avoid punishment. At this point the third structure, the *superego*, comes upon the scene.

Superego

Recall that when we discussed the resolution of the Oedipus conflict we mentioned that to reduce castration anxiety the child identifies with the same-sex parent and adopts his or her values. Freud conceptualized the superego as the repository for these *internalized* values, ideals, ethics, and morals.

The formation of superego is again analogous to cell division for it "splits off" from parts of ego and id, deriving its energy from id and its access to the reality of the outside world through the mediation of ego.

A PART OF SUPEREGO IS CONSCIOUS

The superego is the judge or arbiter of our behavior. Like ego, the superego is partly conscious, partly preconscious, and partly unconscious. The values and ideals we can readily think about are at the conscious level, those less readily available are at the preconscious level, and some that we don't even know we have are at the unconscious level. As with everything unconscious, it is difficult to imagine what unconscious values might be. Acts from which we refrain without knowing why, such as incest and cannibalism, might serve as an example.

GUILT, PRIDE, AND THE EGO IDEAL

Unlike ego the superego has no access to the external world. It gets its ideas of right and wrong from ego's (sometimes painful) discoveries about the rules and values of society and it enforces its judgments by influencing ego's actions. To do that superego has a powerful punishment, *guilt*, and a potent reward, *pride*. To serve as a reference point for its judgments, superego maintains within itself the *ego ideal*. That, essentially, is the person's notion of what he or she ought to be.

"Ought" and "should" are the vocabulary of superego.

A Delicate Balance

The interaction of the three structures—id, ego, and superego— and their relationship to the outside world can be thought of as follows: Id makes a demand, ego seeks to meet it, the outside world may or may not make it possible, and superego may or may not approve it. Keeping these often incompatible requirements in balance is yet another, and extremely important, task for busy ego.

THE THREAT OF DISINTEGRATION

Not only is ego responsible for the various cognitive functions, but it must also (and often at the same time) obtain judgments of right and wrong from superego, restrain the impulses of id, and check the expectations, rules, and opportunities of the outside world. Should id become too demanding, the reality of the world too stressful, or superego too punishing, the delicate balance that the ego is responsible to maintain would disintegrate. With ego thus overwhelmed it could no longer carry out its functions effectively and the person would experience what in Freud's day was called "a nervous breakdown."

ANXIETY AND THE DEFENSE MECHANISMS

Whenever there is a threat to the delicate balance ego is charged to maintain, it receives an alarm signal. That signal is *anxiety*. Anxiety is an emotion similar to fear, except that fear has a specific target, whereas anxiety is a more general, vague feeling of dread.

Defense Mechanisms

Anxiety is an unpleasant sensation and, like all unpleasant sensations and experiences, the person's ego seeks to avoid or escape from it. To do so, ego resorts to one or more strategies that serve to reduce anxiety and forestall the threatened disintegration of which the anxiety is a signal. The strategies are known as *ego defenses* or *defense mechanisms*. They defend against anxiety and serve to maintain the integration of personality, permitting ego to continue carrying out its many functions.

Before we look at some of the defense mechanisms, it is important to stress that ego's use of them takes place at the unconscious level. We do not resort to them intentionally, nor are we aware of using them. In fact, because many of these defenses are ways of deceiving ourselves, they would lose their effectiveness if we were to become aware of using them.

REPRESSION

Repression is ego's most fundamental, first line of defense. It consists of simply pushing unacceptable impulses and disturbing memories below the level of awareness and holding them at the unconscious level. Repressed material is never destroyed and is likely to rise to the conscious level when ego lets down its guard. That is the case during sleep when (as Freud taught) repressed material manifests itself in dreams, or when the person is under the influence of a repression-inhibiting drug, such as alcohol, so that repressed impulses can find expression.

Maintaining repression of id's many unacceptable impulses would require a lot of ego's energy and not leave enough for taking care of its many other important functions. It is therefore fortunate that ego has additional defense mechanisms available that it can use to reduce or divert the pressure of repressed material. (These are the safety valves from the hydrodynamic model).

PROJECTION

When *projection* is used as a defense mechanism, the person's own unacceptable impulses are attributed to ("projected onto") others. Once such projection has taken place, the individual often expends a great deal of energy persecuting those on whom his or her own impulses have been cast off. It seems that ego, unable adequately to deal with the inner impulses, feels better equipped to deal with those others presumably have. That, of course, is usually untrue and shows that projection is not an effective defense. Nor is it a constructive defense for it ruins one's relationship with other people.

Like all defense mechanisms projection is unconscious, but one can imagine it working as if the person were saying, "It is not *I* who is interested in pornography, it is *they*, and because pornography is bad, there ought to be a law prohibiting it so that they can be punished."

REACTION FORMATION

In *reaction formation* ego again provides an indirect outlet for the pressures exerted by a repressed impulse. This time, however, the unconscious impulse is turned into its direct opposite, and finds expression at the conscious level. A mother's impulse to hurt her child, unacceptable to both superego and society, might, through reaction formation, find expression in overly concerned, overprotective, energy-consuming "smothering." Such behavior usually impairs the child's social development so that the mother's reaction formation may be as damaging as the impulse against which it was meant to defend. Like projection, reaction formation is neither effective nor constructive.

SUBLIMATION

Not all defense mechanisms have such pernicious consequences as projection and reaction formation. *Sublimation* is usually effective and constructive. Here the energy of the unacceptable impulse is converted into socially acceptable behavior and given expression in this refined form. An unacceptable aggressive impulse, for example, might be given an outlet in chopping wood or racing a speedboat; the infantile (and severely punished) anal impulse to play with feces might be sublimated through working with clay or oil paints. Freud saw all cultural endeavors or achievements as the consequence of sublimated primitive impulses. It should be noted that explaining the origin of a painting in this fashion does not diminish the artistic value of the picture or one's ability to admire it.

DENIAL

When the defense mechanism of *denial* is used, the source of anxiety is usually a perception that, if its true meaning were recognized, might overwhelm ego's ability to function. An example of denial can be seen in a woman who feels a lump in her breast, but refuses to acknowledge that it might be cancer and therefore fails to consult a physician. If denial were put into words (which it isn't because the defense is unconscious), it would be, "It just isn't true." That, of course, shows that denial is yet another defense which can have dire consequences.

RATIONALIZATION

Related to denial is the defense mechanism of *rationalization*. Ego resorts to it when the person's *self-image* is threatened. The self-image, as we said earlier, is maintained by ego and consists of the ideas one has about oneself. When a student with the self-image of being the best in her class does poorly on an exam and blames it on the teacher's unfair grading, she is using rationalization.

This "sour grapes" strategy of finding a rational-sounding reason for one's failures or failings is again an unconscious device and not a consciously made-up excuse. The difference between a rationalization and an excuse is that the individual who uses it honestly believes the rationalization, whereas he or she knows that the excuse hides the real reason.

Is rationalization a constructive defense? Not if it keeps the student in our example from preparing herself better for the next exam.

DISPLACEMENT

With *displacement* we are again dealing with an id-originating impulse that ego, having consulted superego and checked the external reality for likely consequences, finds unacceptable. If the impulse were given expression, either superego or the environment or both would mete out punishment and would threaten the integration of the personality so that ego would experience anxiety. This mechanism is thus designed not to escape from already existing anxiety, but to avoid it.

An example of displacement is the behavior of a man who is angry at his boss. If he expressed that anger by attacking the boss he would be fired (an external reality). He therefore represses his anger and takes it home. There he might let out the anger toward his wife, but that would make him feel guilty (a superego consequence) or she might refuse to cook his dinner (another external reality). At that point he comes across the family dog and kicks him "for no apparent reason" because the reason was his unconscious displacement of the anger he could not let out at the boss. Constructive? Well, he kept his job and got his dinner, but pity the poor dog.

Defense Mechanism	Operation of the Mechanism
Repression	Threat is pushed below level of awareness
Projection	Unacceptable impulse is attributed to others
Reaction Formation	Unacceptable impulse is turned into its opposite
Regression	Returning to an immature developmental level, usually one at which fixation occurred
Displacement	Aggressive impulse is expressed toward a safe target
Sublimation	Unacceptable impulse is given socially acceptable outlet
Rationalization	Giving an acceptable reason for unacceptable behavior or a failure to have behaved appropriately
Denial	Refusal to accept threatening information

Table 3.2 The major mechanisms of defense postulated by Freud

REGRESSION

Some people defend by *regression* against the anxiety associated with actual or potential trauma, such as the loss of a loved one, dismissal from a job, the house burning down, the loss of a limb, or failure in an important task. This typically finds expression in immature behavior that was appropriate at an earlier stage of development, but is maladaptive at the person's present age. An adult's regression to early childhood may take the form of inordinate dependency, excessive eating or drinking, or an increased desire to sleep.

Regression often reveals the developmental stage at which the individual had experienced *fixation*. That, as discussed earlier, was seen by Freud as the consequence of an uneven transition from one developmental stage to the next. Inasmuch as immature behavior is by definition maladaptive, regression is another mechanism that is other than constructive.

Combinations of Defenses

Although we discussed these defense mechanisms one at a time, they do not necessarily occur alone. As already pointed out, repression is usually the first line of defense, with other mechanisms being called upon to defuse the explosion-threatening state. These other mechanisms often work in unison, each supporting the other, as if shoring up a tottering structure.

"I get a kick out of chopping wood" (sublimation) may be said by the same man who tells us, "I'm not hostile, he is" (projection) and says, "I do not despise him, I really respect him" (reaction formation), "but I can't stand his brother" (displacement) and who later reports, "I had to hit him or he would have killed me" (rationalization).

PSYCHOPATHOLOGY

Two Sources

Freud saw two possible ways in which psychological disorders, *psychopathology*, might come about: Either the defense mechanisms fail and ego is overwhelmed by anxiety and unable to function, or anxiety is so great that one or more of these mechanisms comes to operate in an exaggerated fashion.

WHEN EGO DEFENSES FAIL

When the defense mechanisms fail to defend ego against the anxiety that signals a disintegration of the carefully maintained balance of id demands, superego commands, and the reality of the environment and ego is overwhelmed by anxiety, it ceases to cope adequately with the demands of everyday life. This might manifest itself in the extreme and disabling fears called *phobias*. In the extreme case, when ego loses control over id impulses and repressed memories, these may emerge in very primitive behavior, *delusions* or *hallucinations*, in which case the individual is considered to be *psychotic*.

Just as ego can come to be overwhelmed by id impulses, it can also become the victim of an excessively strict and punitive superego. As a result, ego experiences strong and irrational guilt that it must constantly seek to assuage. To accomplish this, ego might cause the person (unconsciously) to seek punishment in the form of frequent accidents or so-called *masochistic* behavior. People like this often have the feelings of worthlessness and sadness that are marks of *depression* and can lead to suicide—the ultimate punishment.

WHEN DEFENSES WORK OVERTIME

In the second scenario, that where one or more of the defense mechanisms works excessively to reduce anxiety, different disorders may result, depending on the mechanism involved. If the mechanism is projection, for example, a man may come to see other people as hostile and in need of being carefully watched lest they do him harm. This *paranoid* behavior is typical of one form of *schizophrenia*. When denial is the excessive defense, the individual may develop a physical ailment that has no medical cause. Freud called this *conversion hysteria*; it is now referred to as *conversion disorder*. An example of this is *hysterical blindness*, which would keep the individual from seeing threatening scenes and permit their existence to be denied.

PSYCHOANALYSIS

Patients and Subjects

Freud, as we said earlier, developed the technique of *psychoanalysis* both as a tool for investigations of personality and as a method for treating the disorders of personality he called *neuroses*. Those on whom he used psychoanalysis were, with one exception, individuals who had come to his consulting room for help with problems that prevented them from functioning as well as they wished. These people thus were both his patients and the subjects for his study of personality. The one exception was Freud himself because he became his own subject when he performed a unique "self-analysis." In addition to using psychoanalysis with living persons, Freud also employed it to explore the personality of the long-dead Leonardo da Vinci, using an approach that has come to be known as *psychobiography*.

The Basis of the Method

Psychoanalysis as a treatment for psychological disorders is based on the assumption that they have their origin in unconscious conflicts among id, ego, and superego. As developed by Freud and practiced by *psychoanalysts* who still use his traditional method, the treatment is an intensive and time-consuming attempt to bring these conflicts to the conscious level so that ego can resolve them with the help of the psychoanalyst.

Principal Features

The principal features of psychoanalysis, whether as therapy or investigative method, are *free association, interpretation, resistance,* and *insight*. These features, together with the individual who lies on the famous couch and hour-long sessions four or five times a week, are the identifying characteristics of psychoanalysis. There are many other forms of *psychotherapy* that employ Freudian principles and have some of these features, but the term "psychoanalysis" should be applied only to a treatment that has these traditional characteristics.

FREE ASSOCIATION

At the beginning of psychoanalysis the patient (or "analysand") is instructed and taught to say whatever comes to mind, even if it doesn't make sense, is impolite, embarrassing, indecent, or unimportant. Such *free association* is difficult because most of us have learned early in our childhood to censor what we say, so that it is logical, polite, and proper. To facilitate this difficult task, the analysand lies on a couch and the psychoanalyst (or "analyst") sits at its head, out of the patient's sight.

INTERPRETATION

By listening to the patient's free associations the analyst detects unconscious material as it surfaces in disguised or symbolic form. Though silent most of the time, the analyst occasionally offers an *interpretation*. This consists of telling the patient the meaning of what she or he has brought forth. *Dreams* play a role in psychoanalysis in that the analysand also free-associates to their content. Inasmuch as dreams are already closer to unconscious material than waking thoughts, they are particularly useful in psychoanalysis.

Transference. In the course of as intense an experience as psychoanalysis, the patient inevitably develops feelings about the analyst. These may be positive or negative. When they are inappropriate or excessive they are referred to as a *transference*. These are thought to be a form of *displacement* of feelings the patient has or had toward significant figures (a parent, spouse, or boss) in his or her life. Like all other material the patient brings to therapy, the analyst uses the transference as the basis for interpretation.

RESISTANCE

Recall that memories and impulses at the unconscious level were repressed because ego found them threatening. When the psychoanalyst now attempts to bring such unconscious material to awareness the patient often shows *resistance*. This can take the form of not reporting a disturbing dream, of coming late to a therapy session, of denying the accuracy of an interpretation, or of impeding treatment progress by a strong negative transference— that is, by hating the therapist and engaging in verbal attacks. If therapy is to progress, resistance must be overcome and the method for doing this is to interpret it.

INSIGHT

After much work psychoanalysis advances to the point where the patient is able to accept more and more of the analyst's interpretations. Such acceptance, called *insight*, must not only make sense at an intellectual level; it must also feel right at the emotional level. When that happens the treatment is moving forward. Eventually the patient's strengthened ego should be able to deal with the old conflicts in a mature fashion and to lay them to rest instead of having to resort to maladaptive defense mechanisms in dealing with them. Applying the insights gained in treatment and making use of them in daily life is called *working through*.

PSYCHOANALYTIC THEORY IN PERSPECTIVE

At the beginning of this chapter we said that Freud's is the most comprehensive formulation of personality ever produced and praised the magnitude of his achievement. It does not detract from this achievement to point out that the formulation is not without shortcomings. This should not come as a surprise considering the fact that *The Interpretation of Dreams*, the first of Freud's many books in which he outlined his psychoanalytic theory, was published in 1900, almost one hundred years ago.

Strengths and Weaknesses

Research conducted since Freud's time has confirmed that people are often unaware of the motivations that influence their behavior and that they engage in thoughts and actions that reduce anxiety and guilt. It is also well established that experiences encountered in childhood can profoundly influence a person's adult behavior and that family relationships are sometimes wrought with conflict.

On the other hand, there are many concepts and assumptions in Freud's formulations that are stated in such ambiguous fashion that their validity cannot be put to an empirical test. This limits the utility of the theory. How, for example, is one to ascertain whether there is such a force as libido or a guiding rule like the pleasure principle? What precisely is meant by castration anxiety, and how can one find out whether statements patients produce during free association do indeed reflect material from the unconscious level?

Many of the shortcomings of Freud's theoretical formulations stem from the fact that they are inferences based on observations he (and he alone) made in his clinical practice on a relatively small number of people who had come to him for help with problems they considered to be psychological. Not only that, but these people came from a highly educated, financially comfortable segment of Viennese society who may or may not have been representative of the general population. Freud's conclusions about the Oedipus conflict and the development of superego, for example, might thus have been correct in the case of his disturbed patients, but it is unlikely that they apply to all four-year-old children, regardless of where they live and who their parents are.

Freud paid little attention to the role brothers and sisters play in a child's development. Nor did he consider how a child might acquire gender-appropriate behavior when the same-sex parent is absent. His view of the behavior and role of women was singularly biased and his ideas about the causes of such disorders as depression and schizophrenia neglected the important role of biological factors. Much of this inevitably reflects the time in which Freud lived and we are no doubt as limited now as he was then in knowing what the world will be like a hundred years hence. In that connection it is important to recognize that Freud continued almost to the last days of his life to modify and revise his theory, which he always saw as an edifice under construction and not as a finished product.

Sigmund Freud's psychoanalytic theory has had a tremendous influence on Western culture. He used psychoanalysis both as a method of treatment and as a technique for studying personality. His fundamental concepts—instincts (or drives) and libido (or sexual energy)—are based on a hydrodynamic model. In formulating psychological development Freud placed great emphasis on sexual impulses and how these are aroused and satisfied in the course of the mother's care of her child. From this stem the notions of the oral, anal, and phallic stages. The Oedipal conflict and its resolution are seen as the basis of the person's superego, which, together with ego and id, make up the structure of personality.

A person's adult personality depends on how she or he passed through the various stages of psychosexual development. Fixation at any of these stages may result in the person having an oral, anal, or phallic character, while failure to resolve the Oedipus conflict may cause later difficulties in relating to the opposite sex.

An important aspect of mental life is that a large part of it goes on at an unconscious level where much of our behavior originates. Id, which is entirely unconscious, constantly seeks outlets for its primitive impulses that ego seeks to repress. Ego's many tasks of engaging in cognitive processes, checking the reality of the environment, and controlling id are complicated by the commands emanating from superego, which punishes infractions with guilt.

When the carefully maintained integration of personality is threatening to come apart, ego experiences anxiety against which it uses a variety of defense mechanisms, such as repression, projection, reaction formation, and sublimation, to list a few.

When these defense mechanisms don't work or work excessively, the person may develop a psychological disorder or psychopathology. Freud used psychoanalysis to treat such disorders. That treatment entails free association, interpretation, transference, resistance, and insight.

Viewing psychoanalytic theory in perspective and with the benefit of nearly a hundred years of hindsight, one can recognize it for the tremendous accomplishment it represents while acknowledging its many shortcomings. The latter led to modifications and revisions of the theory which we will examine in the following chapter.

Selected Readings

Freud, S. 1965. *The Psychopathology of Everyday Life*. New York: Norton. (Original publication in 1901).

_____. 1966. *Introductory Lectures on Psychoanalysis*. New York: Norton. (Original publication in 1917).

Gay, P. (ed.). 1989. *The Freud Reader*. New York: Norton.

_____. 1988. *Freud: A Life for Our Time*. New York: Norton.

Gilman, S. L. (ed.). 1982. *Introducing Psychoanalytic Theory*. New York: Brunner/Mazel.

4

Psychoanalytic Theory: Dissent, Revisions, and Elaborations

*S*igmund Freud's theory won both supporters and dissenters who proposed
*alternatives, revisions, or elaborations. Some of these dissenters objected
to Freud's insistence that the basic motivation is of a sexual nature, with
the Oedipus conflict a central feature of human development. Others found
his exclusive focus on the immediate family too limiting or believed that he
had neglected important cognitive processes in his stress on unconscious
conflicts.*

*Carl Jung and Alfred Adler were among the first of Freud's contem-
poraries to dissent from his views. Jung formed his own comprehensive
theory of personality, whereas Adler was primarily concerned with expanding the interpersonal aspects of Freud's work. Adler questioned whether
conflicts over sexual impulses were the basic source of anxiety. He pointed
to the infant's small size and helplessness as crucial to personality development. Karen Horney, who made a similar point, also objected to Freud's
male-oriented point of view and proposed a reformulation of the Oedipus
conflict.*

*Erich Fromm elaborated psychoanalytic theory from a sociopolitical
perspective, moving the emphasis from the individual to society as a whole.
Interpersonal relationship was also the principal focus of the revisions
proposed by Harry Stack Sullivan. Following Anna Freud's lead, Heinz
Hartmann and Erik Erikson broadened the scope of psychoanalysis to*

include more detailed concern with ego's cognitive functions. More drastic modifications of Freudian principles were advocated by Melanie Klein, Margaret Mahler, and Ronald Fairbairn, the object relations theorists, who introduced novel formulations about the early interactions between mother and infant in explaining later personality development.

The various elaborations, revisions, and modifications to Freud's theory broadened its perspective to cover social and intellectual aspects of human behavior, but they often introduced concepts that defy objective definition.

AREAS OF DISSENT

A few years after Freud had begun work on his psychoanalytic theory there gathered around him a small group of young physicians who were interested in studying his treatment method. Freud also maintained an active correspondence with physicians in other parts of Europe, particularly Wilhelm Fliess [pronounced: FLEES] in Berlin and Carl Gustav Jung [pronounced YOONG] in Switzerland. In the course of these exchanges some differences of opinion emerged.

These differences focused primarily on the importance of libido theory, the premise that sexual motivation is responsible not only for human development, but is also the source of conflict, anxiety, and neurosis. Freud regarded that premise as basic to his theory and was unwilling to modify, let alone abandon, it. As a result, several of his early followers left him and developed their own theories, which, at Freud's insistence, they gave names other than "psychoanalysis." The first of these dissidents was the Swiss psychiatrist Carl Gustav Jung (1875–1961), who named his theory *analytic psychology.*

JUNG'S ANALYTIC PSYCHOLOGY

Although Jung, like Freud, had studied medicine, his interests encompassed theology (Western as well as Eastern philosophy and religion), archaeology, anthropology, spiritualism, mythology, and several other areas of scholarship. These interests are reflected in his theory, which rivals Freud's in comprehensiveness and surpasses it in complexity.

Human Motives

Jung rejected Freud's insistence on the centrality of sex and postulated that human beings are motivated as much by their aims and aspirations as by their sexual urges. The *attainment of self-hood*, a *striving for growth*, and *creative self-actualization* were to him the basic motivations of human behavior. This *humanistic* orientation mirrors Jung's wide-ranging interests as much as Freud's theory reflects the struggles of the patients to whose free associations he listened in his consulting room.

The Components of Personality

Jung saw personality as composed of three basic units: *ego*, a *personal unconscious*, and a *collective unconscious* containing *archetypes*.

EGO

Unlike Freud's ego which is only partly at the conscious level, all of Jung's *ego* is conscious. It contains the feelings, thoughts, perceptions, and memories of which we are aware. Ego provides us with our sense of identity and continuity as a person, with the "I" feeling, and—as in Freud's theory—it is responsible for managing our affairs.

THE PERSONAL UNCONSCIOUS

The *personal unconscious* is in many ways similar to what Freud viewed as the preconscious aspect of ego. Here are stored the half-remembered events, names, and fleeting perceptions that can be brought to conscious awareness without too much difficulty. When some of this content is organized around one particular person or event, it forms a *complex* that may come to dominate the individual's personality. For example, a man who has a "mother complex" guides his actions by what his mother would like and her image is uppermost in his mind.

THE COLLECTIVE UNCONSCIOUS

The *collective unconscious* is a unique and highly controversial feature of Jung's personality theory. Whereas the personal unconscious contains memories from the individual's own life, the collective unconscious represents, in Jung's words, the "ancestral experience from untold millions of years" and "the echo of prehistoric world events to which each century adds an infinitesimally small amount."

Jung saw the collective unconscious not only as the source of much of our vitality and creativity, but also as the basis of neurotic and irrational behavior. Inasmuch as all humans share a collective unconscious, it accounts for universal tendencies to react with the same feelings to specific situations, figures, and symbols, so-called *archetypes*.

ARCHETYPES

Archetypes are images that evoke powerful emotions, based on experiences humankind has shared since time immemorial. All human ancestors experienced a mother, felt pain, saw death and darkness, and the rising of the sun. These memories live on in each of us and make us react to them and to the words and symbols that stand for them in similar ways.

Among Jung's archetypes are deity, child, hero, great mother, witch, and wise old man. The universality of these archetypes can be traced in dreams, myths, religion, and primitive art. Four archetypes Jung considered of particular importance. They are animus and anima, the shadow, the persona, and the self.

Animus and *anima* are the archetypical images women and men have of each other. Her animus is a woman's innate notions about men, whereas his anima is a man's innate ideas about women. Moreover, animus represents the masculine side of a woman's personality, just as anima stands for the feminine side of the personality of a man.

The archetype of the *shadow* is the evil, animalistic side of human nature. It accounts for our aggressive, cruel, and immoral aspects. The *persona*, on the other hand, is the socially acceptable mask people wear in public, and the *self* represents the innate tendency to seek a balance and integration among the various elements of the personality. To a certain extent, Jung's self and shadow function like Freud's ego and id.

Symbols. Jung put much emphasis on symbols, believing that they represent archetypical ideas that cannot be fully expressed in words. For example, he maintained that still waters, the full moon, or the inside of a church arouse feelings of awe or devotion in us because they are mother-symbols. To analyze a symbol one must consider two aspects. One is its meaning in terms of the past of the person and the species; the other is its meaning in terms of the future of humankind.

Two Personality Types

Jung proposed that in their relationships to others people employ one of two basic attitudes or orientations: *extraversion* and *introversion*. The extravert tends to be a sociable, friendly, outgoing person who is involved with the outside world. The introvert, on the other hand, is likely to be reserved and withdrawn, interested more in his or her own ideas than in interactions with others.

Jung saw extraversion and introversion as inborn characteristics that can be modified through experiences in later life. The archetype of self, in fact, does not become fully formed until a person's adult years. In this, Jung differs from Freud, who viewed a person's character to be determined through experiences in early childhood and subject to later changes only with the greatest of difficulties.

Type	Function	Basis for Action	Example
Extravert	Thinking	Intellectual considerations	A social activist
	Feeling	Expectations of others	A conformist
	Sensing	Search for pleasant sensations	A connoisseur
	Intuiting	Guesses and hunches	A speculator
Introvert	Thinking	Self-generated ideas	A philosophical hermit
	Feeling	Profoundly felt revelations	A religious hermit
	Sensing	Subjective sensations	A creative artist
	Intuiting	Personal images	A visionary prophet

Table 4.1 Jung's personality types and functions

FOUR FUNCTIONS

Extraversion and introversion interact with four psychological functions—*thinking, feeling, sensing,* and *intuiting*—to produce eight ways of relating to the world and making sense of one's experiences. Three examples: the extraverted thinking type, the introverted thinking type, and the extraverted feeling type. Both extraverts and introverts who use thinking interpret their experiences by reason and logic, whereas those who use feeling judge events as to whether they are pleasant or unpleasant. Those who employ sensing rely on their sensations, and those who use intuiting react in terms of their hunches.

A Research Method

Although much of Jung's theorizing was based on his studies of such esoteric sources as ancient myths, modern fairy tales, alchemy, astrology, mental telepathy, and clairvoyance (Hall and Lindzey, 1978), he also employed a clinical procedure that is still in use: *word association.* He presented lists of words to his patients to determine which produced irregularities in breathing and changes in the electrical resistance of the skin. From these signs he inferred that a word was disturbing the patient, pointing to a *complex.*

Analytic Psychology in Perspective

Jung's emphasis on striving for growth, attainment of self-hood, and creative self-actualization makes his contribution a welcome alternative to Freud's rather dismal view of human nature. The concepts of introversion and extraversion he highlighted continue to generate research, and his focus on symbols fascinates many. However, by the criteria of utility and parsimony we discussed in chapter 2, Jung's formulations cannot be viewed as a theory. His provocative notion of the collective unconscious, the concept of universal archetypes, and the idea that symbols hold connotations about the future are not only impossible to put to an empirical test, but they are also incompatible with contemporary knowledge in biology, genetics, psychology, and the philosophy of science.

THE INDIVIDUAL PSYCHOLOGY OF ALFRED ADLER

Cooperation, not Conflict

Alfred Adler (1870–1937) had been a member of the original group of young physicians who regularly met with Freud and who helped him found the Vienna Psychoanalytic Association. Like Jung, Adler took issue with Freud's almost exclusive emphasis on sexual impulses as the source of human motivation and his focus on the conflict between these impulses and the dictates of society. Adler maintained that it is a basic aspect of human nature to be cooperative, to be interested in the welfare of other people, and to seek perfection both in themselves and in society. Thus, where Freud saw biological forces placing the individual into inevitable conflict with society, Adler saw familial and social factors shaping the individual. Freud refused to accept the modifications Adler advocated, and they parted company under what seems to have been rather acrimonious circumstances. In 1933 Adler emigrated to the United States.

TRACES OF PERSONAL CONCERNS

Just as Jung's formulation of analytical psychology reveals many traces of his personal interests in such topics as mythology, religion, and astrology, so does Adler's *individual psychology* bear the hallmarks of his personal concerns.

Adler had been a weak and sickly child. He almost died from pneumonia and suffered from a calcium deficiency that softened his bones and made joining in physical activities with his friends a strain and an effort. He went to medical school to become a physician in an effort to conquer death and his own fear of death. While practicing medicine he developed a theory that states that people deal with *organ inferiority*—that is, with a weakness in any part of their body—by compensating and at times *over*compensating for that weakness. Someone with a weak arm, for example, might compensate by many hours of exercise and overcompensate by becoming a champion weight lifter.

Inferiority, Superiority, and Birth Order

In developing his personality theory, Adler extended the notion of organ inferiority in the physical realm to a *sense of inferiority* in the psychological realm. He believed that everyone has a sense of inferiority and that this sense motivates people to compensate for it by *striving for superiority*. That, it should be stressed, is not a competitive striving to be better than others, but a positive seeking for overcoming imperfections and personal completion.

The reason for Adler's belief that a sense of inferiority is a normal and universal human condition is that all of us are born small and weak into a world of larger and stronger adults. Moreover, our position in the *birth order*, whether we are an only, middle, or youngest child, may lead to other comparisons that make one feel inferior, as may comparisons of one's own family with those of others.

Style of Life

Depending on the source of one's sense of inferiority, the innate, compensatory striving for superiority will take a distinct, individualized form and determine one's *style of life*. There are, of course, some people who either overcompensate or fail fully to compensate for the sense of inferiority. That condition, which Adler called an *inferiority complex*, manifests itself in impaired personal adjustment or difficulty in interpersonal relationships.

Social Interest

Striving for superiority is at first based on the need to overcome one's own sense of inferiority. Once the healthy individual has achieved superiority, however, the motivation for completion and perfection comes to extend to the welfare of others and to the institutions of society. Adler viewed *social interest* as the distinguishing characteristic of the well-adjusted person and as the goal of treatment for those who seek therapeutic help.

Creative Self

Although we are by nature disposed to have a sense of inferiority and innately inclined to compensate for this by striving for superiority, the style of life we adopt and how we express our social interests are matters of *personal choice*. Unlike Freud, who saw behavior determined by dark, unconscious forces, or Jung, who postulated primordial experiences that control how we relate to the world, Adler maintained that we are able consciously to choose our actions and our goal. He labeled this ability the *creative self*, thus placing a conscious self at the core of personality.

Individual Psychology in Perspective

Much of Adler's contribution reflects his personal background and his social philosophy and political convictions. Individual psychology contains many value judgments with which one might agree or disagree, but they are not capable of being put to an empirical test. For that reason one hesitates to call Adler's work a theory that might be judged by the criteria of utility and parsimony.

Nevertheless, individual psychology stands as an attractive alternative to the mechanistic formulations of Freud and the mystic pronouncements of Jung. Adler's is an optimistic formulation that endows the human with altruism, cooperation, creativity, uniqueness, and awareness. It is a socially oriented, humanistic statement about personality and, as such, the forerunner of others.

THE CONTRIBUTIONS OF KAREN HORNEY

The Shifting Focus

The shift of focus from internal, basically biological motivations to external, essentially social determinants that characterize Adler's formulations continues in the contributions of *Karen Horney* (pronounced HORN-eye) (1885–1952). Horney was born and educated in Europe, received psychoanalytic training in Berlin under two of Freud's early followers, and came to the United States in 1932 in the depths of the Great Depression.

Horney soon discovered that the patients she saw in her psychoanalytic practice were far more troubled by concerns about keeping or finding a job than about problems in the sexual realm. This led her to question the universality of Freud's formulations about unacceptable sexual impulses and the Oedipus conflict. She focused instead on the individual's relationship to her or his social environment.

Basic Anxiety

Central to Horney's theorizing is the concept of *basic anxiety*. She defined this as the child's feelings of being isolated and helpless in a hostile world. Basic anxiety bears some similarity to Adler's feelings of inferiority, but there is an important difference. Where, for Adler, inferiority is the unavoidable result of being smaller than those around you, Horney saw nothing inevitable about feeling isolated and helpless, for that depends on your perceiving the world as hostile. When the world, which for the young child consists of the immediate family, is perceived as warm, accepting, affectionate, and consistent, the child will feel loved and secure, not isolated and helpless.

THREE STRATEGIES

Psychological difficulties in adulthood emerge only when childhood experiences lead to the development of basic anxiety that the person must defend against by resorting to certain strategies. These strategies, Horney maintained, manifest themselves in *neurotic patterns* of relating to other people. These can take one of three forms: *moving toward people* (seeking affection by submission and dependency), *moving away from people* (seeking independence by isolation and withdrawal), or *moving against people* (seeking power by aggression and attack).

The healthy adult seeks certain amounts of affection, independence, and power. It is when one of these needs comes to be the central, all-encompassing theme of the person's way of interacting with others that his or her relationships will suffer. That is what concerned Horney.

Her theoretical contribution is thus more a formulation of how people become disturbed than a comprehensive view of personality, such as Freud and Jung had attempted.

REFORMULATION OF THE OEDIPUS CONFLICT

Among Freud's formulations that Horney challenged are the centrality and universality of the Oedipus conflict in establishing a person's gender identity. Although she agreed that around the age of four or five many children manifest jealousy, rivalry, and mixed feelings of love and hatred for their parents, she felt that this behavior was not a sexual phenomenon but a manifestation of the child's attempts to cope with basic anxiety. That anxiety, as already stated, stems from the child's helplessness in the face of parental domination and lack of acceptance. Here, as elsewhere, Horney interprets as deviant and avoidable what Freud had seen as normal and inevitable.

Feminine Psychology

Another area in which Horney challenged Freudian assertions was in the psychology of women. As early as 1923 she wrote *Feminine Psychology* (Horney, 1967), in which she took issue with some of Freud's more blatantly sexist assertions about the motivations of women. He had maintained, for example, that (all) girls are severely traumatized when they discover that they lack a boy's penis, causing them to have *penis envy* and to wish being as well equipped as the more fortunate males.

Motivated by penis envy, girls will first seek to possess their father (the Electra conflict mentioned in chapter 3) and, failing that, wish to give birth to male children who could symbolically furnish them with a penis. Moreover, declared Freud, because they lack a penis women are anatomically destined to be (or feel to be) inferior to men.

Horney rejected all of this, declaring that the status of women is determined by culture and not by anatomy. She pointed out that where men dominate the resources and rewards of society, women may wish to want to be like men, not because they want penises but because they want to share the benefits and privileges enjoyed by men.

THE CONTRIBUTIONS OF ERICH FROMM

*A Social
Scientist*

Like Horney, Erich Fromm (1900–1980) was born in Germany, where he received psychoanalytic training before fleeing Hitler's regime in 1933 and emigrating to the United States. Unlike Horney, Adler, and Freud, however, Fromm was not a physician with an M.D. degree, but a social scientist with a Ph.D. degree and training in sociology, political science, and philosophy. That background, tempered by humanistic convictions and Marxist theory, influenced most of Fromm's writing.

*Basic Human
Striving*

Continuing the move from Freud's biological orientation to an emphasis on socio-cultural determinants of personality, Fromm maintained that human personality was best understood as resulting from interactions between the individual and society.

Human beings, so Fromm asserted, basically strive for freedom and autonomy but they also need to feel connected and related to others. How this conflict between the need to be free and the need to belong is resolved depends on the economic structure of society. A capitalist system emphasizes the individual's opportunity, freedom of choice, and personal responsibility at the price of intense feelings of isolation and loneliness. People deal with this *alienation* in different ways, and much of Fromm's work concerns this issue.

ESCAPE FROM FREEDOM

One way of coping with the personal loneliness Fromm saw as the product of a capitalist society is to trade the individuality and choice it offers for an authoritarian system in which the individual is submerged in the group and told what to do by a powerful leader. Fromm (1941) referred to this as an *escape from freedom*. Here we can again detect the influence of personal experience on the theorist's theory. Living in Germany, Fromm had seen Hitler's rise to power firsthand, and his hypothesis about escape from freedom helped him explain why the German people behaved as they did.

FIVE ORIENTATIONS

In later writings, Fromm (1947) elaborated on his notion that humans' need for freedom and autonomy conflicts with their desire for being connected and related to others. To deal with the loneliness that the economic system engenders, people adopt one of the following five *orientations* or character types. Only one of these (the last) is constructive and productive in terms of self and society.

Receptive. In adopting this orientation, the individual passively leans on support from such outside agents as the state, the church, parents, colleagues, or friends.

Exploitative. Here the person takes advantage of others, either by outwitting them or by the use of force. Everybody is seen as an object to be exploited and the person's prevailing attitude is one of hostility and manipulation, coupled with envy, jealousy, and cynicism.

Hoarding. The person who has adopted this orientation equates security with acquisition and refuses either to share or to spend. Other people, such as a spouse, are viewed as possessions; the future is seen as uncertain, and thoughts generally dwell on an idealized past.

Marketing. From the standpoint of the person with this orientation nothing has intrinsic value. People's worth is defined by how much money they have; possessions, by how much they cost or would bring if sold. Being "well liked" is a prime consideration, and the person therefore engages in whatever behavior is deemed to bring success.

Productive. This orientation is adopted by the healthy, mature, fully functioning person who makes optimal use of his or her abilities and strengths, striving for personal growth and the betterment of society. Fromm describes such a person as rational, creative, loving, optimistic, and forward-looking.

THE CONTRIBUTIONS OF HARRY STACK SULLIVAN

An American Physician

The contributors to psychoanalytic theory discussed thus far had all been born in Europe, although Adler, Horney, and Fromm did much of their work in the United States or (in Fromm's case) in Mexico. In Harry Stack Sullivan (1892–1949) we meet the first among these dissidents who was born in the United States. Like the others (with the exception of Fromm), Sullivan was a physician, but unlike all the others, who concentrated their clinical activity on relatively well functioning neurotics, Sullivan practiced psychiatry in mental hospitals where he treated severely impaired schizophrenics.

Sullivan differs from Jung, Adler, Horney, and Fromm in yet another respect. He wrote only one book, *The Interpersonal Theory of Psychiatry*, published in 1953. This work outlines much of Sullivan's theory, but for the rest one must rely on his notes and lectures which some of his students and followers compiled and published after his death.

An Interpersonal Theory

In the work of Adler, Horney, and Fromm one can detect a trend away from Freud's focus on the personal and intrapsychic to an increasing emphasis on the environmental and social. This trend culminates with

Sullivan's contributions, for, as the title of his book reflects, his was a thoroughly *interpersonal theory*.

Sullivan maintained that it is meaningless to speak of personality independent of the individual's interpersonal relationships. From the moment we are born and throughout the rest of our life we are a part of an interpersonal situation that influences our thoughts and actions even when we are completely alone.

DEVELOPMENT OF THE SELF

The importance of the interpersonal situation in forming our personality lies in the fact that we evaluate ourselves in terms of the way others evaluate us. Thus the *self* is formed. When we sense others as evaluating us as good, we form a good-me self; if we perceive them as evaluating us as bad, we form a bad-me self. Major aspects of the self are established in the early years of childhood and modified in the course of becoming an adult.

THE EGO PSYCHOLOGISTS

Anna Freud and Heinz Hartmann

The trend, represented by the theorists just discussed, to place ever-increasing importance on the social environment in forming personality was accompanied by another tendency. Ever since Adler, these dissidents have increasingly concerned themselves with the functions of the ego at the expense of involvement with the demands of the id that, to Freud, had been at the root of personality.

The focus on ego functions that characterizes *ego psychology* can already be detected in *The Ego and the Mechanisms of Defense* (A. Freud, 1966), the major work of Sigmund Freud's daughter, Anna Freud (1895–1982). Trained and analyzed by her father, Anna Freud made important contributions to psychoanalytic formulations about children and adolescents.

The origin of ego psychology is generally credited to Heinz Hartmann (1894–1970), who worked with Anna Freud for many years and who, with her and others, founded the influential annual series, *The Psychoanalytic Study of the Child*. In *Ego Psychology and the Problem of Adaptation* (1958) and in many other works Hartmann spoke of an *autonomous ego* that develops and remains partially independent of the id. He maintained that there is a *conflict-free sphere* of the ego where thinking, perceiving, and learning can take place without engaging in a constant struggle with id, superego, or external reality.

FOCUS ON HEALTHY BEHAVIOR

Unlike all other theorists in the realm of psychoanalysis, ego psychologists such as Hartmann are more concerned with understanding normal development and healthy human behavior than with trying to explain and treat the behavioral aberrations of disturbed individuals. This orientation enabled these theorists to relate psychoanalytic ego psychology to the research on cognitive processes being conducted in the laboratories of mainstream academic psychology.

Erik Erikson

PSYCHOSOCIAL THEORY

Like Anna Freud, who trained him in psychoanalysis, Erik Erikson (b. 1902) is one of the few nonmedical contributors to psychoanalytic theory. Born in Germany, he had been an art teacher in a progressive private school in Vienna before he emigrated to the United States in 1933. In *Childhood and Society*, published in 1950 and revised in 1963, Erikson introduced a theory of *psychosocial development* that stands in marked contrast to Freud's formulation of psychosexual development. Erikson links ego psychology to cultural influences on personality development. He might thus be viewed as bridging the orientation of Erich Fromm and the perspective of Heinz Hartmann.

EIGHT STAGES OF DEVELOPMENT

Central to Erikson's psychosocial theory of development is the notion that personality develops according to the *epigenetic principle*. That principle is a genetically determined "blueprint" following which an organism develops complex characteristics out of an initially undifferentiated state. As Erikson applied this principle to personality, he viewed the individual as moving in stages into wider and wider social interactions.

There are eight of these stages. At each stage the individual encounters a *developmental crisis*. This crisis takes the form of an interpersonal dilemma that can be solved in a positive or a negative fashion. If the solution is positive the person is prepared to tackle the next crisis, but if the solution is negative it is likely to interfere with the resolution of the crises that will be encountered at later stages.

Erikson's stages bear a certain resemblance to those postulated by Freud, but not only is their focus on such ego processes as personal and social attitudes instead of conflicts based on id impulses, but they also cover the entire life span with particular emphasis on adolescence and adulthood. We shall present the eight stages, indicate when they occur, and outline the crisis each presents.

Stage	Age (approx.)	Crisis	Outcome	
			Success	**Failure**
Infancy	0–1	Basic trust vs. basic mistrust	Confidence in satisfaction of needs	Skepticism about need satisfaction
Early childhood	1–3	Autonomy vs. shame and doubt	Confidence in own abilities	Sense of needing help
Play age	4–5	Initiative vs. guilt	Acting on own urges and desires	Conscience restrains action
School age	6–11	Industry vs. inferiority	Satisfaction in activity	Inadequacy in skills
Adolescence	12–19	Identity vs. identity confusion	Self-confidence	Uncertain about role
Young adulthood	20–25	Intimacy vs. isolation	Fusing identity with another	Unable to love another
Adulthood	26–65	Generative vs. stagnation	Guiding the next generation	Lack of progress in career
Old age	66–death	Ego integrity vs. despair	Satisfaction with accomplishments	Hopelessness and disgust with life

Table 4.2 Erikson's stages of development, their crises, and outcome

Infancy: Basic Trust versus Basic Mistrust. In the context of the mother-child relationship, and depending on its quality, the infant develops either a feeling of basic trust (the positive solution) or a sense of basic mistrust (the negative solution) with respect to other people.

Early Childhood: Autonomy versus Shame and Doubt. As the child's ability to walk, climb, push, and talk matures he or she should develop a sense of autonomy that might be expressed as "I can do it." Failing this, the child will leave this stage with feelings of shame and doubt ("I am inadequate and incompetent"). Again, the direction in which this crisis is resolved depends on the nature of the parent-child relationship, because a feeling of autonomy can develop only when parents permit their child to try doing things on his or her own. Note also that this is more likely to be the case when the child has arrived at this stage with a feeling of basic trust ("She won't let me get hurt") already established.

Play Age: Initiative versus Guilt. Here the dilemma is between developing the ability and inclination to initiate activities and the feeling of being no good and unworthy. The working of the epigenetic principle should again be apparent, for one must already have acquired basic trust and a sense of autonomy if one is to develop an attitude of initiative and self-sufficiency.

School Age: Industry versus Inferiority. This is the age Freud labeled the latency period when presumably nothing of developmental interest is taking place. Erikson, on the other hand, stresses the importance of this stage. It is here where, in interaction with other children and teachers, children must learn to apply themselves industriously to work and play, thus developing a sense of competence. Failing that, they will emerge from this stage with damaging feelings of inferiority.

Adolescence: Identity versus Identity Confusion. Erikson referred to the task to be solved at this stage as *identity crisis*. Here young people must work out who and what they are, especially in terms of what other people think of them. At this stage the self becomes consolidated and many adolescents feel that they must "find themselves." Unless they do, they leave this stage in role confusion, unsure of who they are.

Young Adulthood: Intimacy versus Isolation. Once an identity has been established, the person is ready to move to the next stage in psychosocial development: the stage where one should be able to relate to another person with affiliation, commitment, and love. The alternative is to avoid close contacts, withdrawing into oneself, and developing a feeling of isolation.

Adulthood: Generative versus Stagnation. The relationship established in the previous stage should have prepared the individual to contribute to the next generation by raising a family or by being productive and creative in other ways that benefit society. Generativity (a word Erikson coined) should be based on the wish to be needed and not on selfish motives. A failure to solve this crisis in a positive fashion results in stagnation and boredom.

Old Age: Ego Integrity versus Despair. This stage represents the culmination of life. If all or most of the previous crises have been satisfactorily resolved, the individual should be able to look back with a feeling of contentment and satisfaction at having made even a small contribution to humankind. Disappointment, resentment, disgust, and despair will be felt by those who have grown old and approach the end of life realizing that there are no accomplishments to which they can point.

OBJECT RELATIONS THEORY

Object relations theory is an outgrowth of psychoanalytic ego psychology, to which it is closely related. Neither of these orientations has much to say about internal conflicts among id, ego, and superego. They focus instead on the individual's interactions with the social environment and ask how the helpless infant who is so dependent on others develops into an independent, more or less self-sufficient adult.

Melanie Klein

One of the first to concern herself with the question of the infant's social development was Melanie Klein (1882–1960). Originally a follower of Sigmund Freud, she later dissented from his views and entered into an intensely antagonistic relationship with the more orthodox Anna Freud.

INFANT AND MOTHER

The "object" in object relations can be a person, an animal, or an inanimate item such as a blanket or toy. Klein asserted that the newborn infant's first object is the mother; but not the whole mother, only some part of her, such as the breast. To this the infant forms an attachment that is accompanied by two conflicting feelings. On the one hand, the infant wishes to possess the object, but on the other, it is hostile and fearful toward it. This leads to a necessary developmental step: The child categorizes the world into good and bad objects.

This earliest form of object relations is followed by a stage of development in which the child begins to integrate objects. Now the mother is perceived as a whole person, but this is accompanied by the realization that this single object has both good and bad aspects. As a result, the child comes to have both positive and negative feelings about the mother, and these *ambivalent* feelings must be resolved. The resolution leads the child to the awareness that the mother is a separate figure and oneself a separate person, although one who is dependent on the mother.

In a warm, loving, and protective mother–infant relationship the steps just outlined lead eventually to constructive and productive social relationships, whereas a relationship that is marked by neglect and rejection provides the basis for envy, hostility, and anger.

Margaret Mahler

Another psychoanalyst who speculated about what goes on in the infant's mind long before language permits communication was Margaret Mahler (1897–1985). A pediatrician by training, Mahler became interested in the very close relationship between mother and child. She maintained that at birth infants do not differentiate between self and nonself but view the mother as a part of themselves. Mahler called this primitive phase *symbiosis*.

Gradually, the child forms mental images or representations of significant objects such as breast, bottle, mother, and father. This *internalization* carries with it the feelings and attitudes toward the object and these can later be elicited by either the object or by its mental image.

SEPARATION–INDIVIDUATION

Based on extensive observations Mahler divided the process by which the child separates from the mother and achieves personal autonomy into four subphases. Roughly between the fourth and eighth month of life, in the subphase of *differentiation*, the infant begins to explore the environment, using the mother as a safe base whose continued presence is frequently checked. During the next ten months, in the *practicing* subphase this exploration is expanded to a wider environment and temporary separation from the mother increases.

A critical period for future development is the *rapprochement* subphase which takes place in the second half of the first year. Now the child is torn between wanting to be close to the mother but fearing to be engulfed by her. This conflict between dependence and independence must be resolved, a rapprochement must be found, and it is here that the mother's ability to "let go" becomes crucial, lest the child fail to develop an interest in independent activities and other people.

The final subphase, *consolidation of individuality*, starts around the third year of life and, in a sense, continues into later development. It marks the beginning of what Mahler called *emotional object constancy*. This is the sense that objects have permanence that comes from having mental representations of the objects. Thus, even when mother is absent, the child knows that she continues to exist, for together with her love and approval, she is symbolically present as an internalized object.

Ronald (W. R. D.) Fairbairn

A MARKED DEPARTURE

The object relations theory advanced by the Scottish psychoanalyst Ronald Fairbairn (1889–1964) represents a marked departure from Freud's psychoanalytic theory. Fairbairn (1952) proposed that there is no id, only a *central ego* which is present at birth and has its own source of energy. Moreover, he asserted that people's primary motivation is *object seeking*, not tension reduction and pleasure seeking, as other psychoanalytic theorists had maintained.

STAGES OF DEVELOPMENT

Fairbairn believed that personality development moves through distinct stages from undifferentiated *infantile dependence*, through a *transitional stage*, to *mature dependence*. Mature or adult dependence is marked by the capacity to be a differentiated individual who is able to maintain cooperative relationships with other differentiated individuals.

EGO SPLITTING

Like other psychotherapists who sought to create a personality theory, Fairbairn wanted to explain how psychological disorders come about. Also like others, he postulated a conflict, but, there being no id, the conflict he proposed stems from the person's discordant experiences in relating to objects.

According to Fairbairn, an infant's relationship to the mother has both gratifying and ungratifying aspects. The ungratifying aspects, however, entail not only rejection and deprivation, but also enticement and promise. In the infant's view, the mother thus is composed of (1) a *gratifying mother*, (2) a *rejecting mother*, and (3) an *enticing mother*.

To cope with these conflicting aspects of the real mother the infant *internalizes* her as a mental image. The gratifying mother becomes a part of the central ego where it takes the form of an *ideal object*. Her comforting aspects become one of the person's goals.

The rejecting and enticing aspects of the internalized mother, however, can only be dealt with by *splitting the central ego*. Because ego must now devote a part of its energy to these internalized objects, the infant's normal development will be impaired. The ultimate goal of development, *mature dependence*, can be reached only if the internalized objects that caused ego to split are expelled so that the ego's entire energy can be applied to coping with the external world.

THE DISSENTERS IN PERSPECTIVE

Sigmund Freud's psychoanalytic theory of personality inspired other theorists to advocate revisions and elaborations or to propose their own formulations. With the possible exception of Jung's contribution, none succeeded or even attempted to produce as comprehensive and integrated a theory as Freud's.

Unfortunately, none of the dissenters addressed the major shortcoming of Freud's theorizing: the loose and ambiguous nature of his concepts that makes most of them impossible to evaluate with the tools of science. If anything, such notions as Jung's archetypes and collective unconscious, Horney's basic anxiety, Erikson's epigenetic principle, the internalized object of Mahler, and Fairbairn's ego splitting have contributed further obfuscation to a field that is badly in need of objective definitions and testable propositions.

Theorist	Principal Contributions
Carl Gustav Jung	Collective unconscious Archetypes Extraversion-Introversion Word Association Test
Alfred Adler	Sense of inferiority Birth order Social interest Creative self
Karen Horney	Basic anxiety Interpersonal strategies Feminine psychology
Erich Fromm	Character types (orientations) Emphasis on economic system
Harry Stack Sullivan	Focus on interpersonal relationships Development of self
Anna Freud and Heinz Hartmann	Emphasis on ego functions Focus on healthy behavior
Erik Erikson	Life-long development Developmental crises Identity
Melanie Klein	Infant–mother relationship
Margaret Mahler	Separation–Individuation
Ronald Fairbairn	Ego splitting

Table 4.3 Principal contributions of the revisionists of Freud's psychoanalytic theory

On the other hand, the theorists discussed in this chapter have helped broaden the scope of the Freudian system by recognizing that interpersonal events are at least as important as intrapsychic conflicts, that sex is not the only source of human motivation, and that confrontations with brothers, sisters, playmates, and teachers may be as important to the formation of personality as rivalry with the same-sex parent. Moreover, Jung's identification of introversion and extraversion, Adler's stress on the birth order, Horney's rejection of Freud's male-orientated formulations, Hartmann's emphasis on healthy human behavior, and Erikson's recognition that personality development is a life-long process have increased the relevance of psychoanalytic personality theory to contemporary life.

Although Sigmund Freud continued to make modifications in his psychoanalytic theory throughout his life, he was not receptive to changes suggested by his students and followers. As a result, those with divergent ideas had to develop and advocate them without Freud's approval and often against his opposition.

Carl Gustav Jung early rejected Freud's emphasis on the primacy of sexual motivation. His analytic psychology stresses the motive of self-actualization and adds a collective unconscious to the structure of personality. Other aspects of Jung's theory are archetypes such as animus, anima, shadow, and persona. He introduced introversion and extraversion as personality types and developed the word-association test as a research method.

Alfred Adler was the first of the dissidents to emphasize the individual's relationship to other people. He, too, objected to Freud's libido theory and in his individual psychology spoke of overcoming feelings of inferiority as the key to human motivation. The social orientation that sets Adler's theory apart from Freud's is also found in the contributions of Karen Horney, who identified three strategies that people use to cope with the feeling of being isolated and helpless in a hostile world. The focus of the individual's relationship to society dominates the work of Erich Fromm, who saw the basic human conflict as one between personal freedom and interpersonal connectedness.

The move from Freud's intrapsychic, libidinal focus to ever greater emphasis on environmental and social factors may be said to culminate in the interpersonal theory of Harry Stack Sullivan, who maintained that we form our self on the basis of how other people evaluate us. Paralleling the increasing focus on social factors, theorizing about personality also saw a move from Freud's preoccupation with unconscious conflicts to a concern with cognitive functions. Ego psychologists, such as Heinz Hartmann, offered formulations that stress healthy, adaptive behavior, and Erik Erikson proposed a stage theory in which personality development is viewed as a life-long process.

Whereas most of the dissidents who offered their own theories of personality had accepted some of Freud's conceptualization, the object relations theorists deviated more drastically from the traditions of psychoanalysis. Melanie Klein and Margaret Mahler offered novel ways to conceptualize the mother–infant relationship which they saw as wrought with hostility and conflict. Ronald Fairbairn reformulated Freud's three-part personality structure, insisting that there is only an ego, but an ego that is capable of splitting so that it can deal with the negative aspects of experiences to which the infant is exposed.

We pointed out that the various modifications to and elaborations of psychoanalytic theory broadened its scope by recognizing important human motivations and relationships that had been ignored or neglected in Freud's conceptualizations. At the same time, these dissidents did little to make their personality theories scientifically useful by offering clearly defined and testable constructs. Indeed, from Jung's archetypes through Fairbairn's ego splitting, many of the dissidents added yet more obfuscation to Freud's already esoteric system.

Selected Readings

Coles, R. 1970. *Erik Erikson: The Growth of His Work*. Boston: Little, Brown.

Fromm, E. 1941. *Escape from Freedom*. New York: Rinehart.

_____. 1974. *Man for Himself*. New York: Rinehart.

Hall, C. S., and G. Lindzey. 1978. *Theories of Personality*. 3rd ed. New York: Wiley.

Hall, C. S., and V.J. Nordby. 1973. *A Primer of Jungian Psychology*. New York: New American Library.

Horney, K. 1950. *Neurosis and Human Growth: The Struggle Toward Self-realization*. New York: Norton.

Jung, C. G. 1970. *Four Archetypes: Mother, Rebirth, Spirit, and Trickster*. Princeton, NJ: Princeton University Press.

_____. 1971. *The Portable Jung*. New York: Viking.

Manaster, G. J., and R. J. Corsini. 1982. *Individual Psychology*. Itasca, IL: Peacock.

Orgler, H. 1963. *Alfred Adler: The Man and His Work*. New York: Putnam.

Roazen, P. 1975. *Freud and His Followers*. New York: Knopf.

_____. 1976. *Erikson: The Power and Limits of a Vision*. New York: Free Press.

5

Phenomenological Theories

*T*he principal emphasis of phenomenological theories of personality is on how the individual views his or her world at the present moment. This emphasis is combined with a forward-looking concern for people's ability to reach—to actualize— their potential. This orientation distinguishes them from psychodynamic theories which emphasize the person's past experiences and present disabilities.

The American psychologist Carl Rogers is generally considered to have pioneered the phenomenological approach to the study of personality. He considered it an indisputable fact that the human being is born with the motivation to actualize his or her potential and thus become a fully functioning individual. To help people whose environment prevented them from accomplishing this, Rogers developed a form of psychological treatment, client-centered therapy, in which the therapist is nondirective and accepting.

Abraham Maslow also approached personality from a phenomenological point of view. He proposed that people have a series of needs that range from the concrete physiological to the abstract idealistic and pointed out that unless the more basic needs are met, the idealistic ones cannot be reached. Because of his concern for the betterment of the human condition and his focus on people's positive characteristics, Maslow's is usually considered a humanistic orientation.

George Kelly developed a phenomenological theory of personality that placed the emphasis not on people's feelings about themselves, as Rogers and Maslow had done, but on their ideas about themselves and their environment. He proposed that human life centers on making sense of the world around us. To do this, human beings form constructs about their world and use them to anticipate events. In this they are like scientists who form *hypotheses that they test in experiments. Like the scientist's hypotheses, if the constructs are confirmed, they are adopted; if they are not confirmed, they are modified or rejected. Kelly coined the term "constructive alternativism" to label this process.*

Phenomenological theories have both strengths and weaknesses. In contrast to most psychodynamic theories they have the appeal of presenting an optimistic view of human nature and of looking at the here and now. At the same time, they can be faulted for neglecting the less desirable human characteristics and for saying little about the influence of the past on people's present behavior.

INTRODUCTION

"Phenomenological" Defined

A *phenomenon* (pronounced: fe-NOM-ah-non; plural: *phenomena*) is an observed fact or event. It can be an object or an aspect of an object (a rose or the fragrance of a rose). The crucial part of the definition is that the fact or event is observed, that we know about it through one of our senses. A phenomenon is not something we imagine or conjure up in our thoughts, although observing involves thinking.

PRIVATE PERCEPTIONS

The moment an object impinges on one of my sense organs as a *sensation*, I process it through my thoughts. I interpret it and give it meaning in terms of expectations, attitudes that are based on my past experiences. The sensation thus becomes my *perception* of the phenomenon. It is my private perception of the phenomenon and it may or may not coincide with your private perception of the same phenomenon.

This notion of the privacy of a person's perception is central to the *phenomenological approach to personality*. Those who adopt this approach contend that a person's actions, emotions, and thoughts are determined by his or her private perceptions. They therefore ask in each case: How does the world appear to this particular individual at this particular time?

CONTRASTING THEORIES

You will recognize the contrast between this individualized approach to the study of personality and that taken in the various psychoanalytic theories we discussed in the previous two chapters. There theorists asserted that all boys view their father as a sexual rival, that all children feel insecure or helpless, that infants see the world as hostile or their mother as only a breast. The phenomenological theorist makes no such generalized assertions.

FOCUS ON THE PRESENT

There are two other ways in which the phenomenological method differs from the psychodynamic approach to personality. Whereas the psychoanalyst investigates what events in the individual's past shaped her or his present personality, the phenomenologist asks how the individual perceives his or her world today. This emphasis on the present is reflected in the fact that phenomenological theorists focus primarily on how people are functioning as adults. Almost all psychoanalytic theorists, in contrast, had much to say about early childhood and personality development.

THE PERSON'S POTENTIAL

The other difference between these two theoretical approaches lies in the phenomenologists' concern for what the individual is able to become. The phenomenological question "How does the world appear to this particular individual at this particular time?" could thus be amended to include "And where is that person capable of going from here?" From this it follows that where therapists with a psychodynamic orientation are largely interested in restoring impaired functions, phenomenological helpers seek to enable the individual to reach his or her full potential, to achieve what they call *self-actualization.*

Humanism
The focus on the individual's private perceptions, the respect for these perceptions, the emphasis on the here and now, and the concern with self-actualization combine to make the phenomenological orientation a *humanistic* approach to understanding personality. That is not to say that advocates of other orientations have not also been guided by humanistic values. We spoke of humanistic convictions in discussing the work of both Fromm and Adler. For that matter, anyone who takes an optimistic view of human nature and seeks to better the human condition deserves to be classed as a humanist.

THE PERSON-CENTERED THEORY OF CARL ROGERS

Carl Rogers (1902–1987) was born and educated in the United States. He became a psychologist and received his Ph.D. degree from Columbia University. Rogers developed a method for treating psychological disorders and a theoretical framework in which it is anchored. Both center on the individual's perception of his or her world. Treatment and theory reflect Rogers's fundamental optimism about human nature and a conviction that we can help our fellow humans find and achieve the good that is within them. This outlook makes Rogers a thoroughly humanistic phenomenologist.

Self-Actualization

Central to Rogers's theorizing is the notion that it is in the nature of being human to seek the actualization of one's potential. Like other humanistic personality theorists, Rogers considered *self-actualization*—the inborn propensity to bring out to their fullest the qualities and capacities with which one is born—to be a self-evident truth, an *axiom*. As an axiom, self-actualization requires neither proof nor justification. There is nothing wrong with basing a theory on an axiom; both mathematics and the sciences employ axioms, but the problem is that what is self-evident to one person may not be so to another. In a sense, this is a phenomenological problem in itself: Whether you believe in self-actualization depends on your view of human nature.

THE INDIVIDUAL'S POTENTIAL

Like one's perception of the world, self-actualization is a very personal matter so that the potential that is to be actualized differs from person to person. Inasmuch as a potential is something that lies in the future it is impossible to know what someone's potential is. Nor can one ever say that a person's potential has been reached, for even greater achievements and better deeds may well lie in the future. From the point of view of the individual the principle of self-actualization exhorts one to keep striving, for great things may lie ahead.

Self-actualization can be impeded by environmental conditions or personal difficulties. For that reason Rogers urged that we create conditions in our society that facilitate everyone's self-actualization and he developed a form of counseling to help those who, because of problems of their own, can't fully actualize themselves. We shall speak of that treatment in a moment.

The Fully Functioning Person

Rogers considered an individual who is engaged in actualizing his or her potential to be a *fully functioning person*. Whether a child develops into such a person depends on his or her social environment during the important formative years when the way we see ourselves is greatly influenced by the way others act toward us.

UNCONDITIONAL REGARD

If parents fully accept and respect their child as a person regardless of his or her behavior, the child has the crucial experience of receiving *unconditional positive regard*. Such a child can then grow up with *unconditional self-regard*, which is an important aspect of being a fully functioning person. Children, on the other hand, who experience negative evaluations or conditional regard by parents or other influential adults will not be able to actualize their potential fully.

CONDITIONS OF WORTH

The notion of unconditional regard, whether by a parent toward the child or by the person for himself or herself, is a central feature in Rogers's perspective. Regard is conditional rather than unconditional when a child perceives the mother as implying something like "You are worthy of my positive regard only on the condition that you behave in ways of which I approve." Such a mother is placing conditions on the child's worth, and these *conditions of worth* will become a part of the child's self-perception and self-regard.

Client-Centered Therapy

Rogers described the ideal, fully functioning person as one who is open to experience, has accurate awareness, lacks defensiveness, possesses unconditional self-regard, and maintains harmonious relations with others. To help those whose move toward that ideal has been thwarted, Rogers developed a form of therapy he called *nondirective counseling* or *client-centered therapy.*

In line with the theoretical propositions just outlined, the client (Rogers preferred this term to "patient") is assumed not to have experienced unconditional positive regard, thus having been prevented from becoming a fully functioning person. The task of the therapist therefore is to enable the client to experience such regard. This means that the therapist is nonjudgmental, nondirective, and fully accepting of the client's perceptions, feelings, and actions.

Although in principle the therapist is unable to experience the world through the eyes of the client, he or she seeks to convey *empathy*, and to give the client the feeling of being understood. By experiencing the therapist's unconditional positive regard, acceptance, and empathy, the client eventually becomes more open to experiencing real feelings, to be less defensive, and to gain positive self-regard, thus being better able to establish harmonious interactions with others. That is to say, treatment facilitates becoming a fully functioning person.

THE HUMANISM OF ABRAHAM H. MASLOW

The philosophy of humanism provided the foundation for the work of Abraham H. Maslow (1908–1970). A native of Brooklyn, New York, Maslow had a Ph.D. degree in psychology. He taught that subject at Brooklyn College and Brandeis University.

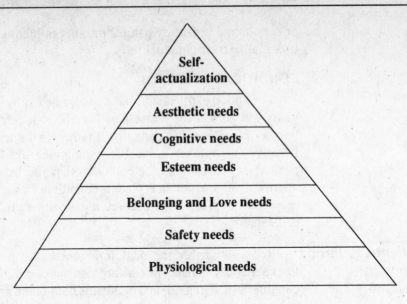

Fig. 5.1 Maslow's Hierarchy of Needs

A Focus on the Normal Person

Unlike all the theorists discussed thus far, Maslow's interest in personality did not stem from working with disturbed individuals. This may account for the fact that his theoretical contributions focus on healthy, normal, functioning behavior. He said little about psychological disorders and nothing about psychotherapy.

Maslow's humanism led him to the conviction that an understanding of personality requires one to concentrate on people's positive characteristics. He was convinced that by studying normal people one would discover ways to prevent psychological problems. This strategy is the exact opposite of that followed by theorists since the days of Freud, who studied disturbed individuals in hopes of discovering how normal people develop and function.

A Hierarchy of Needs

Like Rogers, Maslow maintained that self-actualization is a basic aspect of human nature, but unlike Rogers, he did not view it as the sole source of our behavior. Maslow offered a theory of motivation that centers around a hierarchically organized series of innate needs that lend meaning and satisfaction to life.

This *hierarchy of needs* might be visualized as a pyramid (Fig. 5.1) in which the physiological needs—such as food, water, sleep, sex, and elimination—provide the base and self-actualization lies at the top. Between the base and the pinnacle Maslow placed (in ascending order) safety needs, needs for belonging and love, needs for esteem, and cognitive and aesthetic needs.

According to Maslow, the needs at the lower level of this hierarchy must be met before those at the higher levels can be satisfied. Thus, unless the basic physiological needs and the needs for safety are taken care of, the needs for belonging and love, esteem, knowledge, and appreciation of beauty cannot be considered, and self-actualization is out of the question.

Note that the lower on the hierarchy a need is located, the more we depend on the actions of others. We must rely on them to provide such essentials of life as food, shelter, and security. We need them for feelings of love and belonging, and even esteem is largely an interpersonal matter. When we reach the needs for aesthetic enjoyment, knowledge, and understanding, we can be relatively self-sufficient, but only in achieving self-actualization are we truly independent.

A GOOD SOCIETY

When one imagines the need hierarchy as a pyramid, it is easy to recognize that reaching self-actualization requires a climb that is aided by the support and cooperation of others. In Maslow's view, the reason relatively few people are able to actualize their human potentials lies in the imperfections of society.

From this it follows that to enable more of us to reach self-actualization we must build a society where everyone's needs for food, clothing, safety, and shelter are met so that they can experience belongingness, love, and esteem and can afford to appreciate cognitive and aesthetic pleasures. That is Maslow's humanistic prescription for a good society.

The Actualized Person

Maslow reasoned that to discover the maximum height to which humans are able to grow, we would not study people's average height and certainly not those whose growth had been stunted. We would seek instead the tallest among us and examine them in detail. In line with this notion, Maslow picked thirty-eight historical figures, contemporary persons of distinction, and individuals among his own acquaintances, all of whom he considered self-actualized. His list included Abraham Lincoln, Walt Whitman, Ludwig van Beethoven, Albert Einstein, and Eleanor Roosevelt. After examining these paragons in detail, Maslow described the characteristics that distinguish them from ordinary humans (whom he did not study).

According to Maslow, self-actualized persons have a need for privacy, a realistic orientation, and an acceptance of themselves, of others, and of the world as it is. They have a great deal of spontaneity, are problem-centered, autonomous, and independent. They identify with humanity, appreciate people and things in a fresh rather than a stereotyped fashion, and have had profound mystical or spiritual, so-called *peak experiences* of ecstasy or awe. They maintain profound, deeply felt, intimate relationships with a few specially loved people, and possess a philosophical sense of humor. They do not confuse means with ends, have a great fund of creativeness, resist conformity to the culture, transcend their environment, and hold democratic values and attitudes. Maslow found adjectives like *meaningful*, *challenging*, and *exciting* to be more appropriate than *happy* and *satisfied* for describing the lives of such people.

Some have pointed out that this picture of the self-actualized person may be more a reflection of Maslow's personal ideals and value system than of the actual characteristics of people like Beethoven. That misgiving, however, should not be limited to Maslow's contribution. Freud's pessimism, Horney's feminism, and Fromm's Marxism are but three examples of personal concerns coloring a theorist's formulations.

THE PERSONAL CONSTRUCT THEORY OF GEORGE A. KELLY

George A. Kelly (1905–1966) was born in Kansas and spent most of his professional life as a psychology professor at Ohio State University, where he developed his *personal construct* theory of personality.

A Formal, Cognitive Theory

In contrast to the more casual fashion in which Rogers and Maslow had presented their views, Kelly's is a formal theory with a fundamental postulate and eleven explicit corollaries. Like the theories of Rogers and Maslow, Kelly's is phenomenological in that it asks how the individual perceives his or her world. But where the primary concern of the two humanistic phenomenologists was with how people feel about themselves, Kelly focuses almost exclusively on their thoughts about themselves and the world around them.

His can thus be viewed as a cognitive theory.

The Human as Scientist

The model on which Kelly based his theory was that of the scientist whose goal is to understand, predict, and thus control the events under study. That goal, Kelly asserted, is not unique to scientists; it is shared by all humans and in that sense every human is a scientist. According to that view, all of us are constantly seeking to improve our understanding of our world so as to be better able to anticipate (predict) events and thus cope with (control) them. Ambiguities and uncertainties make us uneasy and we seek to replace them with knowledge and understanding.

PERSONAL CONSTRUCTS

In the process of trying to understand our world we formulate ideas about it, we *construe* how it works, we form *constructs*. Because different people have different experiences, the constructs they form will differ; they are *personal constructs* and these form the core of the individual's personality.

Inasmuch as each of us construes experiences in different ways, it is meaningless to ask what things are "really" like. For Kelly, reality depends on people's constructions. The same reasoning holds for the meaning of an event: Events have no inherent meaning. Their meaning depends on how they are construed.

Constructs Guide Actions. Our constructs of the world and of ourselves determine how we anticipate events and thus they guide our actions. That is the essence of Kelly's *fundamental postulate*. Once we have construed other people as hostile, we will approach them in a fashion that would be different had we construed them as friendly. If I have construed myself as shy, I will enter a gathering in a manner that would be different had I construed myself as outgoing. Furthermore, the constructs I have formed about myself will also determine how I explain my experiences. If I construe myself as incompetent and discover that my watch is missing, I am likely to think that I have lost it. If I construe myself as competent, however, I am likely to believe that someone stole it.

CONSTRUCTIVE ALTERNATIVISM

Personal constructs are for the person what hypotheses are for the scientist; they are predictions that must be tested to see if they are correct. As with a hypothesis, if the prediction is confirmed, the construct is retained. If it is not confirmed, the construct should be modified or rejected. Constructs thus have alternatives, both in terms of the individual who can adopt different constructs and in terms of different people construing the same event in different ways. Kelly called this *constructive alternativism*.

INDIVIDUAL DIFFERENCES

One of the implications of personal construct theory is that it places major emphasis on *individual differences* inasmuch as everybody has his or her own set of personal constructs. That is the *individuality corollary* in Kelly's formal theory. It leaves no room for personality types or similar generalizations about people.

PERSONAL RESPONSIBILITY

Another implication of the theory derives from the fact that personal constructs are a function of the person's own cognitive processes. Each of us forms his or her constructs, tests them against experiences, and adopts or modifies them on the basis of these experiences. Inasmuch as constructs are of our own making, we are responsible for them. Moreover, inasmuch as our constructs guide our actions, we are responsible for these actions and we shape our own destiny.

In thus placing responsibility for our fate on our own shoulders, Kelly is also in the humanist tradition. His humanism is more demanding than that of Rogers and Maslow, however, for where they tended to blame a failure to self-actualize on imperfections of society, Kelly would fault a person's personal constructs for his or her difficulties.

The Properties of Constructs

Constructs are *dichotomous*, that is, they always have two poles even when the second pole exists only by implication. That is the *dichotomy corollary* of Kelly's theory. The good–bad dichotomy can serve as an example. I may be construing the people I meet as being good people or bad people, but even if I said, "All my friends are good," the statement implies that they might also be bad.

The two poles of a construct may vary. They may be different for different people and different for the same person on different occasions. Whereas I use good–bad in construing people, someone else may use good–selfish for the same purpose. Similarly, I may use my good–bad dichotomy in categorizing people, but employ good–spoiled when tasting food.

According to the *range corollary* of the theory, constructs have a *range of convenience* that defines the limits within which they apply. In my use of good–bad it has a wide range of convenience for I employ it to categorize people, pets, books, weather, movies, beaches, and much more. As I use clever–stupid, on the other hand, it has a very narrow range of convenience for I apply it only to people, dogs, and inventions. Most of the time, and most appropriately, however, I apply clever–stupid to people. In Kelly's terms, that is where the *focus of convenience* of that construct of mine is located.

Constructs also have the property of *permeability*. This refers to the degree of a construct's flexibility to encompass events not previously encountered. Permeability is closely related to range of convenience. My good–bad construct has a wide range of convenience and is likely to be able to encompass (be permeable to) most new experiences I might encounter. If I took up skiing and found myself on a ski slope, I could quickly construe the snow as either good or bad. At that point snow would be included in that construct's range of convenience.

Some constructs are *preemptive*. This means that they are so rigidly maintained that they preclude the use of any other construct. A preemptive construct is like a strong prejudice. Having construed broccoli as "awful," a boy will refuse to eat that vegetable, no matter how it is prepared because, based on that construct, he predicts that it will also be awful. In fact, should he construe brussels sprouts as similar to broccoli, he would not eat that either.

The Role Construct Repertory (REP) Test

Kelly emphasized that to understand a person one must know both poles of his or her constructs and also their range of convenience. To that end he developed a psychological instrument, the *Role Construct Repertory Test*, with which one can ascertain how an individual construes the important people in his or her life.

A person who takes the REP test is instructed to identify individuals who play or have played important roles in his or her life. The form used for this test specifies that, in addition to the self, these individuals are to include twenty-one people, such as parents and siblings, a current and a former friend, an "admired person," a "pitied person," a "threatening person," a "successful person," and so forth. Next, the individual is to indicate for all possible combinations of three people on this list in what important way two of them are alike and how the third one differs from the other two.

The similarities and differences among these triads of people are typically expressed by such adjectives as rigid–flexible, masculine–feminine, and dependent–independent. When the test results are later analyzed, these adjectives reveal not only the constructs the person who took the test employs with respect to important individuals, but also the two poles of these constructs and their range of convenience.

Emotions

Personal construct theory deals primarily with a person's cognitions because constructs are ideas we form about the world, but Kelly's formulation also touches on the emotional states of threat, fear, guilt, anxiety, and hostility. These are experienced when a prediction based on one or more personal constructs has failed to be confirmed, calling for a change in the construct system.

Threat is experienced when the disconfirmation concerns a major aspect of the person's construct system. A man who has construed himself as a highly competent architect and good provider for his family would experience threat if he were dismissed from his job because a building he designed had collapsed. When a more peripheral aspect of one's construct system has been disconfirmed—as when a "punctual" student is late for class—Kelly calls the emotion one experiences *fear.*

Guilt stems from an awareness that one's behavior consistently deviates from the way one has construed oneself. A student would experience guilt if she has construed herself as conscientious and responsible, but finds that she repeatedly fails to do her homework, and cheats on her exams.

Anxiety results from an awareness that one's available constructs cannot cover a newly encountered, hence strange, person or situation; that the experience lies outside the range of convenience of one's construct system. Because everyone is occasionally faced with new and strange people or situations, most of us are familiar with the tense, uneasy feeling (the anxiety) one experiences under these circumstances.

Suppose that for the first time in your life you meet someone who does not speak English and therefore does not understand what you are saying. If your constructs about people include that everybody understands English and that the only people who don't understand you are hard of hearing, this experience will make you anxious because your constructs do not cover it.

You could handle your anxiety effectively by modifying your constructs so as to include the fact that not everyone understands English. But there are also less adaptive ways of responding to your anxiety. One would be to escape from the anxiety-arousing situation by turning away from the stranger and henceforth avoiding contact with people who don't speak your language. That is maladaptive because it restricts your range of activities and experiences.

Another maladaptive way of dealing with the anxiety is to try making the situation conform to your constructs. Inasmuch as you construe as hard of hearing anyone who does not understand what you are saying, you would start shouting to "make" the person understand. Kelly referred to such behavior as *hostility*.

Fixed-Role Therapy

In keeping with his theory that places personal constructs at the core of an individual's personality, Kelly viewed any psychological difficulty as the result of discrepancies between constructs and experiences. Treatment for such difficulties would therefore have to focus on modifying a troubled person's constructs. As a technique for accomplishing this Kelly developed *fixed-role therapy*.

This treatment approach begins with a thorough assessment of the client's construct system. Based on this assessment, the therapist then prepares for that client a *fixed-role sketch*. That sketch describes a fictitious individual who, though similar to the client, has some constructs that differ, thus enabling him or her to engage in behavior with which the client is having difficulty.

PLAYING A ROLE

The client is then asked to *play the role* of the person in the sketch for a limited length of time. By thus engaging in behavior they had previously avoided because it made them anxious, many clients discover that their constructs are faulty. With the therapist's encouragement and help they then proceed to modify these constructs, making them more like those of the person whose role they had played.

PHENOMENOLOGICAL THEORIES IN PERSPECTIVE

Contrasts

During the years when Rogers, Maslow, and Kelly created their theories, the formulations of Freud and his followers dominated the field of personality psychology. In a sense, the phenomenological theories represented a reaction to psychoanalytic theory, and when one compares the two approaches one finds many aspects that are diametrically opposed. Freud had been pessimistic about human nature; Rogers and Maslow were optimistic. Freud emphasized unconscious processes; Rogers, Maslow, and Kelly focused exclusively on thoughts and feelings of which people are aware. Freud saw primitive id impulses as the source of human motivation; Rogers and Maslow spoke of a motive to self-actualize or, in the case of Kelly, to make sense of the world.

There are other differences. Freud wrote extensively on how personality develops; Rogers, Maslow, and Kelly said almost nothing about that. Freud saw the determinants of current behavior to lie in the person's past; the phenomenologists believed that a focus on present perceptions suffices to explain how a person acts.

The contrast is most conspicuous when one compares the approaches to psychotherapy of Freud and Rogers. In psychoanalysis the patient's defenses are expected to have led to distorted perceptions; in client-centered counseling the client's perceptions are accepted as representing reality. In psychoanalysis the therapist is the authority who interprets the meaning of what the patient brings to the treatment sessions. In client-centered counseling the therapist avoids giving the client instructions and tries to convey the experience of understanding and acceptance.

Strengths and Weaknesses

In these contrasts lie both the strengths and the weaknesses of phenomenological theories, for in offering alternatives to some of the extreme positions of the psychoanalysts, Rogers, Maslow, and Kelly have, at times, taken extreme positions of their own.

It was certainly an improvement to recognize that humans interpret their experiences, make choices, and seek to better themselves instead of viewing them as driven by forces of which they are not aware and over which they have little or no control. On the other hand, it is not warranted to assume that we are at all times fully aware of the reasons for our actions.

The same can be said about the idealist view of human nature held by Rogers and Maslow. Though it corrects for Freud's pessimism, it fails to admit that not all of us are at all times striving for the betterment of ourselves and society. Nor, for that matter, are we always able to verbalize what we are thinking and how we feel in such a clear and valid fashion that another person (such as a Rogerian therapist) can gain empathic understanding.

There are also some specific strengths and weaknesses in the formulations of the three theorists discussed in this chapter. Rogers and Kelly expressed their views with considerable clarity, and Kelly attempted to present them in a formal framework. Both, however, employ assumptions that are difficult, if not impossible, to test. Examples of these are Kelly's postulating that all we do is controlled by the way we anticipate events, and Rogers's notion of self-actualization as an innate tendency.

Finally, Maslow's work is difficult to classify as a theory of personality. It seems best to view his contribution as a statement of a personal value system and philosophy of life. As such, many would endorse it.

Phenomenological theories of personality focus on how the individual perceives the world at the present time. Because people's perceptions may differ widely, the phenomenological approach to personality stresses individual differences and refrains from generalizing about people. Another characteristic of this approach is that it emphasizes the individual's potential for personal growth and improvement. For that reason this approach is often referred to as humanistic.

Carl Rogers asserted that it is in the nature of our being human that we seek to actualize our potential. Self-actualization is the goal of life, and the individual who reaches it is a fully functioning person. To become such a person one must experience unconditional positive regard from other people, particularly from those who are important, such as one's parents. To make self-actualization possible people need an accepting environment, and to help those whose personal growth has been impeded Rogers developed client-centered counseling. In that form of treatment the therapist tries to understand how the client experiences his or her world and seeks to provide the unconditional positive regard that the client has presumably failed to receive elsewhere.

Abraham Maslow differs from most of the earlier personality theorists in that his focus is on the normal person. His contribution, therefore, does not include a therapeutic approach. Like Rogers, Maslow spoke of self-actualization, but he asserted that only a few people can reach this goal because it lies at the summit of a hierarchy of needs that is so constituted that the basic needs must be satisfied before the higher needs can be met. This notion led Maslow to the conviction that we must build a society that enables everyone to satisfy such basic needs as food, clothing, shelter, and safety so that as many as possible can reach self-actualization. Based on his study of self-actualized individuals, Maslow drew a picture of what such ideal people are like.

The theory of George Kelly is built around the image of the human as a scientist who forms hypotheses about nature and proceeds to test them. Kelly referred to these hypotheses as personal constructs that people form to make sense of their experiences. Kelly's is a cognitive theory because personal constructs involve people's thoughts. Constructs have a number of characteristics. Among these are their dichotomous property, their range of applicability, and their flexibility. Kelly viewed such emotions as anxiety and guilt as arising when a construct fails to provide meaning for one's experience. To assess people's personal constructs Kelly developed the Role Construct Repertory Test, and to help those whose constructs lead them into difficulty he devised fixed role therapy.

In contrast to the rather pessimistic, past-focused psychodynamic theories of Freud and his followers, the phenomenological theories are markedly optimistic and future-oriented. Instead of stressing unconscious processes, they emphasize feelings and cognitions of which we are aware. Instead of the resolution of inner conflicts, they place self-actualization and improved perceptions at the center of human endeavor. At the same time, phenomenological theories tend to slight the influence the past has on present behavior, fail to recognize that we are subject to influences of which we are not aware, and say very little about personality development.

Selected Readings

Bannister, D., and F. Fransella. 1971. *Inquiring Man: The Theory of Personal Constructs.* New York: Penguin Books.

Hoffman, E. 1988. *The Right to Be Human: A Biography of Abraham Maslow.* Los Angeles: Tarcher.

Kirschenbaum, H. 1979. *On Becoming Carl Rogers.* New York: Dell.

Maslow, A. H. 1987. *Motivation and Personality.* 3rd ed. New York: Harper & Row.

Rogers, C. R. 1961. *On Becoming a Person.* Boston: Houghton Mifflin.

6

Dispositional Approaches to Personality

*D*ispositions are pervasive tendencies that are believed to cause a person to behave in a similar fashion under a wide variety of circumstances and over an extended period. Many different personality theories employ dispositional constructs.

After showing that dispositional notions have been with us since the days of ancient history, we turn to more contemporary formulations and explore the theory of traits proposed by Allport and the categorization of traits which were contributed by Cattell using the statistical technique of factor analysis. We follow this with a review of Eysenck's theory of personality types in which personality is tied to physiology and genetics.

The chapter ends with an examination of Murray's motivational theory, which declares that a person's needs interact with environmental factors to produce behavior. Studies conducted on some of the needs Murray had identified have shown that they can be used to predict how people will behave under specified conditions.

INTRODUCTION

Traits and Types

When you ask someone what another person is like, the answer will probably contain adjectives that describe how that person typically behaves. You may hear such terms as friendly, careful, relaxed or excitable, petty, and irresponsible. In other words, you will be told how that person is *disposed* to act; you will be given a dispositional statement about his or her personality. *Dispositions* are often called *traits*. They can be defined as stable and enduring internal characteristics that dispose or incline an individual to act in recognizable ways.

People have different traits and different combinations of traits, but many traits go together. That makes it possible to classify people who have similar combinations of traits and to speak of different personality *types*. Note that different pictures come to mind when one person is described as friendly, careful, and relaxed, and another is labeled as excitable, petty, and irresponsible. These combinations of traits characterize different types of people.

Because dispositions are straightforward descriptions in everyday language of how a person behaves, the lay person's *implicit personality theory*, mentioned in chapter 2, employs the dispositional approach. For the same reason, that approach was also used at the very beginning of the study of personality.

HISTORICAL ANTECEDENTS

A Matter of Survival

We can speculate that at the dawn of human existence two of our ancestors left their cave and followed the course of their river into the valley below. When they came to a bend in the river they saw some other cave dwellers. The two stopped and, in whichever way they communicated, one asked the other about the strangers' disposition, "I wonder what they are like. Are they friendly or hostile?" Knowing the answer to that question would have had a great deal of survival value for our ancestors. To this day it can be a matter of survival to know the disposition of a stranger who approaches one on a dark street or in a deserted park.

Theophrastus, Hippocrates, and Galen

CHARACTERS

One of the earliest dispositional personality theories is that of the Greek philosopher Theophrastus (372–287 B.C.), who wrote a book entitled *Characters*. In it he described many different types of people. Most of these were unpleasant, undesirable types, like the flatterer, the dissembler, the mean, the tactless, the avaricious, and the garrulous. Theophrastus believed that one could use one's reasoning power to will oneself to be one character or another. People, he asserted, could therefore be held personally responsible for the kind of character they were.

TEMPERAMENTS

Another early Greek who employed a dispositional approach to explain human behavior was the physician Hippocrates (460?–377? B.C.). He has been called "the father of medicine" and his Hippocratic Oath is still pledged by every graduating medical student. Hippocrates taught that physical illness is the result of an excess in one of four basic body fluids; *humors*, they were called. These humors not only caused disease, they were also thought capable of influencing one's *temperament* and, through it, behavior. The four body fluids and the temperamental dispositions they produced are: blood made people sanguine (optimistic); phlegm made them phlegmatic (lethargic); black bile made them melancholic (mournful); and yellow bile made them choleric (hot-tempered).

The classification Hippocrates proposed was limited to four types of people: the sanguine, the phlegmatic, the melancholic, and the choleric. Some 500 years later another Greek physician, Galen (A.D. 131–201), expanded this fourfold system. He described nine temperamental types, each of which was closely tied to a physical condition.

A CONTEMPORARY NOTION

Although the classifications offered by Hippocrates and Galen have long been discarded, words like *sanguine* and *phlegmatic* are still in our vocabulary. Moreover, it is a very contemporary notion that personality is influenced by such physical entities as genes that control brain functions, metabolism, hormones, and—ultimately—behavior. We shall return to that issue later in this chapter.

Gall and Phrenology

The ancient idea that there is a relationship between aspects of the body and an individual's personality traits emerged again in 1796 when the physician Franz Joseph Gall (1758–1828) began a series of lectures. Gall was born in Germany. He later settled in Vienna, where he practiced medicine and studied the anatomy of the brain. In the course of these studies it struck him that anatomical differences among people's brains might explain individual differences in people's behavior. Together with his student and later associate Johann Kaspar Spurzheim (1776–1832), Gall developed a conceptual scheme they called *phrenology*.

A REVOLUTIONARY IDEA

Phrenology is based on the premise that the abilities and tendencies that find expression in behavior are the functions of specific areas of the brain. That in itself was a revolutionary idea in those days for it proclaimed that the mind, which had been viewed as independent of the body, is, in fact, a function of the brain, that the brain is the organ of what we call the mind.

FLAWED REASONING

After establishing this premise, Gall proceeded to develop a list that covered feelings, aptitudes, and sentiments, as well as intellectual, perceptive, and reflective faculties. Next he had to find where in the brain these personal characteristics were located. Here he faced the limitation that there was then no way of finding out how the living brain functions. Gall had the idea that the shape of the brain might tell him something about what was going on inside, but inasmuch as he also lacked the tools for looking at the shape of a living person's brain he thought that the shape of the person's skull was a way of finding out. With the hindsight of two hundred years we can recognize the fallacies in this reasoning and call it primitive, yet Gall also committed what we can now recognize as gross errors in the method he used in his studies.

Having judged a man as extraordinarily proud, for example, Gall would examine the shape of that man's skull. Then, having found this proud man and others like him to have a bulge on a particular part of the skull, Gall would conclude that the location of pride was in the part of the brain that lay under this protuberance. This and similar conclusions about the location of faculties and propensities were later used to ascertain these personality characteristics by analyzing a person's skull. If you had a bump on the part of the head where pride was thought to be located, you were judged to be proud, for example.

The errors Gall made are now obvious to us. He should have checked the validity of his judgment of the man's pride by obtaining the independent judgments of others. Moreover, the judgment of pride and the examination of the man's skull should have been done by different people so that the knowledge of his pride could not bias the anatomical finding. There is also the unverified assumption that the shape of the skull accurately reflects the configuration of the brain. That relationship should have been independently assessed by studying the brains of people who had died. We also know that the correlation of two phenomena, such as a psychological disposition and an anatomical feature, does not provide a basis for conclusions about the location of the disposition.

THE FATE OF PHRENOLOGY

Phrenology was soon rejected by Gall's scientific contemporaries, but the general public accepted it with enthusiasm. Gall, Spurzheim, and their followers lectured in Europe and the United States. Charts and three-dimensional models of heads showing the location of the various faculties and propensities sold widely, and people paid to have their heads examined so that their personalities could be analyzed. Soon charlatans appeared at places like county fairs to entertain people with demonstrations of phrenology. What had begun as a serious, albeit flawed, scientific attempt to explain individual differences had ended as a subject of ridicule. Phrenology is a curious detour on the road to understanding personality, but we can still profit from Gall's mistakes by being sure to avoid them.

Kretschmer

The idea that there is a relationship between how an individual behaves and his or her body was also the basis of the system for classifying body types proposed by the German psychiatrist Ernst Kretschmer. Based on observations he had made in his work with severely disturbed psychiatric patients, Kretschmer identified three basic types of *physique*, or body build. The plump he called *pyknic*, the muscular *athletic*, and the slender *asthenic*. Unusual cases that did not fit any of these categories he referred to as *dysplastic*. To apply this system Kretschmer developed a checklist that included objective measurements of various parts of the body. He then classified 260 psychotic patients according to their physique and found that the pyknic had predominantly been diagnosed as manic-depressive, whereas the asthenic and athletic had almost always been diagnosed as schizophrenic.

As we could with Gall's work, we can, given today's knowledge, point to a major flaw in Kretschmer's study. He failed to control for the effect of his patients' age. Schizophrenia is usually diagnosed much earlier in people's life than manic-depressive disorder so that the schizophrenics among Kretschmer's patients were probably younger than the manic-depressives. As people age they tend to become flabby and to gain weight. The association of a plump body with manic-depressive states and of the muscular or slender body with schizophrenia might thus have been a function of age and not due to a "biological affinity," as Kretschmer thought.

Although Kretschmer believed that psychotic states lie on a continuum with normal conditions, he offered no observations to support the contention that his classification system could also be applied to healthy people and their personality. That, as described in chapter 1, was done by William H. Sheldon, who built on Kretschmer's contribution, extending and refining it.

ALLPORT'S TRAIT APPROACH

With Gordon W. Allport (1897–1967) we leave the historical antecedents of the dispositional approach to the study of personality and begin to examine more contemporary contributions. Like any drawing of a line between the past and the present, this one is arbitrary and there may be some who consider Gordon Allport a part of the history of psychology.

Allport is generally viewed as having been the first in the United States to employ the trait approach in the study of personality. He was born in Indiana and spent nearly all of his professional life at Harvard University, which had awarded him a Ph.D. degree on the basis of a dissertation entitled "An Experimental Study of the Traits of Personality."

Fundamental Assumptions

Allport (1961) defined personality as "the dynamic organization within the individual of those psychophysical systems that determine his [or her] characteristic behavior and thoughts." Let us examine this statement.

The key term in this definition is *psychophysical systems*. It reflects Allport's view that personality is a blend composed of both mental and physical aspects and that these are so fused that it makes no sense to ask whether personality is a psychological or a physiological entity.

These psychophysical systems, the definition further states, do not float around inside the person in a random fashion. They are systematically arranged, organized in a dynamic fashion, which means that the organization is constantly undergoing transformation. As a result an individual's personality has both continuity and malleability, that is, the capacity to change.

That the dynamic organization is *within the individual* reflects Allport's belief that personality is not an abstraction, a construct that summarizes our observations of a person's actions, but that there actually is such an entity within individuals that *determines* their *behavior* and *thought*.

People's behavior and thought, moreover, are *characteristic* of them; they make one person different from the next, thus accounting for *individual differences*. These individual differences are a major theme in all of Allport's work. He maintained that no two people are alike and considered it far more instructive to study the individual than to search for laws governing human behavior.

Traits and Their Dimensions

In examining Allport's definition of personality we met his notion of the fusion of the psychological and the physiological—of mind and body. We find this idea again in his definition of a *trait* to which he referred as a *neuropsychic structure*. Note the word "structure" for it implies that for Allport traits are not mere adjectives that label various behaviors; they actually exist somewhere within the body. These structures, Allport proposed, have the capacity to make many stimuli *functionally equivalent*.

Having that capacity means that traits can influence an individual's perceptions and therefore his or her behavior. Depending on their traits, two people might thus see the same situation in different ways and react to it differently. A good-natured, easygoing wife, for example, might view a game of chess as an occasion for relaxing enjoyment regardless of whether she wins or loses. Her aggressive, competitive husband, on the other hand, would see the same game as a contest that he can enjoy only when he wins.

TWO VIEWS OF TRAITS

Allport differentiated between *common traits* and *individual traits*. That does not mean that there are two kinds of traits, merely that the same trait or combination of traits can be viewed from two perspectives. When traits are viewed as common traits they are characteristics that permit one to compare one person with another and to speak of groups that share certain traits. Viewed as individual traits, they are a person's unique characteristics. Individual traits do not lend themselves to comparisons with other people or to statements about groups. As we shall see in a moment, the trait terms used are the same for both common and individual traits.

We are describing a *common trait* when, returning from a trip abroad, we tell our friends that the people in the country we visited were friendly. That means neither that everyone we met was friendly, nor that the friendly ones were all equally friendly. What we are doing is to generalize about the trait of friendliness in a group of people. Another example of common traits might be an office manager who wants to hire a bookkeeper. Knowing that this position calls for someone with the trait of accuracy, she might interview several candidates for that job, compare them for accuracy, and hire the one she deems to be the most accurate.

Staying with the example just used, picture the person who won the job. He was the most accurate among the candidates, but he undoubtedly also possesses other traits. He may also be neat, punctual, and conscientious. That is to say that the trait of accuracy forms a *pattern* with other traits. That pattern comprises this man's *individual traits*. Some of the people not chosen for the job might also have been neat, punctual, and conscientious in addition to being accurate, but because each of these traits varies in degree (one can be more or less punctual, for example), the *pattern* differed. It is here that the unique characteristics of the individual of Allport's definition of personality come into play.

DIMENSIONS OF INDIVIDUAL TRAITS

Individual traits may be a more or less pronounced aspect of a person's personality. The most pronounced or pervasive traits Allport referred to as a person's *cardinal disposition*. A cardinal disposition dominates an individual's personality to such an extent that it is recognized by anyone who interacts with that person. Few people possess a cardinal disposition, but those who have one often come to be identified with that disposition and vice versa. For example, cardinal dispositions are associated with the names of such historical figures as Mahatma Gandhi, J. P. Morgan, Florence Nightingale, Albert Schweitzer, St. Francis of Assisi, or Abraham Lincoln.

More frequent than the rare cardinal dispositions are *central dispositions*. Everyone has a few of these. They are the relatively small number of traits that come to mind when one tries to describe a person. Usually there are between three and ten of them. The patterns these central dispositions form are highly characteristic of a person; they might be said to represent a major aspect of his or her personality.

The third dimension of individual traits that Allport described is *secondary dispositions*. These are characteristics that are more peripheral to the individual's personality and less crucial to its description. Secondary dispositions are likely only to be displayed under special circumstances. An example of secondary dispositions controlling behavior might be an otherwise reserved and dignified man who at football games predictably jumps up on his seat, waves his arms wildly, and cheers loudly for his team.

Motivation

Recall that in Allport's definition of personality mention is made of psychophysical systems within the individual that determine a person's characteristic behavior and thoughts. The word *determine* implies motivation; people behave in a certain way because internal "neuropsychic structures" (that is, traits) cause them to do so. Indeed, Allport equated traits with motives, and for him motives had four important characteristics.

CHARACTERISTICS OF MOTIVES

Allport argued that motives are *contemporaneous*. This means that the motivation for a thought or action is present at the time when that thought or action takes place. The origin of that motivation does not lie in the person's childhood, as Freud proposed, or in the individual's ancestral history, as Jung might have asserted. According to Allport, another characteristic of motives is their *diversity*. Each action is determined by a combination of several motives, not by just one, such as sex or striving for superiority, as Freud or Adler proposed.

Yet another characteristic, Allport insisted, is that motives are *purposeful*; they involve cognitive processes, such as planning and intention. Here again he diverges from Freud and his followers, who considered most actions to be determined by unconscious motivation. Lastly, and in line with Allport's championing of individual differences, he viewed each person's pattern of motivation to be *unique*.

FUNCTIONAL AUTONOMY

Allport introduced the concept of *functional autonomy of motives*. That, he felt, encompassed the four characteristics of motives just mentioned: contemporaneity, diversity, purposefulness, and uniqueness. Functional autonomy means that human motivation is self-sustaining and that it does not derive, directly or indirectly, from earlier and more basic motives. According to Allport, people engage in actions for their own sake, not because they seek to satisfy a biological or social need, or because they were given an incentive or expected a reward.

With the notion of functional autonomy Allport diverges from personality theorists who postulate that human motives are derived from basic physiological needs either through sublimation, as Freud would have it, or via conditioning, as learning theory proclaims. Not surprisingly, the notion of functional autonomy has been widely questioned and attacked.

The Proprium

Allport's desire to distance himself from earlier personality theorists is also reflected in his avoidance of terms like "ego" or "self." He felt that these had the connotation of an internal agent, almost a tiny person or *homunculus*, who organizes and directs the personality system. Such a view was clearly incompatible with the notion of functional autonomy. Yet Allport also recognized that the individual has a sense of being distinct from other people, of having self-esteem and self-confidence—a sense of self. To encompass these aspects of the individual he coined the term *proprium,* which is related to "property" and shares with it the Latin root that connotes something that belongs to one, something one owns.

SEVEN ASPECTS

The proprium, Allport (1961) wrote, is not something we are born with. It develops in the course of becoming an adult and has seven aspects. During the first three years of life we begin to develop a sense of *bodily self*, a sense of *self-identity*, and *self-esteem*. Starting at age four the child goes through a self-centered period Allport called *extension of self*. It is marked by extreme possessiveness and generally subsides by age six. Also between four and six the *self-image* emerges, to be joined at age twelve by the *self-awareness* of being able to cope with the demands of the environment through reason and thought. Lastly, there emerge during adolescence the intentions, long-range plans, and distant goals that Allport referred to as *propriate strivings*.

A Profusion of Traits

Allport had developed his theory in the course of intensive study of individuals and their lives. He used trait labels to describe these people and traits to explain their behavior. Although he declared that traits are organized, he did not describe that organization, because he felt that it differed from individual to individual. Questions such as how many traits there are and how they relate to one another thus remained unasked and unanswered. Allport (Allport and Odbert, 1936) once reported that there are close to 18,000 trait-related words in an unabridged English dictionary. Even with synonyms (such as affable, amicable, congenial, and friendly) replaced by one word, the remaining trait terms would still be too many to be useful for a personality theory. We now turn then to the contribution of a personality theorist who reduced the plethora of trait terms to a manageable number.

CATTELL'S FACTOR THEORY OF TRAITS

Raymond B. Cattell, a psychologist who retired from the University of Illinois after serving on its faculty for nearly thirty years, used the statistical method of *factor analysis* to bring the number of available trait names to a workable size.

Factor Analysis

As mentioned in chapter 2, factor analysis is a technique that permits an investigator to discover which of a large number of data, such as trait labels or scores from different tests, correlate with one another, forming so-called *clusters*. These clusters indicate that the correlated tests or traits have something in common, that they relate to the same ability or characteristic. The characteristic thus identified is referred to as a *factor*, and it is up to the investigator to give that factor a name. Cattell considered the factors he extracted to be trait characteristics that he first labeled A, B, C, and so forth and then gave names, many of which are somewhat outlandish.

THREE SOURCES OF DATA

Cattell (1957) used three sources of data in his studies of personality. These he labeled *L-data, Q-data, and T-data.* L-data consist of information gathered from a person's life history as it is reflected in school records and work history. Q-data are based on responses to questionnaires and interviews given to the individual being studied or his or her acquaintances. T-data are obtained from tests administered to the individual.

Having gathered such data (he called them *trait elements*) from a large number of people, Cattell would correlate the information from each data source with the information from every other data source. This resulted in a *correlation matrix* which he then factor-analyzed to determine how many factors would account for the various intercorrelations.

Categories of Traits

Cattell considered traits to be the building blocks of personality, and he conducted many studies to learn more about them. These studies led him to identify several categories of traits. We shall examine two of them, *source traits* and *surface traits*.

SOURCE TRAITS

Source traits are the basic, underlying structures of personality that constitute its core. They are the causes of human behavior and they account for our consistency from one situation to another and from one time to another. Cattell concluded that there are sixteen source traits and that everybody has each of these to a greater or lesser degree. The *Sixteen Personality–Factor Questionnaire (16 P–F)* mentioned in chapter 2 is based on these factors. It is used to assess individuals and compare groups.

Each of the sixteen source traits has two poles. Factor E, for example, ranges from Dominance to Submissiveness; factor B from Intelligent to Unintelligent. Unfortunately, not all of Cattell's factors carry such easily understood labels. For most of them he coined entirely new words. In the following sentence their equivalent in everyday language is shown in parentheses. Factor H, for example, ranges from Parmia to Threctia (venturesome to shy), factor I ranges from Premsia to Harria (tender-minded to tough-minded), and factor M ranges from Autia to Praxernia (imaginative to practical).

Each source trait subsumes a variety of specific behaviors. A person whose scores fall on the high, Parmia pole of factor H, for example, would not only have the characteristic of being venturesome. He or she might also be carefree and overtly interested in sex. Similarly, someone with the source trait of Autia on factor M might not only be imaginative, but also eccentric, complacent, and self-absorbed. Another way of looking at this is to remember that the source trait Autia was discovered through a factor analysis that was based on the correlations of observations and test scores that reflected such characteristics as imagination, eccentricity, complacency, and self-absorption. The intercorrelation or clustering of these characteristics then emerged from the factor analysis as factor M, which Cattell chose to label Autia.

CIRCULAR REASONING

It is well to note here that there is a *circularity* in the sequence just described. Remember that Cattell viewed source traits as causing human behavior. An imaginative person would thus be said to be so because of the source trait Autia. Autia causes a person to be imaginative. What happened originally is that people were observed to be imaginative. The correlation coefficients of their imaginativeness and related characteristics then underwent a factor analysis out of which emerged source trait M, "Autia." To then turn around and say that Autia causes people to be imaginative is not an explanation of that characteristic.

Autia and the other source traits are *explanatory labels* because behavior was observed and given a label that was then used to explain the behavior that had been observed. Whenever behavior is attributed to traits in the absence of independent evidence to the effect that the trait did indeed cause the behavior, the danger exists that one is engaging in circular reasoning.

SURFACE TRAITS

Two or more source traits can interact to form *surface traits*. Unlike the source traits, which are limited in number and play an important explanatory role in Cattell's formulations, surface traits are more numerous, more superficial, and merely descriptive. Anyone can observe surface traits and recognize that they are correlated without the aid of tests or complicated statistical analyses. We all know someone who is friendly, cheerful, generous, and talkative, who loves beer parties and loud music, readily hugs both men and women, and immediately calls everyone by his or her first name. There is no one source trait that subsumes all of these surface traits. In Cattell's view several source traits contribute to making such a person act in this fashion.

EYSENCK'S THEORY OF TYPES

We turn now to a personality theorist who can also be classified as following the dispositional approach to personality theory and who, like Cattell, makes extensive use of factor analysis in his research. Unlike Cattell, however, Hans J. Eysenck, a German-born psychologist working in England, speaks not of many, relatively independent traits but of a limited number of traits that are subsumed under no more than three personality *types*. Another way in which Eysenck's approach differs from that of Cattell's is that he uses factor analysis not to discover the composition of personality but to test explicit hypotheses.

The Hierarchical Model

Eysenck has proposed that personality is organized in a hierarchical form. A hierarchy is like a pyramid; it has a broad base and a narrow top. Most organizations have hierarchies. At the top is a chief executive or president. Immediately under her is a small number of vice-presidents, each of whom is responsible for a larger group of department heads who, in turn, are in charge of many section chiefs. At the bottom of this hierarchy, supervised by the section chiefs, are the numerous people who work on whatever the organization produces.

THE HIERARCHY

With this image in mind we can now examine Eysenck's hierarchical model of personality as depicted for the case of extraversion in Fig. 6.1. Starting at the bottom we find a person's *specific responses*. Two or more of these specific responses combine to form the next level of the hierarchy, the level of *habitual responses*. Let us assume that we are examining the personality of a specific man. His specific responses upon meeting someone new might be to smile, hold out his hand, and say, "Hi, I'm Joe." If we observe that he does this every time he meets a stranger, we can say that in this situation that behavior is his habitual response. There probably are other habitual responses that this man can be observed to make. He may enjoy lively parties, seek the company of other people, and talk a great deal. Such

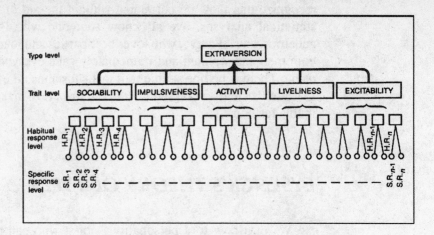

*Fig. 6.1 The hierarchical organization of personality
in the case of extraversion
(From H. J. Eysenck, The Biological Basis of Personality, 1967.
Courtesy of Charles C Thomas, publisher, Springfield, IL)*

a collection of habitual responses forms the next level of the hierarchy, the level of *traits*. In the case of Joe, the trait would be *sociability*. There would, no doubt, be other traits that Joe displays and correlates with his sociability. He might also be impulsive, lively, excitable, and highly active. That cluster of traits combines to define *extraversion*, a *type* that constitutes the top of this particular hierarchy. Other types in Eysenck's system are similarly constituted, but by different specific and habitual responses, and different traits.

Dimensions of Personality

Eysenck (1953) construes types not as independent categories to which people can be assigned, but as continuous *dimensions* along which people differ. As with a trait which can be more or less characteristic of a person, so it is with a type. Because introversion and extraversion are endpoints of a single dimension, one is not either an *introvert* or an *extravert*. Most people, in fact, fall somewhere near the middle of the introversion–extraversion dimension. This is not unlike the dimension of height, where the endpoints could be called giant and midget, but where relatively few people are at either of these extremes.

There are only two dimensions in Eysenck's system. The poles or endpoints of these dimensions are the *types*, and the dimensions are identified by their endpoints. *Introversion* and *extraversion* are the poles of introversion–extraversion dimension; emotional *stability* and *instability* are the poles of the stability–instability dimension. Eysenck conducted factor-analytic studies that revealed these two dimensions to be statistically independent. They can therefore be conceptualized as lying at right angles to one another.

FOUR QUADRANTS

Imagine the face of a clock where instability is located at twelve o'clock and stability at six o'clock, extraversion at three o'clock and introversion at nine o'clock. Now draw an imaginary line that connects stability and instability and another line that connects extraversion to introversion. You now have formed four quadrants: one between noon and three o'clock, and three others between three and six, six and nine, and nine and twelve. A well-known figure that Eysenck used in many of his works (e.g., Eysenck and Rachman, 1965), shows that these four, statistically derived quadrants coincide with choleric, sanguine, phlegmatic, and melancholic, the four "humors" which Hippocrates proposed some twenty-four hundred years ago! (Fig. 6.2.)

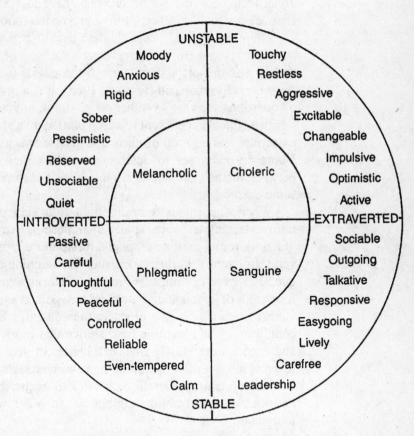

Fig. 6.2 The two dimensions of personality as conceptualized by H. J. Eysenck, and their relationship to the four temperaments proposed by Hippocrates. (From H. J. Eysenck & S. Rachman, The Causes and Cures of Neurosis. *San Diego, CA: EDITS/Robert R. Knapp, publisher, 1965. Reproduced with permission. All rights reserved.)*

The four quadrants formed by the types or poles of Eysenck's two dimensions also permit the display of the specific traits from whose factor-analyzed intercorrelations the dimensions had emerged. In the quadrant formed by instability and extraversion one finds such trait terms as *touchy, restless, aggressive, excitable, impulsive, optimistic*, and *active*. Between extraversion and stability appear such trait terms as *carefree, lively, talkative, outgoing*, and *sociable. Passive, thoughtful, controlled, reliable*, and *calm* can be found in the quadrant formed by introversion and stability, while the fourth quadrant (between introversion and instability) contains such trait labels as *quiet, reserved, rigid, anxious*, and *moody*.

Research Support

In discussing the work of Cattell we mentioned the circularity of labeling behavior with trait names and then using these labels to explain the behavior. To attribute behavior to traits one must have independent evidence, we said. Eysenck has such evidence for his extraversion-introversion dimension.

There are several psychological tests that make it possible to group people into introverts and extraverts on the basis of where on this dimension their test scores place them. One of these tests is the *Eysenck Personality Inventory* (Eysenck and Eysenck, 1963). It is a questionnaire composed of 57 questions such as "Do other people think of you as very lively?"

In a typical experiment research participants are divided into a group of extraverts and a group of introverts. These two groups then participate in laboratory exercises to determine whether their responses discriminate between them. Time and again this turns out to be the case. We shall cite some examples.

When one shines a bright light into subjects' eyes, the pupils of introverts contract more rapidly than those of extraverts, but when placed in a dark room, extraverts' pupils dilate more rapidly than those of introverts. In lengthy, boring tasks, such as watching a radar screen for infrequently appearing "blips," introverts perform better than extraverts. When four drops of lemon juice are placed on a person's tongue, introverts secrete almost twice the amount of saliva than do extraverts. Studies of memory, conditioning, and learning have shown that introverts learn more quickly and forget more slowly than extraverts. In general, it seems, introverts respond more readily to stimuli than extraverts. Conversely, the extraverts' nervous system appears to be slower to excite than the introverts'. The extraversion–introversion dimension, in other words, has a biological foundation.

The Neurophysiology of Extraversion–Introversion

Eysenck offers a neurophysiological postulate to explain the results of experiments such as those just cited. It has to do with the transmission of nerve impulses. The transmission of these impulses from one neuron to another Eysenck calls *excitation*. The blocking of such transmission he calls *inhibition. Dissipation* is the term he uses for the eventual subsiding of the effect of a transmitted impulse.

According to Eysenck, extraverts are individuals in whom excitation develops slowly and is weak, whereas their inhibition develops quickly, is strong, and dissipates slowly. Introverts, conversely, are individuals in whom excitation develops rapidly and is strong, whereas inhibition develops slowly, is weak, and dissipates quickly. Hypotheses based on this formulation have been repeatedly confirmed. For example, extraverts and introverts react differently to drugs that are known to affect the function of *neurotransmitters*. Depressant drugs make introverts behave more like extraverts, whereas stimulant drugs make extraverts act more like introverts.

These basic differences between the two personality types strongly suggest that there might be a genetic base for them. Eysenck believes that this is the case and research tends to bear him out.

GENETIC INFLUENCES ON EXTRAVERSION–INTROVERSION

When the co-twin method, which we mentioned in chapter 1, is used to investigate the genetics of human behavior, test scores of identical twins are compared with test scores of same-sex fraternal twins. Identical twins have identical genes, whereas fraternal twins have only half their genes in common. When these twin pairs are reared in the same environment and the test scores of the identical twins are more similar (correlate more highly) than those of the fraternal twins, the difference can be attributed to genetic factors.

Twin studies have shown that the correlations of extraversion–introversion test scores of identical twins are considerably higher (.54) than those of fraternal twins (.21).

There have also been studies on personality characteristics that are related to the extraversion–introversion dimension, such as sociability and activity level. Here, too, genetic factors seem to play a major role. For example, an investigation of adopted infants showed their sociability to be more similar to that of their birth mothers, whom they had never known, than to that of the adoptive mothers by whom they were being raised.

MURRAY'S THEORY OF NEEDS

Of the modern dispositional theorists discussed thus far, Allport studied what people do and attributed their actions to traits, whereas Eysenck sought to classify people by types and attributed these types to biological factors. We turn now to a dispositional theorist who focused on *motivation* to explain what it is that disposes people to behave in certain ways.

An Interactionist

Unlike the psychologists Allport, Cattell, and Eysenck, Henry A. Murray (1893–1988) had studied medicine and biochemistry, earning both an M.D. and a Ph.D. degree, but he devoted almost all of his life to the study of personality. *Explorations in Personality*, a work Murray and his collaborators published in 1938, represents a major contribution to that field, because it explicitly acknowledged that forces both from within the individual and from his or her environment must be taken into account in explaining human behavior. Murray was thus an *interactionist*. The forces stemming from within the individual Murray designated as *needs*; the environmental forces he called *press* (this word is both singular and plural).

NEEDS (*n*)

Murray construed *needs* as forces that organize and direct thoughts, feelings, and behavior to the end of changing an unsatisfactory condition to a satisfactory one. He recognized two kinds of needs: *primary needs* and *secondary needs*. Primary needs are biological, such as the need for oxygen, water, food, sex, and physical safety. There are twelve of these needs and because they are innate all humans possess them. There are twenty-seven secondary needs. These are learned in the course of an individual's life. People will therefore differ both in the number of their secondary needs and in the strength of each of these needs.

The twenty-seven secondary needs can be grouped into five major categories. They are ambition, defense of status, response to human power, affection between people, and exchange of information. Murray used the lowercase *n* as an abbreviation for need. Some needs in the category "ambition" are *n* Achievement, *n* Recognition, *n* Order, and *n* Construction. Examples of response-to-human-power needs are *n* Dominance, *n* Aggression, and *n* Abasement. This last is defined as a need to apologize, submit, or surrender. *n* Affiliation, *n* Nurturance, and *n* Succorance are examples from the category "affection between people," and *n* Counteraction is one of those in the category "defense of status."

PRESS AND THEMA

Satisfying a person's internal needs may be facilitated or frustrated by external circumstances. These circumstances, called *press*, can take many forms. Murray differentiated between two kinds of press. *Alpha press* are an objective aspect of the environment. Losing one's job is an Alpha press. *Beta press* are based on the individual's subjective impressions. An example might be a man's unsubstantiated belief that his boss plans to fire him. Because of the wide variety of circumstances that may facilitate or frustrate people in the satisfaction of their needs, Murray had to develop different lists of press for different purposes. An example of a press is the presence of friendly companions which, because it facilitates a person's *n* Affiliation,

Need	Goal of Need
Abasement	Submission to external forces
Achievement	Accomplishment
Affiliation	Establishing friendship
Aggression	Overcoming opposition
Autonomy	Freedom from constraint
Counteraction	Compensating for failure
Defendance	Defense against criticism
Deference	Admiration of a superior
Dominance	Control over one's environment
Exhibition	Impressing others
Harmavoidance	Avoiding physical injury
Infavoidance	Avoiding humiliation
Nurturance	Caring for the helpless
Order	Maintaining an orderly environment
Play	Enjoyment and fun
Rejection	Disregarding another
Sentience	Enjoyment of sensual feelings
Sex	Copulation
Succorance	Being taken care of by another
Understanding	Obtaining answers to questions

Table 6.1 Examples of Murray's Secondary Needs

is identified as *p* Affiliation. Similarly, someone who refuses to be dominated and thereby frustrates *n* Dominance would represent *p* Dominance.

It is, of course, possible for several needs to coincide and to interact with one or more press. An instance of such interaction is called a *thema*. A person's motivational system is composed of such themas. To identify these and thus to study a person's needs and press, Murray and his collaborators developed the *Thematic Apperception Test* (TAT) we discussed in chapter 2.

Research on Need for Achievement

Murray's theory of needs stimulated a great deal of research designed to investigate the ramifications of specific needs. The need for achievement, *n* Achievement, was explored in great detail by David C. McClelland and his colleagues (McClelland, Atkins, Clark, and Lowell, 1953).

The typical procedure used by this research group was to take groups of largely male college students and stimulate their achievement need by telling them that they were about to be given an important examination. Following this, the subjects were instructed to write stories to a limited number of TAT pictures that had been selected for their relevance to personal achievement. These stories were then analyzed and scored for *n* Achievement so that the investigators could identify individuals with high or low achievement needs. Groups of high and groups of low *n* Achievement were then exposed to various experimental conditions so that the relationship of achievement motivation to different aspects of behavior could be studied.

Using the procedure just outlined, McClelland's group found that individuals with high *n* Achievement are more ambitious, get more enjoyment from competitive situations, and tend to be more persistent in finding solutions to problems. High *n* Achievement individuals do best in college courses that they perceive as relevant to their future careers, and they tend to choose occupations with higher social prestige than do individuals with low achievement needs. When stress is placed on excellence in performance, research subjects with a high need for achievement outperform those with low achievement motivation, but such performance is not found under relaxed experimental conditions that do not seem to stimulate achievement need. In tasks that can be graded from simple to extremely difficult, persons with high need for achievement tend to choose an intermediate level of difficulty. This suggests that they find no challenge in tasks where success is virtually guaranteed and that they prefer not to become involved in tasks in which the chances of success are exceedingly small.

POWER NEED

Another motivation that has been studied by McClelland (1975) is the need for power. This need is measured in a fashion quite similar to that used for measuring *n* Achievement. Most of the research participants have again been men. Studies of *n* Power have shown that compared to their peers with low need for power, male college students high in that need more often hold office in campus organizations, write more letters to the campus newspaper, and are more frequently elected to important campus committees. They are also more likely to participate in or to watch vigorous competitive sports, to consume more alcohol, and to engage in exploitative sexual activity.

There is an interesting relationship between *n* Power and alcohol consumption. With the ingestion of alcohol, power themes in TAT stories increase, but the type of power themes depend on the amount of alcohol a subject has consumed. Small amounts of alcohol increase the frequency of such socially acceptable power themes as using power for the benefit of others, whereas larger amounts bring out more primitive, selfish themes of power, including those involving exploitative sexual and aggressive behavior.

DISPOSITIONAL THEORIES IN PERSPECTIVE

Dispositional theories of personality cover a wide range of approaches, from Allport's theory of traits, to Cattell's statistical analyses, through Eysenck's work on types, and Murray's interest in motivation. Each has its weaknesses and its strengths.

The trait approach risks circularity, and factor analysis entails subjective judgments on the part of the experimenter. The focus on extraversion–introversion tends to leave little room for environmental influences on behavior, and the interaction of needs and press is not stated in a systematic, testable fashion.

At the same time, Allport's focus on the individual, Cattell's statistical rigor, Eysenck's emphasis on biological factors, and Murray's stress on human motivation have all contributed to expanding our conception of personality and its components. Moreover, the research on *n* Achievement and *n* Power has shown that when one has identified these needs, one can predict how people will behave in laboratory experiments and in real life.

Even the ancient Greeks attempted to categorize people on the basis of their behavior or to explain behavior by postulating internal entities that control it. They spoke of a limited number of characters and temperaments. Gall attempted to determine people's traits by the shape of their skull. In modern times the dispositional personality theories have become more sophisticated. Allport proposed that traits provide the key to personality and worked out a detailed theory of how they determine behavior.

The statistical method of factor analysis permitted Cattell to reduce the very large number of adjectives denoting traits to only sixteen bipolar traits. The same method was employed by Eysenck to identify two dimensions of personality, one ranging from extraversion to introversion, the other from instability to stability. Eysenck and others have shown that these dimensions are related to biological and genetic factors.

The chapter ends with an outline of Murray's motivational theory and mention of research showing that with knowledge of people's needs one can predict how they will behave under specified circumstances. Each of the theories reviewed has some strong and some weak points. Together they have had a major impact on contemporary views of personality.

Selected Readings

Allport, G. W. 1965. *Letters from Jenny*. New York: Holt, Rinehart and Winston.

Cattell, R. B., and P. Kline. 1976. *The Scientific Analysis of Personality and Motivation*. New York: Academic Press.

Eysenck, H. J. 1982. *Personality, Genetics, and Behavior*. New York: Praeger.

Murray, H. A. 1962. *Explorations in Personality*. New York: Science Editions.

Plomin, R. 1990. *Nature and Nurture: An Introduction to Human Behavioral Genetics*. Pacific Grove, CA: Brooks/Cole.

7

Learning-Based Approaches to Personality

The second half of the twentieth century saw the development of several theories of personality that employ principles based on laboratory studies of learning. Like the research that had spawned them, these theories follow the behavioral tradition then dominant in American psychology. This tradition requires that the object of study be what people do—their observable behavior—and that constructs dealing with unobservable events inside the person be defined in terms of that behavior.

Dollard and Miller developed a personality theory that applied to human behavior principles discovered in studies of learning in animals. In so doing, they leaned heavily on formulations offered by Freud which they translated into learning-theory terms. They maintained that all behavior is motivated by drives and that learning results from the reduction of these drives.

Skinner held that inferences about what goes on inside the person are unnecessary. He insisted that human behavior can be explained by the detailed analysis of the relationship between the behavior and its environmental consequences.

Rotter believed that to understand human behavior one must take people's thoughts into account, particularly those that have to do with their expectations and evaluations of the rewards for their actions. This "cognitive focus" was further developed by Bandura, who stresses that much of what we learn is learned by observing others, and that how we see our own capabilities plays a decisive role in how we act and what we do.

The chapter ends with a brief look at behavioral approaches to the treatment of psychological disorders.

THE BEHAVIORAL TRADITION

At the beginning of the twentieth century *introspection* was the dominant method for studying mental processes. This meant that highly trained observers were presented with carefully controlled sensory stimuli and asked to describe their own mental experiences. John B. Watson (1878–1958) judged that psychology had made little progress using this approach. In his view, the proper object of study for psychologists was not something as elusive as people's minds, but the objectively observable things people do, their behavior. With an article entitled "Psychology as the Behaviorist Sees It," Watson (1913) founded *behaviorism*. It became a highly influential orientation in American psychology and remained so for more than sixty years (Baars, 1986).

Two Kinds of Behaviorism

Although Watson and his students published a few studies that dealt with the fears of young children, most of the research of the early behaviorists was concentrated on animals, mainly rats, whose behavior can be closely observed and experimentally controlled. It was not until mid-century, with the publication of *Personality and Psychotherapy*, by John Dollard and Neal Miller (Dollard and Miller, 1950), that behavioral psychologists turned their attention to human personality.

In a sense, it is paradoxical for a behaviorist to talk about personality. Watson had insisted that psychology could legitimately study only observable, overt behavior. That rules out the thoughts, memories, feelings, and emotions that seem to be such an integral part of what most people consider to be personality. Watson and his followers did not say that these covert processes do not exist; they merely pointed out that they neither lend themselves to objective research, nor are they relevant to the study of human behavior.

Extreme views such as these continue to be held by those who subscribe to a radical behaviorism. More compatible with the study of personality, as usually conceived, are those who subscribe to methodological behaviorism. Here cognitive and emotional processes are recognized as legitimate objects of study, provided their conceptualization ties them closely to observable events and overt behavior. When Dollard and Miller (1950) chose as the subtitle for their book the phrase "An Analysis in Terms of Learning, Thinking, and Culture," they declared themselves to be methodological behaviorists.

DOLLARD AND MILLER'S DRIVE-REDUCTION THEORY

Like many other psychologists, Dollard and Miller considered *personality* to be a short way of saying *the integrated total of overt and covert human behavior in its interaction with the environment*. What they offered was thus not so much a full-fledged theory of personality as a detailed description of the processes through which behavior is learned, maintained, and modified. In analyzing how behavior is modified in psychotherapy, Dollard and Miller relied on Freudian concepts that they translated into the learning-theory terms of their day.

Principles of Learning

The theory of learning on which Dollard and Miller based their formulations owed much to the classical experiments on *respondent conditioning* conducted by Ivan P. Pavlov (1849–1936) and to the contributions of Miller's mentor, Clark L. Hull (1884–1952).

RESPONDENT CONDITIONING

While studying the salivation of dogs, Pavlov had discovered that a previously neutral stimulus that is repeatedly paired with the presentation of a stimulus that naturally elicits a physiological response will eventually gain the capacity to elicit that physiological response even when the natural elicitor is absent. For example, when a light (which does not elicit salivation in dogs and is therefore considered "neutral") is repeatedly presented together with food (which does elicit salivation), it will eventually become capable of eliciting salivation, even when no food is offered. As is widely known, Pavlov referred to the food as the *unconditioned stimulus* (UCS), to the light as the *conditioned stimulus* (CS), to the natural salivation as the *unconditioned response* (UCR), and to the newly acquired salivation to the light alone as the *conditioned response* (CR). (Fig. 7.1.)

Before Conditioning		
UCS (food on tongue)	→	UCR (salivation)
CS (e.g., a light)	→	no relevant response
During Conditioning		
CS (light) + UCS (food on tongue)		
After Conditioning		
CS (light)	→	CR (salivation)

Fig. 7.1 Procedures employed in respondent conditioning

DRIVE REDUCTION

Building on the work of Pavlov and on his own studies with rats, Clark Hull (1943) had developed a complex theory of learning that applied to all animals, including humans. The theory was based on the notion that all behavior is motivated by a *drive*. There are *primary drives*, such as hunger, that are physiological in nature, and *secondary* or *acquired drives*, such as achievement, that are originally learned through association with primary drives.

According to Hull's theory, a person will learn to engage in a particular action under specific conditions when that action is *reinforced* (rewarded) by *drive reduction*. Technically speaking, when a person who is motivated by a drive makes a *response* in the presence of a distinct *cue* and the response is reinforced by *drive reduction*, he or she is likely to repeat that response when that cue is again present.

Let us assume that you are hungry (drive) and a friend takes you to a fast-food restaurant with a distinct trademark (cue), where you eat (response) a succulent hamburger that satisfies your hunger (drive reduction). This experience will increase the likelihood that next time you are hungry and pass a pair of golden arches you will stop to eat there again. That demonstrates that your eating in that restaurant had been reinforced by your reducing your hunger there during your first visit.

This homely example illustrates an important point about learning. Note that we could not know until your second visit to the restaurant whether your eating there had been reinforced. One cannot demonstrate learning while it is taking place, only later when the earlier response is repeated. It is the same in the classroom. The instructor cannot tell during the lecture whether you are learning anything; that can only be established by giving you a test later on. It is a weakness of reinforcement theory that one can tell only later, from the increased likelihood of a response, that reinforcement had taken place at an earlier time.

CUE-PRODUCING RESPONSES

Thus far we have spoken of cues only as external signs; stimuli that indicate that if a previously learned response were to occur, reinforcement (drive reduction) would follow. Cues are things people notice. People notice not only external events, however; they are also aware of internal events. Dollard and Miller therefore expanded their definition of responses to include thoughts, emotions, expectations, and signals emanating from the person's own body, such as pain and discomfort.

These internal cues are, by definition, not subject to an outsider's observations, and this creates a problem for behaviorists who want to work only with observable events. Dollard and Miller dealt with this dilemma by introducing the concept of *cue-producing responses*. They viewed these as *mediating responses* in that they are responses that intervene (mediate) between the external cues and overt responses, both of which an outsider can observe and therefore study. Like other responses, cue-producing responses are elicited by external cues, but they also have cue functions in their own right. Not only that, they can also serve as acquired drives.

The emotion of fear can serve as an example of a mediating response that has both drive and cue functions. Assume that a small boy experienced pain when a large dog jumped on him and knocked him down. The pain elicited fear and the response the boy made was to let out a loud scream that quickly brought his mother, who picked him up, cuddled him, and reduced both his pain and his fear.

That drive reduction probably reinforced the response of screaming to the internal cue of fear. Whether that assumption is correct, we will see the next time the boy encounters a fear-eliciting situation; a thunderstorm, let us say. If he again screams, we can say that he had learned that response in the dog-pain-fear-scream situation. But what, under these circumstances, would be the drive? The answer is, the fear. It is not only the cue for screaming, but also the drive for the screams; the drive that will be reduced, at least occasionally, by the mother's solicitations.

GENERALIZATION, DISCRIMINATION, EXTINCTION

In the example just given the boy screamed even though neither pain nor dog was present. That is explained by a process called *mediated generalization* through which very different stimuli that elicit fear can lead to the same response: screaming. It is likely, however, that the solicitous mother is present only in the house and not when the boy is playing in the yard or at a neighbor's. With the screaming thus selectively reinforced, that response should demonstrate *discrimination* in that the boy would scream to the cue of fear only when he is in the house.

As long as the boy is small it is likely that his screaming will predictably bring his mother on the run so that this behavior will continue to be reinforced. Later, when that consequence will no longer be occasionally forthcoming, the boy should cease screaming when he is afraid; the absence of reinforcement will have made the response undergo *extinction*.

Conflict

In addition to employing drive-reduction theory to explain how the individual differences that are so important for a discussion of personality might come about, Dollard and Miller also offered an analysis of behavior under *conflict*.

To understand conflict we must first recognize that not all consequences of our actions are necessarily positive, thus motivating us to attain them. There also are negative consequences, such as pain, guilt, or embarrassment, that we would just as soon avoid. When positive consequences beckon, we approach them. When negative consequences threaten, we avoid them. But life would be easy if these alternatives always appeared one at a time. Unfortunately, much of the time we are forced to choose between two consequences, and often one possible action can have both positive and negative consequences.

THREE TYPES OF CONFLICT

When two goals with positive consequences are in conflict, the situation is called an *approach–approach conflict*. When two goals with negative consequences conflict, an *avoidance–avoidance conflict* exists. The third possibility is the *approach–avoidance conflict* when one and the same goal has both a positive and a negative consequence.

Miller and Dollard offered the following five rules that permit one to predict how each of these conflict situations is likely to be resolved:

1) The tendency to approach a positive goal increases the closer one comes to that goal.

2) The tendency to avoid a negative goal increases the closer one comes to that goal.

3) The tendency to avoid a negative goal increases with nearness more rapidly than does the corresponding tendency to approach a positive goal.

4) An increase in the strength of a drive with respect to a goal will increase the tendency to approach or avoid that goal.

5) Whenever two response tendencies compete, the stronger will prevail.

Applying these rules to the approach–approach and the avoidance–avoidance conflicts, one can easily predict what a person would do, but the approach–avoidance conflict calls for a closer look.

APPROACH–AVOIDANCE ANALYZED

The approach–avoidance conflict can be exemplified by a hungry man on a weight-loss diet who is tempted by a high-calorie dessert. Such a situation often results in a "should I or shouldn't I?" vacillation that reflects the person's being torn between approaching and avoiding that food, a state that is known as *ambivalence*. What causes this ambivalence?

The answer can be found in the third of the five rules. It states that the tendency to avoid a negative goal increases with nearness more rapidly than does the corresponding tendency to approach a positive goal. (Fig. 7.2)

Let us apply this rule to our example of the hungry dieter. There the negative goal is represented by eating the food and the associated fear of gaining weight. The positive goal is represented by eating the food and the associated reduction of hunger. Fear, we know, is a learned drive that varies

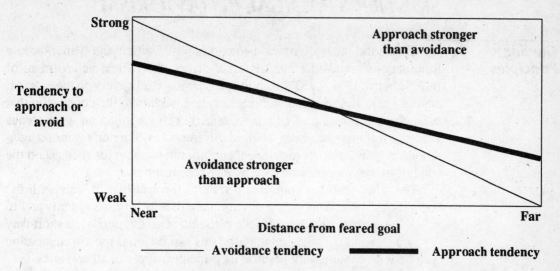

Fig. 7.2   *The Approach–Avoidance Conflict: The distance from the feared goal determines whether it will be approached or avoided.*

as a function of proximity to the feared object. The closer we are, the greater the fear. Hunger, on the other hand, is an innate, internal drive that remains relatively constant regardless of one's distance to food.

Although the tendency to avoid increases with nearness to the goal more rapidly than the tendency to approach, there is a point at which the strength of these tendencies is equal. Picture the hungry dieter, fork in hand, in front of the high-calorie dessert. His fork has come to a stop at that point of equal strengths. Moving it forward increases his fear of gaining weight, so he moves it back to where his hunger is stronger than the fear which drives him forward again. How will this highly imaginary scenario end?

If our friend sits in front of the dish long enough, the hunger will increase, whereas the fear remains the same. According to the fourth rule, the tendency to approach will then win out. That can happen even if we do not postulate an increase in hunger because the man can also fall back on the much-used "I'll start my diet tomorrow," which lowers the fear component of the ambivalence and makes it possible to enjoy the whipped cream-covered chocolate layer cake.

SKINNER'S RADICAL BEHAVIORISM

Guiding Principles

Unlike the methodological behaviorism of Dollard and Miller, whose formulations revolved around internal drives, the radical behaviorism of B. F. Skinner (1938, 1953) had him focus almost exclusively on the external environment. His research with pigeons had led him to the conclusion that *behavior is a function of its consequences*. The emphasis on what comes after the response has been *emitted* differentiates Skinner's *operant conditioning* from Pavlov's respondent conditioning, where the focus is on the conditions that precede and thereby *elicit* the response.

The term *operant conditioning* reflects the fact that it deals with the "operations" or actions on the environment that the organism emits and to which the environment provides the consequences. *Organism* is a short way of saying "human or other animal" and this expression is used in connection with operant conditioning because its principles apply to all creatures.

As pointed out earlier, radical behaviorists do not deny that internal events exist. They study external events because these are immediately available for scientific analysis, whereas internal events can be studied only indirectly and by inference. The external events that Skinner chose to study are the observable characteristics of the environment, the *stimuli* that control overt behavior, the *responses*. The focus on stimuli and responses is the reason for this being called S–R approach. The essence of that approach is to discover the lawful relationship between stimulus and response by what Skinner called a *functional analysis*; an analysis, that is, of the function that the *consequence* of a response serves in its relationship to the stimulus. This will become clear in a moment.

Operant Conditioning

Remember that in radical behaviorism one cannot refer to such internal events as desire or disgust, pleasure or pain, expectation or memory. An analysis of human behavior must therefore rely solely on a person's action (the response) and on what is happening in that person's environment (the stimuli) both before and after that action.

REINFORCEMENT

The key to understanding operant conditioning is the concept of *reinforcement*. As was true with the drive-reduction theory of Dollard and Miller, however, one can only tell whether reinforcement has taken place by observing whether a response that has been emitted undergoes a change. Changes in a response can be in probability, frequency, speed, or magnitude, and these may increase, decrease, or remain the same.

Let us go back to the screaming child we met in our discussion of Dollard and Miller and analyze his behavior in Skinnerian terms. We observe a large dog knocking the boy down (stimulus), the boy emits a scream (response), and the mother picks him up (consequence). As radical behaviorists we make no assumptions about pain or fear because we cannot observe these internal events. Nor are we entitled to speculate whether the boy liked being picked up or whether he found it comforting. In fact, we can say very little about this episode until the next time the boy encounters a large dog. When that occurs and he screams more loudly than last time we can say—in retrospect—that the consequence of being picked up had reinforced screaming in the presence of a large dog. Moreover, we can now declare that being picked up by the mother served the function of reinforcing the screaming, of constituting *positive reinforcement*. Technically, this is referred to as a *reinforcing stimulus* because it consists of an event in the boy's environment. As we will point out later, the big dog is technically a *discriminative stimulus*.

We spoke of positive reinforcement in this illustration because the response had increased in magnitude; it had been strengthened by adding something to the boy's environment (being picked up) that had not been there until after he emitted his scream. There is another way to strengthen a response. It is called *negative reinforcement*.

In negative reinforcement something that had been present in the environment when the response was emitted is removed as a consequence of (*contingent* upon) the response, as in the following example. A loud, high-pitched noise (stimulus) comes from the radio. A woman gets up and switches the radio off (response). The noise stops (consequence). If the next time this noise begins the woman gets up more quickly to switch the radio off, we are entitled to consider the cessation of the noise to have served the function of negative reinforcement, strengthening the woman's response. Note that reinforcement, whether positive or negative, always *strengthens* a response. Negative reinforcement is not the same as punishment!

Punishment weakens the response, but again we cannot tell that a consequence was punishing until after we have seen its effect on the response the next time it occurs. If the probability, frequency, speed, or magnitude of the response *decreased*, the consequence had been punishment. Like positive reinforcement, punishment is something that is produced contingent on a response that has been emitted.

Note, incidentally, that the loud noise from the radio which, when turned off, reinforced behavior, could, when turned on, punish a response. If each time the woman turned on her radio it emitted a loud, high-pitched noise, her turning on the radio would soon become less likely. The same environmental event can serve as a punisher at its onset and as a negative reinforcer at its offset.

To summarize, positive reinforcement strengthens a response by producing something, punishment weakens a response by producing something, and negative reinforcement strengthens a response by removing something. There is a fourth possibility. It consists of weakening a response by removing something; it is called *response cost.* Here something is taken away contingent on a response that, when given, is known to provide positive reinforcement. Response-cost procedures can be found in daily life in privileges being suspended or fines being levied, but these should be viewed as response costs only when they have the effect of weakening the responses they follow.

There remains one more condition that can obtain after a response has been omitted: The response can have no effect on the environment so that there is no consequence at all. Under those circumstances the response is unlikely to be repeated, and, if it had previously been reinforced by a consequence, it will undergo *extinction,* eventually dropping out of the person's behavioral *repertoire.*

SCHEDULES OF REINFORCEMENT

Whether and how soon a response will undergo extinction as a result of not being reinforced depends on the frequency and regularity with which that response had been reinforced up to that point. That is known as the *schedule of reinforcement,* and Skinner, together with his students and colleagues, investigated the effect of these schedules in great detail.

When a response is reinforced every time it is emitted, the organism is on a *continuous reinforcement schedule.* Such a schedule leads to very rapid response *acquisition* (learning), but equally rapid extinction when reinforcement is omitted on several successive *trials* (occasions). The reason for this is easy to understand if one does something a radical behaviorist abhors, imagining what a pigeon or person might be thinking under those conditions.

Suppose a vending machine has been dispensing a candy bar every time you dropped in your coins, that is, you were on a continuous reinforcement schedule. If one day the machine failed to deliver, you would quickly realize that it is broken and stop using it, particularly if it also failed to work the next time you tried. Your response is undergoing extinction. However, a week or so later, reasoning that the machine had been fixed, you might try it once again. That is known as the *spontaneous recovery* of an extinguished response. It demonstrates that extinction is not a wiping out of an acquired response, but merely a failure to perform it. Should the machine once again deliver your candy, you would very quickly return to your old *habit* of dropping money into it.

Although a well-maintained machine might deliver reinforcements on every trial, most human behavior and particularly that occurring in social interactions is not on a continuous schedule, but on a *partial reinforcement schedule.* That is, the reinforcement is forthcoming not regularly but intermittently. That is why such a schedule is also known as an *intermittent reinforcement schedule.* There are four types of such schedules. They differ according to the basis on which delivery of reinforcements is determined.

On a *fixed interval schedule* reinforcement is given for the first response that is emitted after a specified period of time has passed since the last reinforcement. On such a schedule the frequency of responses typically increases as reinforcement approaches and falls off after it has been delivered. When reinforcement ceases extinction follows quickly. The weekly paycheck is an example of a fixed interval schedule.

On a *variable interval schedule* the time period between reinforcements varies randomly around a specified time and that time is expressed by an average. Sport fishing has been used as an example of a variable interval schedule, and those addicted to it will tell you that, on the average, they catch a fish every couple of hours. The response rate on such a schedule is steady but relatively low and the behavior is highly resistant to extinction.

On a *fixed ratio schedule* reinforcement is given after a specified number of responses has been emitted. For instance, when a 5:1 ratio is used one reinforcer is provided for every fifth response, regardless of how much time has elapsed. Paying workers on a piecework basis is an example of a fixed ratio schedule. That schedule produces a very high rate of responses and extinction comes slowly ("the faster you work, the more money you make and eventually you'll get paid"). Because of these characteristics this schedule lends itself to the pernicious employment practice of the "speed up" in which the boss "thins out the ratio," demanding ever more production for the same amount of pay.

Lastly, there is the *variable ratio schedule.* Here the number of responses required before reinforcement is delivered varies randomly around a specified average. Of the four partial reinforcement schedules, this regimen produces the highest and steadiest response rate. Gamblers operate under a variable ratio schedule. In an honest game the payoff is determined by chance and the ratio can be determined only when the game has ended. When the game is "fixed," however, as in the case of slot machines, those in control determine the ratio and can manipulate it to their advantage. In either case, gamblers do not know the odds and, unfortunately, many keep at the game until their resources are spent.

SHAPING AND PROMPTING

According to the principles of operant conditioning, a response can be acquired and learned only when it has been reinforced, and reinforcement can take place only after the response has been made. That raises the question how a response originally got its start so that it could be reinforced. There are two answers. One involves the genes; the other, outside helpers.

All members of every species are born with certain inborn, genetically determined responses. Newborn chicks peck, young pigs root, baby birds open their beaks and chirp, and human neonates coo, cry, smile, and move their limbs. These random movements, which Skinner referred to as *free operants*, eventually make contact with something that, by nature, has reinforcing capacity. The chick finds a corn, the pig a truffle, the bird gets a worm, and the infant attracts a caretaker. The innate behavior is thus reinforced and maintained.

The development of human behavior in its complexity fortunately need not depend on chance encounters with the *primary reinforcers* provided by nature. Events that initially lack the capacity to reinforce will, when repeatedly paired with primary reinforcers, become reinforcers in their own right. Thus, a smiling face that the infant sees whenever milk is provided can become a *secondary reinforcer*. Moreover, the environment does not furnish either primary or secondary reinforcers after every response, but selectively, and this leads to the *shaping* of behavior.

The caretaker who approaches the crib responds selectively to the infant's innate behavior. A smile is returned with a smile, cooing is responded to with some words, crying results in being picked up, and so forth. In the course of such interactions, some responses are strengthened and others go unnoticed or are purposely ignored. Such shaping is often carried out in a systematic fashion, as when an adult helps a toddler walk.

Later on, when the child has acquired language (which some believe to follow operant principles), the adult or older child may use *prompts*, suggesting responses and reinforcing these or providing a *model*, demonstrating what one must do to be reinforced. Gradually, over the years, through prompting, shaping, modeling, and the use of primary and secondary reinforcers, we humans acquire behaviors that are far removed from the innate responses with which we are born.

DISCRIMINATIVE STIMULI

Thus far we have spoken of the stimulus in the stimulus-response-reinforcement chain simply as some aspect of the environment in the presence of which the organism emits a response that is followed by a reinforcing consequence. What is the function of the stimulus in that chain of events?

In operant conditioning, as pointed out earlier, the stimulus does not elicit the response, as it does in Pavlovian conditioning. In operant conditioning the stimulus that was present on the previous occasion when reinforcement was experienced now serves as a signal that the same response is likely again to be followed by a reinforcer. Once a response has thus come under *stimulus control*, the stimulus that has this capacity is called the *discriminative stimulus*, because its presence or absence helps the organism discriminate when a response is likely to be followed by reinforcement and when not.

Because the environment does not remain the same, discriminative stimuli are unlikely to be identical from one time to the next. The mother, who has become a discriminative stimulus for reaching up and smiling, won't be wearing the same dress every time she approaches the baby's crib. Fortunately, the normal human infant is capable of *stimulus generalization*, so that any of a range of similar discriminative stimuli can elicit the same response. That response will not be emitted, however, if the stimulus is too dissimilar from the one under which the response had originally been learned. The baby thus comes to *discriminate* between the mother and a stranger.

ROTTER'S SOCIAL LEARNING THEORY

When Skinner (1953) extended the principles of operant conditioning to human behavior he asserted that it could be understood without recourse to such mental processes as thoughts, memories, plans, and expectations. In contrast, Julian B. Rotter (pronounced ROT-er) (1954) insisted that to understand human behavior one must consider not only the effect of reinforcement but also the person's anticipation of that reinforcement and the value he or she places on it.

Four Basic Concepts

Rotter employs four basic concepts that, together, permit one to predict a person's behavior.

BEHAVIOR POTENTIAL

As used by Rotter, the term *behavior* applies to everything a person might do in response to a situation. That includes thinking, talking, gesturing, facial expressions, motor activity, and emotional reactions. Thus, there are a variety of ways in which a person can respond to a situation. When someone insults you, you might respond with anger, reciprocate with an insult, make a disagreeable face, walk away, or think about not losing your temper. Each of these behaviors has a potential for occurrence, a likelihood of happening in that particular situation. The same response may have a high *behavior potential* in one situation, a low one in another. The higher the potential of a particular response relative to that of other available responses, the more likely it is for that response to occur.

REINFORCEMENT VALUE

People are often faced with a variety of activities among which they have to choose. Usually, each of these activities has a different outcome, that is, each has a different reinforcer as its consequence. Which of the activities one chooses depends on which of the reinforcers one prefers, on one's subjective *reinforcement value*. The value of a given reinforcement is always relative to the other available and equally likely reinforcements. If my choice is limited to chocolate ice cream or vanilla ice cream, I would pick chocolate, but if strawberry ice cream were added to the selection, I would choose it.

EXPECTANCY

In determining behavior potential one must consider both reinforcement value and *expectancy*. The behavior potential of my choosing strawberry ice cream was based not only on its reinforcement value being higher than that of chocolate and vanilla, but also on the fact that I expected it to taste as good as I remembered it from an earlier visit to a different ice cream parlor. More formally stated, expectancy refers to the probability that a specific reinforcement will occur if a certain behavior is chosen in a particular situation.

THE PSYCHOLOGICAL SITUATION

The last of Rotter's four basic concepts stresses the fact that all behavior occurs in a *psychological situation* to which the individual brings the three subjective dispositions just discussed and on which that situation has a major impact. The reinforcement value one assigns to various outcomes and the expectancies one has regarding a reinforcement always depend on the situation in which one happens to be. Had I been in a different ice cream parlor, or in different company, or at a different time of year, the result of my choice might have been different.

Individual Differences. Rotter refers to the situation as a *psychological* situation to emphasize that the same objective set of circumstances has a different effect on different people, depending on their personal background, previous experiences, and present condition. Thus, like behavior potential, reinforcement value, and expectancy, the psychological situation is a highly personal concept. With all four varying from individual to individual and for each individual from time to time, it is easy to see that these four basic concepts contribute mightily to the individual differences Rotter's theory was designed to explain.

Locus of Control and Interpersonal Trust

In formulating expectancy Rotter had differentiated between two types, *specific expectancy* and *generalized expectancy*. Thus far the expectancies we referred to were of the specific kind; expectancies about strawberry ice cream, for example.

In addition to such specific expectancies, however, people also have more generalized attitudes toward life, such as to what extent chance governs what happens to us and whether people are basically trustworthy. These are generalized expectancies and Rotter views them as important for understanding a person's behavior.

LOCUS OF CONTROL

What determines whether you succeed or fail in reaching a goal you have been trying to attain? Some people will answer this question by attributing the outcome to their own effort. Others will answer that it depends on whether luck is with them. The difference between these two groups is one of a generalized expectancy about the *locus of control* over the outcome of their actions. Those who attribute success and failure to their own abilities and efforts expect the locus of control to be internal. Those, on the other hand, who attribute the outcome to fate, luck, or outside agents expect the locus of control to be external.

Rotter developed a test, the *I–E Scale*, to assess a person's locus of control. Studies conducted with this scale have shown that those with an internal locus of control—the *internals*, for short—are more likely to seek information about a task, show higher achievement on intellectual and performance tasks, and are less likely to succumb to social pressure than those whose scores on the I–E Scale place them among those with an external locus of control, the *externals*.

Locus of control is seen as a generalized expectancy because an internal will approach a great variety of tasks and situations with the assumption that he or she can influence the outcome in important ways. An external, conversely, will approach the same tasks and situations convinced that the outcome is in the hands of influences over which he or she has no control.

Research results suggest that whether locus of control is internal or external is, at least in part, a function of one's life experiences. People who grew up in an unpredictable, chaotic environment or who live under conditions where success is never achieved, no matter what they do, are not likely to develop or maintain an internal locus of control.

INTERPERSONAL TRUST

Rotter also developed the *Interpersonal Trust Scale*, with which a person's readiness to trust another's promise or assurance can be assessed. Like locus of control, interpersonal trust is a generalized expectancy. High trusters approach others with the expectation that they can be trusted; low trusters are more likely to be on their guard.

Interpersonal trust scores are correlated with socioeconomic status. Among college students high trusters were found to come from higher socioeconomic groups than low trusters. Moreover, trust scores were related to the scores of their parents. These findings strongly suggest that whether one is trusting or guarded in relating to others is influenced by one's childhood experiences. Parents who make promises and are able to keep them because they have the financial resources to carry them out are likely to raise children who become trusting adults.

BANDURA'S SOCIAL COGNITIVE THEORY

Ever since 1959, when he and Richard Walters analyzed adolescent aggression from a learning-theory standpoint (Bandura and Walters, 1959), Albert Bandura has been working toward a comprehensive formulation of personality to which he now refers to as a *social cognitive* theory (Bandura, 1986). In presenting that theory Bandura acknowledges that he had the benefit not only of the earlier contributions of such theorists as Dollard and Miller, Skinner, and Rotter, but also of the work of his own students and colleagues. Bandura has been able to incorporate in his theory many useful constructs others had developed, while avoiding or, where possible, improving upon their more controversial ideas.

Basic Concepts   RECIPROCAL DETERMINISM

A long-standing debate among personality theorists is whether behavior is primarily determined by characteristics, such as traits, that are located within the person and carried from situation to situation, or whether the environment dictates the way in which the person will act. Dispositional theories, like those we encountered in the previous chapter, represent the former viewpoint, whereas Skinner is an exponent of the latter.

Bandura argues that neither of these extreme positions is correct and offers the notion of a *reciprocal determinism* to explain how personality comes about. According to that formulation, the *person*, with his or her characteristic dispositions, expectations, and self-perceptions, interacts with the particulars of the momentary *situation* and engages in *behavior* that, in turn, affects both the person and the situation. In other words, person, situation, and behavior mutually influence one another.

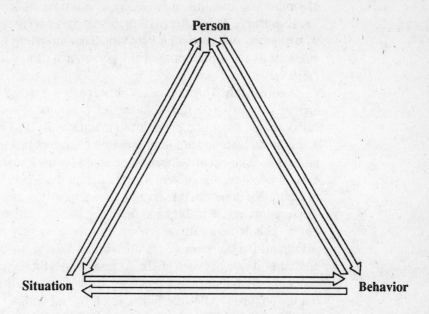

*Fig. 7.3 The mutual influence of person, situation, and behavior
as construed in reciprocal determinism*

ACQUISITION AND PERFORMANCE

Another issue on which personality theorists have disagreed revolves around the role of reinforcement in learning. Is reinforcement essential? When does reinforcement take place? What is it that is reinforced?

Here Bandura offered the important distinction between the *acquisition* of a response and the *performance* of that response. A reinforcing consequence, he argues, is not essential for learning how a certain action is performed, but for a person actually to perform that action, he or she must have the *expectation* that it will lead to a reward.

OBSERVATIONAL LEARNING

The distinction between acquisition and performance as well as the reason why Bandura calls his a *social cognitive* theory are readily apparent in his analysis of *observational learning*.

Without denying that some learning takes place by Pavlovian conditioning and some by operant reinforcement, Bandura points out that many social responses and personal characteristics are acquired by observing the behavior of others and imitating these *models*. Learning by imitation is not an original idea of Bandura's. Miller and Dollard had published a book called *Social Learning and Imitation* in 1941. It is to Bandura's credit, however, that his laboratory research identified the mechanisms that are involved in observational learning, or *modeling*. It is a three-stage process.

Exposure. This is the first stage. In it the *observer* is exposed to a model who engages in a particular behavior. That modeling can be done by a *live model* or by the representation of a person in a film, a story, or a cartoon—a *symbolic model*.

Acquisition. This is the second stage of the modeling process. It is not enough to be in the presence of a model. One must also *attend* to that model's behavior and *store* that behavior in memory if it is to be learned. Note that attention and storage are unobservable cognitive processes. Whether these processes have occurred can be checked by asking the observer after the exposure to describe or demonstrate the model's behavior. Only when that is accurately done can one be sure that acquisition has taken place.

Acceptance. The third and final step in observational learning is *acceptance*. This is demonstrated when the observer performs the model's behavior in a spontaneous fashion without having to be prompted, and in pursuit of his or her own goals. Assume that a three-year-old boy has been watching his father practice putting strokes with golf club and ball on the living-room rug. After the father has left, and without anyone having said anything to the child, the boy takes a stick and tries to hit a small, round object with it. That would be an instance of observational learning, with acquisition and acceptance.

REINFORCEMENT AND PUNISHMENT

Bandura has shown that acquisition and acceptance are made more likely when the observer was exposed to a model whose behavior was reinforced. Conversely, when the model's behavior was punished, the observer is less likely to perform that behavior or more likely to perform its opposite. Because these consequences affect the observer's behavior without the observer having experienced them directly, they are referred to as *vicarious reinforcement* and *vicarious punishment*.

PERCEPTION OF SELF-EFFICACY

In his work on observational learning Bandura described the cognitive processes through which we develop much of our social behavior and many of our personal characteristics. Another of his contributions deals with a cognitive process that plays a central role in determining what actions we undertake. It is the *perception of self-efficacy*. Efficacy has to do with ability and competence, with how effectively one is able to do something. Self-perceived efficacy or perceived self-efficacy is therefore a person's judgment of his or her own efficacy with respect to a specific task.

Through research on the topic Bandura has found that self-percepts of efficacy affect what people choose to do, how much effort they will put into an activity, how long they will persevere when a task proves difficult, and the amount of stress they experience in difficult or threatening situations. A strong sense of self-efficacy not only facilitates good performance; it also helps withstand failure. Moreover, people's judgment of their capabilities influences how they think and feel about a task as they anticipate doing it and while they are carrying it out.

In the course of studying self-efficacy, Bandura developed procedures for modifying people's perceptions of their own competence. He calls it *efficacy induction*. This can be accomplished by modeling, by giving instructions, by exposing a person to carefully managed success experiences, or by combinations of these. Using such procedures Bandura and others have shown that increasing self-perceived efficacy can reduce people's fears, help them better tolerate pain, assist in staying on a diet, or giving up smoking.

LEARNING-BASED FORMS OF THERAPY

Bandura's use of efficacy induction is but one of several instances in which learning-based principles are applied to treat people's psychological problems.

Pavlovian conditioning principles are being used in reducing disabling fears, and the reinforcement principles of Skinner are employed to teach new and more adaptive response patterns. *Biofeedback methods* employ electronic sensors that enable a person to monitor changes in such autonomic responses as blood pressure so that changes in the desired direction can be selectively reinforced. Modeling procedures are used to teach adaptive behavior, and various cognitive principles are employed to help people change their expectations, perceptions, and reactions.

LEARNING-BASED THEORIES IN PERSPECTIVE

The development of the personality theories we discussed in the previous chapters had taken place in settings that had little or no contact with the laboratory tradition of psychological science. These theories had been based on therapists' observations of their patients, on self-reports, on the statistical analyses of psychological tests, or on quasi-philosophical speculations that reflect the theorist's own value system. Learning-based theories, in contrast, derive their principles from basic laboratory research. That lends these theories both their strengths and their weaknesses.

STRENGTHS

Without denying the influence of genetic and other biological factors, the focus on learning helps to explain how the individual characteristics that make up an individual's personality are acquired and maintained. The theorists' behavioral tradition makes them insist on tying their formulations to observable phenomena, and their background in experimental psychology leads them to test their propositions in controlled research. Unlike the often vaguely stated formulations found in other approaches to personality theory, the behavioral approach demands that constructs be objectively defined and capable of being measured.

As far as specific theories are concerned, the one offered by Dollard and Miller had in its favor that it spelled out in great detail just how learning takes place, thereby reducing the vagueness of some Freudian assertions. Skinner's radical behaviorism eliminated all reference to unobservable events, insisting that only controlled laboratory research of observable phenomena can lead to an understanding of human behavior. The social learning theory of Rotter stressed that most of human behavior is learned and expressed in the individual's interaction with other people. With his studies of modeling Bandura filled in the details of how social learning occurs, and through his work on self-efficacy he elaborated on the cognitive aspects of human behavior.

WEAKNESSES

The fact that learning-based theories had their origin in the psychological laboratory also proved to be a source of a weakness, because principles discovered in research on dogs and pigeons are limited in their capacity to explain human behavior. Moreover, the need to partition behavior into single units of stimulus and response makes it difficult to deal with as complex an interacting system as human personality.

One of the reasons the theory of Dollard and Miller lost popularity was their use of drive reduction as the central explanatory concept. For the acquisition and maintenance of many aspects of human behavior it is not at all obvious what the drive is that is being reduced. Skinner's principles, though extremely powerful when applied to the behavior of young children or retarded adults, tend to provide less-adequate explanations for the behavior of intelligent, verbal adults. Moreover, although Skinner provided the tools for analyzing important aspects of human behavior, he did not offer a theory of personality; nor was that ever his intention. The cognitive emphasis of Rotter's and Bandura's theories was a reaction to radical behaviorism's refusal to accommodate cognitive processes. Their contributions are more compatible than Skinner's with the concept of personality, but their formulations lack the elegance and cohesiveness of the latter's principles.

The behavioral tradition, with its insistence on definitions that refer to observable behavior, has spawned several personality theories. At first, these theories employed principles that had been discovered in laboratory studies of animal learning. The earliest of these theories was proposed by Dollard and Miller. They maintained that all learning can be analyzed by identifying drive, cue, response, and reward, and that drive reduction explains why learning occurs.

Skinner's radical behaviorism did away with all inferences about internal processes and focused attention exclusively on observable phenomena. His assertion that behavior is a function of its consequences expresses his belief that what happens after a response is emitted determines whether that response will occur again, change, or undergo extinction. Positive and negative reinforcement maintain behavior; punishment reduces its frequency. Various schedules of reinforcement determine the rate of responding and the speed of extinction.

Rotter also drew on principles of learning in developing his theory, but he recognized that unless one took people's cognitions into account one could never hope to understand them. Expectations are particularly important cognitions because they determine what a person will and will not do. Another set of cognitions to which Rotter's theory calls attention is whether people believe that reaching their goal depends on their own efforts or on circumstances beyond their control.

Bandura took many contributions of other theorists and welded them into a comprehensive system of his own. In it he addresses the argument about the primacy of person or situation and proposes that personality is the result of an interplay between the person's predispositions, the situation, and his or her behavior. Much of our social behavior, Bandura argues, is learned through observing others. He differentiates between the acquisition of a response and its performance and states that no reinforcement is needed for acquisition to take place. Finally, Bandura offers the concept of self-perceived efficacy to explain why we will undertake some tasks and avoid others.

This section reviewed a variety of approaches to personality theory. Each has its strengths and each its weaknesses. We have made progress since the days when Hippocrates proposed that there were four types of people whose temperaments flowed from the liquid substances in their bodies. We have also come a long way since Sigmund Freud speculated about three entities inside the person that fight with one another for control. Nevertheless, we do not have a theory of personality that is universally accepted. The search for one continues. One of the forms this search takes is to investigate specific processes of personality. Some of these we will examine in Part III.

Selected Readings

Baars, B. J. 1986. *The Cognitive Revolution in Psychology*. New York: Guilford.

Bandura, A. 1986. *Social Foundations of Thought and Action: A Social Cognitive Theory*. Englewood Cliffs, NJ: Prentice-Hall.

Skinner, B. F. 1948. *Walden Two*. New York: Macmillan.

_____. 1971. *Beyond Freedom and Dignity*. New York: Knopf.

Part III:
Personality Processes

8

Development of Personality

The personality processes we shall discuss in this section differ from the personality theories presented thus far in that each deals in detail with one important facet of personality. In the personality theories these aspects were usually covered somewhat briefly as one of many other facets, because the focus was on personality as a whole or on the general principles that guide how a person functions.

Another difference between personality processes and personality theory lies in their source. Some personality theories, as we pointed out, were based on the clinical observations of therapists; others on laboratory studies of animals; and some on the administration and analysis of psychological tests. What is known about the psychological processes we are going to cover in this section, on the other hand, is based on research that was specifically aimed at finding answers to questions about these processes. Investigators of personality development, for example, set out to study the development of specific aspects of personality, not personality as a global entity.

Some personality theories include speculations about the beginnings of personality in childhood and its development during the early years of life. As discussed in earlier chapters, Freud and Erikson included in their theorizing rather detailed accounts of the phases or stages of psychosexual development and their influence on the personality of adults. That the behavior that characterizes an individual's personality is acquired during childhood is implied in all of the learning-based contributions to personality theory, but only Bandura's modeling principles detail just how that occurs. None of these theories, however, has looked in detail at the aspects of personality development that researchers have investigated and which we shall explore in this chapter: the development of the self-concept, the development of moral judgment, and the development over the lifespan.

DEVELOPMENT OF THE SELF-CONCEPT

The Sense of Self

The *self-concept* is an important aspect of an individual's personality. It may be the most important aspect of personality because the self-concept deals with the person's own sense of being an individual, distinct from other individuals, and with his or her unique combination of characteristics. The sense of self includes the knowledge that one is alive, an awareness of thinking thoughts and doing things, and a conviction of knowing more about oneself than anybody else can conceivably know. People's self-concept represents their definition of themselves; what they believe themselves to be.

PRIVATE KNOWLEDGE

Because it is a concept, and a concept is something one has in one's head, the self-concept is private knowledge, a cognition to which others have no direct access. This poses difficulties for those who wish to study the self-concept because they are limited to drawing inferences about a person's self-concept from observing what he or she does or says. When it comes to investigating the origins of the self-concept by studying infants, these difficulties are heightened because the route of language is not yet available.

Self-Awareness

The first step in the development of a self-concept is the discovery that one is a separate entity, an individual different from other individuals. That differentiation between self and nonself seems to begin when the infant is around three months old. By the first birthday it is well established. It is, however, one thing to know that I and my mother are two distinct entities; it is quite another to realize that I am I; that is, to be aware of myself. Such *self-awareness* seems to emerge between twelve and eighteen months. We know that from the results of so-called *mirror studies*.

MIRROR STUDIES

Investigators of self-awareness make use of the simple device of placing infants in front of a mirror and watching how they behave. Infants' interest in their own reflections emerges relatively early, but indications that they are recognizing themselves do not appear until after they are fifteen months old, when they engage in *mark-directed behavior*.

To describe mark-directed behavior, let us assume that an examiner wants to find out whether a particular eighteen-month-old boy is capable of that behavior. The examiner would surreptitiously put a spot of rouge on the boy's nose and then place him in front of a mirror. If, upon seeing his reflection, the little boy points to the spot on his own nose, one can infer that he has self-awareness because he must have recognized that the image in the mirror is, in fact, he himself and that the mark is located not on the face of the image but on his own nose.

INDIVIDUAL DIFFERENCES

Studies of the development of mark-directed behavior and of the self-awareness that is inferred from it have shown that there are *individual differences* in both the rate and the quality in which these capacities emerge. No one, however, has reported finding an infant who demonstrated mark-directed behavior before the age of fifteen months, and even at that age self-recognition is found in only about 25 percent of the children studied.

AGE-RELATED CHANGES

To recognize oneself in a mirror and to know that a spot on the nose that is seen in the mirror indicates that one has a spot on one's own nose implies the operation of such cognitive processes as perception, memory, and reasoning. The little boy in our example must have had previous experiences with a mirror from which he learned what his face looks like. In order to touch the spot on his nose in the rouge task he must then have remembered and recalled his features, compared these with the image before him, and realized what it was about his reflection that was different from what he remembered himself to look like. It is remarkable that children as young as eighteen months are able to do all that.

Object Permanence. We know that there are individual differences in the rate and quality in which such functions as perception, memory, and reasoning develop. It is therefore not surprising that research has shown a positive relationship between a variety of cognitive measures and self-recognition. One of the methods used in studies of this relationship is to test whether a child knows that an object continues to exist even when it is out of sight. That is known as *object permanence*.

To test for object permanence the examiner shows the child a toy and then covers it with a cloth or pillow. If the child retrieves the toy she or he is said to have reached the developmental stage of object permanence. Research has shown that there is a fairly high correlation between object permanence and self-recognition and that both develop gradually.

VARIABLES AFFECTING SELF-AWARENESS

The development of self-awareness that is inferred from self-recognition is faster in some children and slower in others. What are some of the variables that contribute to these individual differences? Some that come to mind are the family's socioeconomic status, the mother's educational level, the infant's gender and birth order, and the number of other children in the family. Each of these *demographic variables* has been investigated, but none was found to bear a relationship to the onset of self-recognition. There is, however, a variable involving mother and infant that has been found to bear a relationship to the development of self-recognition and thus to self-awareness. It is *attachment behavior*.

Attachment Behavior

Before we can examine the relationship between self-recognition and attachment behavior we must describe what attachment behavior is and how it is measured.

Around two or three months after birth the infant develops the capacity to discriminate among individuals, between father and mother, between strangers and members of the family. Just about this time there also emerges the beginning of what appears to be a preference for one specific caregiver, ordinarily but not inevitably the mother. A little later, usually during the second half of the first year, the infant begins to organize a series of already available behaviors into a cluster that is directed at this specific caregiver. These behaviors are smiling, looking, visual following, and vocalizing. A little later, clinging and physical following are added to this list. Because all of these actions serve to establish and maintain physical proximity or psychological contact with the caregiver, they are called *attachment behaviors*, *attachment* for short.

A RECIPROCAL RELATIONSHIP

Attachment is a two-way, reciprocal relationship between the mothering person and the child. Smiling, cooing, and looking would do the infant little good if there were not someone who responded to these smiles, looks, and sounds by engaging in behaviors that provide the secure base from which the child can set out to explore the environment. Viewed in this light, attachment is not an attribute of the child, but a quality that permeates the interaction between two individuals. To assess the quality of attachment Mary Ainsworth and her associates (Ainsworth, Behar, Waters, and Wall, 1978) developed a technique called *the strange situation*.

THE STRANGE SITUATION

This strange situation is strange in the sense that it is unfamiliar to the one-year-old infant whose reactions to it are unobtrusively observed in a series of standardized episodes. First mother and infant are alone in a room

Episode	Participants	Events	Time
1	Mother, Infant, Experimenter	Mother with infant is taken into experimental room and given instructions. Experimenter leaves.	30 sec.
2	Mother, Infant	Mother sits looking at magazine while infant explores the room. If infant fails to explore the toys within 2 min., mother is to call attention to them.	3 min.
3	Stranger, Mother, Infant	A woman whom infant has never seen enters, greets mother, and sits silently in a chair for 1 min. She then talks with mother for 1 min., then attempts to interact with infant for 1 min.	3 min.
4	Stranger, Infant	Stranger reduces her interaction with infant. If infant resumes play, she sits quietly in chair. If infant is upset she tries to provide comfort; otherwise, episode ends.	3 min.*
5	Mother, Infant	Mother reenters and stranger leaves. Mother tries to interest infant in toys. When infant seems comfortably occupied, mother gets up, says "bye-bye," and leaves the room.	3 min. or more
6	Infant	As in all other episodes, the infant is observed from an adjoining room by use of a one-way mirror. If infant becomes unduly upset, episode is terminated.	3 min.*
7	Stranger, Infant	Stranger rejoins infant, initiates interaction guided by infant's behavior. If infant engages in solitary play, stranger retreats to her chair.	3 min.*
8	Mother, Infant	Mother reenters, greets and picks up infant while stranger quietly leaves. Mother interacts spontaneously with her infant until end of episode.	3 min.

* or less if infant becomes unduly distressed

Table 8.1 The episodes of the Strange Situation

that contains a number of age-appropriate toys for the child and some magazines for the mother. A female stranger then joins them and tries to interact with the infant. During this the mother quietly leaves the room so that the infant is left with the stranger. After three minutes the mother reenters and the stranger departs so that mother and infant are once again alone. The mother now seeks to interest the infant in one of the toys, and when the infant seems comfortably occupied, she rises, says "bye-bye," and leaves him or her alone. After three minutes, the stranger comes back into the room and, unless the infant is engaged in solitary play, tries to interact with her or him. Three minutes later the stranger again exchanges places with the mother, who greets and picks up the infant for some spontaneous interaction that lasts for another three minutes. Throughout all this trained observers behind a one-way mirror watch and record the infant's movements, posture, looking, crying, smiling, and vocalizing. Should the infant become unduly upset during any of the mother-absent episodes, that condition is immediately terminated.

THREE FORMS OF ATTACHMENT

The primary focus of the observations conducted during the various episodes of the strange situation is on the infant's reactions to the entrances, exits, and absences of the mother and the stranger. It is these reactions, especially those to the reunion with the mother after the two separations, that enabled Ainsworth and her fellow investigators to identify three major classes or groupings of attachment; they named these *secure attachment, resistant attachment,* and *avoidant attachment.* We shall describe each of these, remembering that the terms refer not to the infant, but to the quality of the mother-infant interaction.

Secure Attachment. During the first strange situation episode during which mother and infant are alone and before the stranger enters, infants whose behavior reflects secure attachment will have used their mother as a base from which to explore the room. When the stranger enters, they may scurry back to the mother as if seeking the safety of her proximity. During the separation episodes exploration is reduced and distress becomes likely, and following them one can observe an increase in such attachment behaviors as crying, clinging, vocalizing, and looking. In the reunion episodes, such infants seek contact with and proximity to the mother, or at least interaction with her. Once reunited with their mother, they quickly recover from the distress shown during separation and display no negative emotions, such as anger.

Resistant Attachment. In this form of attachment the infants show signs of anxiety even while they are with their mother in the episode before the first separation. They become intensely distressed by the separation and are difficult to quiet upon reunion. Although they will seek proximity to the mother when she returns, they resist her attempts to initiate contact and interaction with them. They will kick, hit, and squirm to be put down, or push away a toy that is offered to them.

Avoidant Attachment. Unlike the infants in the other two groups, those classified as showing avoidant attachment rarely cry during the separation episodes or upon reunion. What particularly distinguishes them, however, is that they actively avoid their mother when she reenters the room. They ignore her and look away, actually turning their back to her when the mother seeks to establish contact or interaction with them. Occasionally these infants may make abortive approach responses, but throughout the remaining period they fail to resume active exploration. When reunited following the second separation episode, these infants display the same or even greater avoidance of their mother.

STABILITY OVER TIME

Traces of the pattern of attachment behaviors displayed by individual infants in the strange situation when they were one year old have been found in their personality when they were five years old and their teachers were asked to rate their behavior. Those who had earlier been classified as securely attached were now described as spontaneous, enthusiastic, resourceful, curious, self-reliant, and able to maintain appropriate control over their impulses, wishes, and desires. In contrast, those who had been assigned to the avoidant or resistant categories of attachment—collectively referred to as *insecurely attached*—had difficulty with self-control. The children from the avoidant group were described as maintaining too tight a control over their impulses so that they were rigid and lacked spontaneity, whereas those from the resistant group had too little self-control so that they tended to act impulsively and to be unable to delay gratification.

We began this discussion of attachment because we had asked how this important phase in the development of human interaction relates to the development of self-recognition. To that we can now return.

Attachment and Self-Recognition

From the point of view of the development of the child's self-concept one might assume that early emergence of self-recognition is a positive sign. Moreover, because secure attachment would seem to be the most positive of the three forms of attachment, children assigned to that category might be expected to develop self-recognition earlier than children whose attachment is of the avoidant or resistant quality.

AN UNEXPECTED FINDING

In view of this reasoning it comes as a surprise to learn that when this assumption was tested in a major longitudinal study (Lewis, Brooks-Gunn, and Jaskir, 1985), the opposite was found to be true: The insecurely attached group of children produced more appropriate self-recognition behaviors at an earlier age than the securely attached infants. Not that the securely attached were delayed; the insecurely attached were early.

To understand this surprising finding one must remember that self-recognition manifested by the mirror task is used to evaluate self-awareness; early self-recognition can thus be equated with early self-awareness. Why should insecurely attached children develop self-awareness earlier than securely attached children?

A POSSIBLE EXPLANATION

Recall how infants who are classified as showing avoidant attachment behave in the strange situation. During their mother's absence they rarely cry either when she leaves or when she returns. Upon reunion with the mother these children actively avoid her, ignore her, look away and turn around when she attempts to establish contact or to initiate interaction. It is as if these children were displaying *self-reliance*; as if they were saying, "Never mind, I don't need you. I can't rely on you. I can take care of myself."

Attachment provides the infant with a secure, protecting base from which to explore the environment and to which to return when threat is encountered. When that base is not strong and reliable, as it appears to be in the case of insecurely attached children, the exploring infant has to be more self-reliant, more alert to potential dangers.

Early self-recognition may therefore be a reflection of insecurely attached children's need to rely less on their mother and more on themselves, to be wary and vigilant, and to act on their own.

If this were the case early self-recognition would be a desirable sign from the point of view of the developing self-concept. But this is another assumption that is contradicted by the results of research. By the time they are six years old, children who had been early self-recognizers tend to have a less-positive image of themselves than those whose self-recognition developed later. Early emergence of self-recognition can thus not be viewed as a positive sign as far as personality development is concerned.

SELF-AWARENESS AND SELF-CONCEPT

When, at eighteen months of age, a girl looks in a mirror and touches a red spot that has been placed on her nose we can infer that she is aware that what she is looking at is an image of her own face and that something about that face is different from what she knows to be her face. She thus indicates that she knows who she is; that she is aware of herself. That demonstration of self-awareness, however, can tell us nothing about what that girl thinks about herself or of herself; it tells us nothing about what concept she has about herself; nothing about the content of her self-concept. To learn about that we must wait until she has developed the language to talk about herself.

The Self-Concept in Childhood

FROM EXTERNAL TO INTERNAL

Inquiries about children's self-concept reveal a developmental trend inasmuch as the focus of their answers gradually shifts from descriptions of their describing external characteristics to talking about their internal traits and qualities. In the preschool years (ages three to five) children respond to questions about their self-concept by giving their name, their gender, their age, and their address. Prodded to say more, most will add statements about their family, their pets and other prized possessions, physical attributes such as body build, hair, and eye color, what they are good at, and what they enjoy doing.

A statement about what one enjoys doing is about an inner state and it is a forerunner of descriptions of feelings, attitudes, and opinions that become more and more prevalent as the individual moves from childhood to adolescence.

WORDS FOR INTERNAL STATES

Self-concepts are acquired over time through experiences people have in the context of their social and physical environment. It is easy to imagine how a three-year-old learned her name, her address, and that she is a tall, thin girl with brown hair and brown eyes, who is good at throwing a ball, and has a baby brother whose name is Daniel. Someone probably told her these facts. But how did she come to know that she likes ice cream? How, for that matter, did any of us learn to label our internal states, whether that be hunger, anger, jealousy, or liking ice cream?

One possible answer to this is that the labels for private states are learned in the same way we learn the labels for public conditions and concrete objects. Just as Sarah's mother or father taught her to say her name and to learn her address and telephone number, told her that she is three years old and has brown hair, one of them probably saw her consume with gusto a dish of ice cream and said, "My, you sure like ice cream, don't you?" In the same way, she could have learned to label the inner states of likes and dislikes, loves and hates, fears and hopes. Someone saw her hug her baby brother and said, "You love your little brother, don't you?" or, seeing her shed tears over a broken doll, pronounce, "You are sad because dolly lost her arm."

INTROSPECTION

Whereas younger children identify themselves in terms of publicly observable categories, older children and adolescents tend to describe themselves more and more in such private terms as attitudes, beliefs, values, wishes, traits, and feelings. This developmental trend from a focus on external characteristics to one on internal states parallels and depends on an increasing capacity and disposition to think about one's own thoughts and feelings, to engage in *introspection*. Adolescents, at least in Western cultures, are well known for spending a great deal of time and energy exploring their own thoughts and feelings and in speculating about the thoughts and feelings of those around them.

Identification

There are aspects of the self-concept, of the ideas one has about oneself, that derive from one's *identification* with significant other individuals one encountered in the course of becoming an adult. Freud saw identification with the same-sex parent as motivated by the need to reduce the anxiety associated with the *Oedipus conflict*, but contemporary views are more likely to attribute identification to the processes of modeling and observational learning we discussed in chapter 7.

Identification entails adopting as one's own one or more of the attributes of another person. These attributes can be anything from facial expressions and bodily movements to fears, attitudes, values, or political opinions. The earliest model with whom identification can take place is usually a parent, and not necessarily the one of one's own sex. Later on children may identify with older siblings, teachers, sports champions, or television celebrities. The figures who serve as models for identification are almost always older, stronger, more successful, more powerful, or more famous than the individual who identifies with them. Moreover, for older children the model is usually of the same sex.

These tendencies can be explained by Bandura's modeling theory. It states that the reinforced behavior of a model is more likely to be acquired than behavior that is punished or not reinforced and that the more similar a person is to the observer, the more likely he or she is to serve as a model.

Sex and Gender Differences

Among the personality characteristics and self-concept attributes to which identification makes an important contribution are the attitudes, expectations, and behaviors the people in a given society typically associate with the sex of an individual and the gender roles they consequently assign. The word *sex* is here used to denote the biological aspects that pertain to the reproductive organs according to which individuals are classified as *male* or *female*. *Gender*, in contrast, refers to the social and psychological attributes that people associate with being a boy or a man, a girl or a woman.

NATURE OR NURTURE

There are few topics concerning human characteristics about which the question of the relative contributions of heredity and environment—nature and nurture—is more hotly debated and more difficult to answer than in that of sex and gender. Two points should be established at the outset.

One is that a definitive answer to that question will probably never be known because it is impossible to conduct the experiments that are necessary to arrive at such an answer. Such experiments would require that a substantial number of randomly selected, biologically normal male infants be reared by parents who believe them to be females so that, when they are adults, they could be compared with an analogous group of females who had been reared by parents who thought they were males.

The other point is that whatever contribution genetic factors make to observed differences in the psychological characteristics of males and females, that contribution is established by the time the person is born. At the present time, at least, that cannot be altered. What can be altered, however, are the contributions the social environment makes to these differences so that, if we deem it desirable to modify these differences, we will have to focus on the social environment and to study its contribution in great detail.

SEX TYPING

The anatomical characteristics that enable us to classify one baby as a girl and another as a boy are determined by the infant's genes. As soon as that classification has taken place—that is, immediately after birth—the social environment brings its influence to bear by means of *sex typing*.

Sex typing refers to the way others behave toward a child of a given sex in terms of the stereotypes their society associates with that sex. In our society most boys and girls are given distinctively different names, different clothing, different hair styles, different toys. Their rooms are differently furnished and decorated and, later on, they encounter different demands, expectations, rules, and attitudes. It has been shown that even parents who start out with the intention of treating their male and female children alike soon find themselves behaving one way toward the girl and another way toward the boy, often in such subtle ways as how they hold them when they are picked up and the tone of voice they use in speaking to them. Little wonder that male children develop "boyish" behavior, while female children become "typical" girls.

Sex Differences in Human Behavior

Before we look at behaviors in which males and females typically differ, it is important to stress that all of these differences refer to group averages and that there always are individuals in each sex group whose behavior is more like that of the other sex than that of the average for their own sex.

Research has fairly well established that there are sex differences in three areas. These are *verbal abilities*, *visual-spatial abilities*, and *mathematical abilities*. Girls excel in verbal abilities and boys are better in visual-spatial and mathematical abilities. In addition to differences that have been found in these academic skills, it has repeatedly been shown that males are more *aggressive* than females.

The difference in verbal skills first becomes noticeable in elementary school when girls show greater proficiency in reading. Starting around junior high school age girls excel in tests of vocabulary, object naming, grammar, logical reasoning, reading comprehension, and creative writing.

The difference in visual-spatial abilities does not become apparent until adolescence, when studies show fairly consistently that males perform better than females on such tasks as map reading, aiming at targets, or visualizing objects from different perspectives.

For mathematical ability the nature of the sex difference is more complex. Until puberty girls and boys do not differ in their ability to learn quantitative concepts or arithmetic skills. After age thirteen, however, the mathematical skills of boys tend to increase at a faster rate than those of girls. However, when mathematical problems are stated in verbal form, girls perform about as well as boys, whereas boys excel over girls when the problems deal solely with numbers or geometric forms. It thus seems that the differences in verbal and visual-spatial skills play a role in the difference in mathematical skills.

TWO KINDS OF AGGRESSION

It is in the area of aggression that the sex difference is most clear-cut. Not only can it be observed as early as age two, but it is present at every level of development and in every culture where it has been studied. Here it is useful to distinguish between two kinds of behavior that is called aggression. One is *angry aggression*. It is the kind of aggression that is accompanied by anger and that usually serves no function other than making the aggressor feel less angry. The other kind is *instrumental aggression*. It has an external object as its goal; it is a means to an end, the "instrument" by which that end is reached. Instrumental aggression may take the form of hitting another child to obtain a desired toy or calling others demeaning names to make them feel badly. It is that kind of aggression in which males excel.

HORMONES OR SOCIETY?

We said at the outset of this discussion that it is a moot point to ask whether sex differences are due to heredity or to environment. In all likelihood both play a role, interacting to produce the outcome we observe. That interaction can most readily be seen in the case of aggression. There is support from three sources for the assertion that biological factors contribute to aggression. One of these sources is that not only male humans but also male apes and male monkeys show more aggressive behavior than the females in their species. Another is that levels of aggressiveness vary directly with the amount of the male sex hormone *testosterone* in the bloodstream. And third, the greater aggressiveness of males, beginning at a very young age, has been found in widely different cultures.

Biological factors, however, may merely predispose the male more so than the female to develop aggressive behavior under the influences to which his society exposes him. These influences begin very early. Parents relate to boys in a manner that is different from the way they relate to girls. Fathers engage in rough-and-tumble, mock wrestling play with their sons, but not with their daughters. Later, aggression-related qualities such as achievement, competition, self-reliance, and independence are more likely to be expected of boys than of girls. "Stand up for your rights" is more likely to be said to a boy. A girl, by contrast, is more likely than a boy to be expected to share and compromise, to handle conflict by talking it out rather than fighting, to be kind, caring, and well mannered.

MORAL DEVELOPMENT

Whereas there continues to be disagreement as to the relative contribution of heredity and environment to human aggression, there is no such disagreement about how people come to know right from wrong and to act accordingly. *Moral reasoning* is not inherited; we learn it in the course of growing up from the people with whom we live.

The Stage Theory of Jean Piaget

Jean Piaget (1896–1980) (pronounced Pee-ya-ZHAY) was a Swiss child psychologist who, among many other topics that he investigated in the course of his long life, studied the development of moral concepts. To do this Piaget (1932) used observations and interviews aimed at finding out how children arrive at moral judgments and how these judgments change as they mature.

One of Piaget's techniques was to ask children of different ages such questions as "Why should you not cheat in a game?" or "Why do games have rules?," following their answers by asking them for examples of bad or unfair behavior. Another approach was to present a child with a set of two stories. One of these stories might be about a boy who accidentally caused a large amount of damage, whereas in the other a boy intentionally caused a small amount of damage. After presenting these stories Piaget would ask the child which boy was naughtier and why.

STAGES OF MORAL ORIENTATION

Based on methods such as these Piaget concluded that moral reasoning develops in *stages*. Children younger than ten, he declared, have an *objective orientation* to moral issues. That means that they take experiences literally and ignore the subtleties of purposes and intentions. Accordingly, they judge the relative culpability of the two boys in the stories on the basis of the amount of damage done and say that the boy who caused the greater damage was the naughtier of the two.

According to Piaget, children older than ten have a *subjective orientation* to moral issues. Their moral judgments are relative to the situation and the person's motivation. In line with that orientation children of that age take into account that one boy caused damage by accident, whereas the other did so intentionally. They therefore judge as naughtier the one who caused the damage on purpose.

STAGES OF MORALITY

Piaget also identified developmental stages of morality. Prior to age seven or eight he considered children to be at the stage of *moral realism.* There the child is absolute in his or her moral judgment. Lying is always wrong, regardless of circumstances, and the parents' standards are accepted as the criteria for what is right. From approximately eight to eleven he held children to be in the second stage, which he called the *morality of cooperation.* In that stage children believe that fairness means equal treatment, sharing, and reciprocity. Around age eleven or twelve Piaget found children to enter the third and highest stage. He called it *moral relativism.* Now actions are judged as good or bad in the light of what led up to them and the circumstances in which they take place. The subjective orientation mentioned earlier is a reflection of moral relativism.

The Stage Theory of Lawrence Kohlberg

Lawrence Kohlberg carried research on the development of moral judgment beyond childhood (1967). To do this he employed a method similar to Piaget's. He would present a subject with ten stories, each of which involved a moral dilemma. After each story he would ask the subject to state what the protagonist in the story should have done and to give the reason for that judgment.

In a typical story a man needs a very expensive new medicine that might save his sick wife's life. He does not have enough money to buy the medicine, can't borrow the sum, and the pharmacist won't sell it for less. Desperate, the man breaks into the pharmacy at night and steals the drug. Should the man have done this, and why or why not?

Level of Morality	Stage	Focus	View of Others
I Preconventional	1	Avoiding punishment	No appreciating of others' needs
	2	Obtaining goal by trade-off	Others have interest of their own
II Conventional	3	Meeting expectations important to others	Agreements with others take precedence over own needs
	4	Law and order	Responsibility for self and others
III Postconventional	5	Democracy and relativity of rules	Individual rights take precedence over rules and agreements
	6	Self-chosen universal principles	Needs of humanity precede all else

Table 8.2 Kohlberg's Theory of Moral Judgment

STAGES AND LEVELS

On the basis of responses to this and similar stories Kohlberg identified six developmental stages, grouped at three moral levels, as follows:

Level I—Preconventional Morality. At this level young children and very primitive adults perceive rules and regulations as lying outside the self. In Stage 1 the rules are based on *conformity to authority figures*; at Stage 2 they are based on *concrete reciprocal hedonism*. This might find expression in "I did something for you, so you should do something for me."

Level II—Conventional Morality. Most adolescents and many adults operate at this level. In Stage 3 morality is based on good intentions and the *desire for social approval*. At Stage 4 a *law-and-order orientation* serves as the basis for moral judgment, so that good and bad are defined in terms of maintaining social harmony.

Level III—Postconventional Morality. According to Kohlberg, only relatively few people reach this, the highest level of morality, and they do so around the age of twenty. Here morality is seen as based on contractual obligations and the social good. In Stage 5 moral judgments are made on the basis of achieving the *greatest good for the greatest number*, whereas in Stage 6 the person's own *ethical principles* provide the basis for making moral judgments.

UNIVERSAL, INVARIANT, AND IRREVERSIBLE?

As a strict *stage theorist* Kohlberg believed that these stages applied regardless of the culture into which a person had been born; they were *universal*. Moreover, he declared them to be *invariant*, that they always appear in the same sequence in the course of a person's development although most people never progressed beyond the second of the three levels. In Kohlberg's view, the stages were also *irreversible*. Once a given stage had been reached, all the person's moral judgments would be made at that level, never on a lower level. These assertions continue to be subject to controversy, and the results of research studies that were designed to test them have raised questions about their validity.

Delay of Gratification

IMPULSE CONTROL

Gaining the ability to postpone an immediate reward for the sake of obtaining a larger reward in the future is an important step in the development of an individual's personality. Continuing to go to school instead of dropping out and taking a job, saving money instead of spending it, studying for an exam instead of going to a party, waiting until everybody at the dinner table has been served instead of starting to eat the moment the food is on one's plate, are all instances that require a self-imposed *delay of gratification*. Some call it *impulse-control* or *willpower*.

An infant does not delay gratification. Hungry newborns cry until fed; when body waste accumulates it is instinctively eliminated. Waiting for food and retaining body wastes must be taught and are gradually learned. As the child gets older, society expects delay of gratification in areas other than bodily functions, including those that are defined as "polite" behavior. As a result, the ability to delay gratification is sometimes equated with *socialization* and used as a definition of maturity.

A number of psychologists, particularly those with a social learning orientation, have studied the development of the capacity to delay gratification.

THE ROLE OF PRIOR EXPERIENCES

In one series of investigations (Mischel, 1974) children were given the choice between small rewards that were immediately available and larger rewards that would become available after some delay. One of the results showed that whether or not the children chose the delayed reward depended on their prior experiences with similar situations. If they had learned in the past that promises were kept so that the delay would really result in a larger reward, they were willing to wait. *Trust* thus plays a role in delayed gratification. In the absence of trust, children (and people in general) forgo a larger, but uncertain reward for the sake of obtaining gratification when it is available.

EFFECTS OF MODELS

Whether it is learning control over the elimination of body wastes or learning to wait until the hostess has started to eat, delay of gratification is learned from other people. Some of this learning is by direct instruction, but much of it comes from observing the behavior of models. This has been demonstrated by studies in which children were exposed to models who either chose to wait for a larger reward or selected the immediate, but smaller reward. The influence of the model's choice on the choices of the children continued to have an effect four to five weeks later when the children were again put in a choice situation.

PERSONALITY CORRELATES

Several studies have investigated whether the ability to delay gratification at an early age is correlated with other personality characteristics at that time or in later years. The results suggest that such negative characteristics as irritability, aggressiveness, and low tolerance for stress tend go along with a preference for immediate reward, whereas delay of gratification is correlated with resourcefulness, deliberation, cooperation, and social as well as academic competence. Such correlations are difficult to interpret but it seems likely that the same social environment that leads children to delay gratification also fosters the development of other positive personality attributes.

LIFE-SPAN DEVELOPMENT

Most of the research on personality development we have discussed thus far had been conducted with children. But personality development does not end with childhood. In fact, changes in personality occur during adolescence and continue throughout life.

Puberty and Adolescence

Puberty is a biological phenomenon and as such it is universal. All normally developing humans, male and female, in all parts of the world experience the relatively rapid biological changes that mark puberty, and they have done so throughout the history of our species.

Adolescence begins at the same time as puberty, but unlike it adolescence is neither rapid nor universal. It is a social phenomenon comprising the fairly lengthy period of transition from childhood to adulthood and it varies from society to society, depending on its structure and customs. There were times in human history when adolescence did not exist—when a child became an adult from one day to the next, with the transition often marked by an initiation ceremony.

PHYSICAL CHANGES AND PSYCHOLOGICAL EFFECTS

Puberty entails spurts in growth, increased physical strength, the maturation of the sex organs, and the development of *secondary sex characteristics* such as body hair and the deepening of the male voice. Girls enter puberty about two years earlier than boys, and there are individual differences in its onset within the sexes. Differences in the rate of physical maturation have an effect on individuals' *self-esteem* and *self-image*. Boys who mature earlier than their peers tend to earn both their envy and admiration, making them feel good about themselves. In contrast, girls who are early maturers tend to feel unattractive and ashamed.

AUTONOMY AND CONFORMITY

Adolescence is often thought to be a time of trouble, but this is not inevitable. Whether it is or not depends a great deal on the opportunities, expectations, and tolerance of the individual's social environment.

In our society the role of the child is fairly well defined. This is particularly true regarding the *power relationship* in which the child is dependent on the adult. When childhood comes to an end with the onset of puberty, the role of the young person becomes ambiguous. Has dependency ended? What are the rights and privileges of the adolescent? What are the rules and expectations? Both adolescents and adults are often uncertain about the answers to these questions.

INDEPENDENCE STRIVINGS

The adolescent typically rejects the dependence of childhood and strives for independence. Many feel that they have to tell the world that they are no longer children and do not want to be treated as such. Adolescents use hair styles, dress modes, and even language to differentiate themselves not only from children but, even more so, from adults. In their desire for *autonomy* from the rules of parents and the parents' generation, adolescents look for the support of their peer group and in so doing often display a remarkable *conformity* to the behavior of that group.

IDENTITY

The ambiguity of the adolescent's role brings with it an ambiguity about his or her *identity*. "I am no longer a child, but I am not yet an adult" leads to the questions "Who am I?" and "Who do I want to be?" Theorists such as Erik Erikson, whose view we discussed in chapter 4, consider the so-called *identity crisis* as the principal developmental event of adolescence. Many young people in that age group try out various identities, hoping to find out who they "really" are. This is what makes eccentric religions and peculiar cult groups attractive to adolescents and why smoking and the use of alcohol and other health-impairing drugs tend to flourish in that age group. Eventually most of these explorers "find themselves," establish an identity, and grow into adulthood.

Adulthood

Adulthood is the least-studied stage of personality development. For a long time, in fact, it was believed that personality development ceased when a person became an adult and that no further changes would occur until old age brought the deterioration of functions. Recent studies, however, have shown that adult personality does undergo developmental changes, but, unlike the changes in childhood and adolescence, these are no longer associated with physical maturation but with changes in the social environment.

ENVIRONMENTAL CHANGES

There are many environmental changes that may have an effect on an adult's personality. Some of these are marriage, divorce, becoming a parent, losing or changing jobs, becoming responsible for an infirm parent, having children leave home, promotions or other career achievements, moving to a different community, retirement, and loss of a loved one.

Not all of these events will necessarily produce a noticeable change in the individual who experiences them, nor will every individual be affected by such events. Much depends on the personality characteristics that the individual brings to such an experience. As we know by now, some people have more, others less, stability, so that a crisis, such as the loss of a loved one, will affect them differently.

This interaction between the individual's personality and significant experiences is not unique to adults. It can be found at any age level, because personality development is a cumulative progression, not an additive sequence of independent events.

The Contribution of Daniel J. Levinson

Of the relatively few studies conducted on adult development, those of Daniel J. Levinson (1978) are among the most widely known. Unfortunately, due to a lack of funding these studies were limited to men.

THE AGE-THIRTY TRANSITION

Levinson proposed that after entering adulthood in his early twenties a man typically explores a variety of alternatives (in jobs, life-styles, and companions) before getting married and choosing a career. This is followed by what Levinson calls the *age-thirty transition*. He describes this as a particularly stressful time for many men who discover that their earlier choices of spouse or occupation were not satisfactory and require change.

THE MIDLIFE CRISIS

In the next adult stage, which lasts until a man is about forty years old, the focus is on settling down, on realizing one's goals and aspirations, on building a home and family. There follows the *midlife transition period*. This can again be stressful, for many men now ask themselves whether they are achieving what they set out to do. When the answer is negative they may experience the turmoil and despair of a *midlife crisis*. This is aggravated by the recognition that half or more of life is already over so that there may not be "enough time" to make changes.

LATE ADULTHOOD

As with any crisis, some men resolve it successfully by accepting their loss of youth and limiting their aspirations or by starting a new career and approaching it with renewed energy and purpose. Others, however, emerge from this crisis discouraged and defeated, resigning themselves to a life of decline with little hope for improvement. They enter *late adulthood* depressed and defeated and assume a pessimistic stance toward the aging process. Those who successfully resolved their midlife crisis or never experienced one are generally able to make constructive use of that next stage of life.

Old Age

Whereas adolescence begins and ends for most people at more or less the same time and the physical changes of puberty are the same for everyone of the same sex, the start of *old age* is difficult to specify, and the physical changes that accompany it vary from individual to individual. This limits the generalizations one can make about this age group.

RESPONSIBILITY AND MORTALITY

The results of an experimental study by Rodin and Langer (1977) have far-reaching implications for one group among the aged, those residing in nursing homes and similar institutions.

Rodin and Langer had the administrator of a nursing home give one group of its elderly residents a talk that emphasized the responsibility they had for themselves. Each member of this group was given a plant for which to care. A control group of residents in the same institution was given a similar talk but that one stressed the staff's responsibility for them. Each member of this group was also given a plant, but these were to be watered by the staff.

There were both immediate and long-term effects of this simple manipulation of responsibility. Compared to the control group, those who had been given responsibility for themselves and their plants became more active, displayed an increased alertness, showed a greater interest in social activities and contests, interacted more with friends and staff members, and reported feeling happier.

These effects were still evident among the survivors when a follow-up evaluation was conducted eighteen months later. The self-responsibility group were judged to be more sociable, involved, self-initiating, and vigorous than the control group. Even more remarkable is that there had been significantly fewer deaths among the responsibility-induced group than among those who had been given no responsibilities. Being given and accepting responsibility for oneself appears to have the most salutary consequences not only for one's personality, but also for one's health and longevity.

DEVELOPMENT OF PERSONALITY IN PERSPECTIVE

An Inherent Handicap

Development, by definition, is an ongoing process, characterized by change. To study this process one ought to observe the changes as they are taking place. As we have seen, personality development is a life-long process. To study it one should therefore observe the changes from the moment of birth until death. That is an impossible task. As a result no one has ever conducted a life-long, *longitudinal study* of personality development, and it is unlikely that anyone ever will.

What we know about the development of personality is pieced together from studies conducted by different investigators on different people at different phases of their life. Such *cross-sectional studies* are occasionally supplemented by a *follow-up study* in which subjects who had been examined at an earlier time are reexamined a few months or a few years later. None of these approaches, however, can provide a fully satisfactory picture of how the development of personality proceeds.

Are Stages Real?

In this chapter we met several formulations that conceive development as occurring in fairly distinct *stages*. It is conceivable that these stages are an *artifact*, the incidental result of the cross-sectional research on which these theorists based their conclusions. If, instead of following the development of a group of children from birth to age ten, one compares a group of one-year-olds with a group of two-year-olds and these with a group of three-year-olds and so forth, one might well get the impression that development proceeds in a step-wise fashion when it could be going up a smooth incline. We just don't know and, in view of the impossibility of conducting life-long longitudinal studies on representative groups of people, we may never know.

Are Subjects Representative?

There is another problem that plagues research on personality development. It is the difficulty of obtaining adequate numbers of randomly selected subjects who are available for the length of time required to conduct a detailed study. Much of Piaget's work, for example, was conducted on his own children or on children he happened to encounter on his walks in the park. Other studies mentioned in this chapter used children enrolled in nursery schools attached to universities, college students taking a course in introductory psychology, or elderly women residing in one nursing home. Such highly selected samples greatly limit the applicability of the results if one wants to speak about human development.

Moral Judgment or Moral Behavior?

Lastly, a comment about the studies on the development of moral reasoning. You will have noticed that the method used in these studies entailed presenting subjects with a story and asking them for their opinion on what the person in the story did or should have done. Although it is interesting to know about these *judgments* and to learn that subjects of different ages make different judgments, they tell us nothing about what *action* these subjects themselves would take if they were placed in a moral dilemma. That, it seems, would be more relevant to knowing about the development of morality than answers to hypothetical questions. The research on delay of gratification placed children into actual choice situations and observed their behavior. More work like that is needed if we are to gain meaningful knowledge about personality development.

*O*ne *of the important processes in the realm of personality, probably the most important, is its development. Various aspects of this have been studied. One of these is the development of the self-concept.*

Before one can develop a concept of oneself one has to be aware of oneself, but self-awareness begins to develop so early in life that one cannot find out about it by verbal means. Investigators therefore rely on observational methods. One of these is the mirror test in which a small amount of rouge is placed on babies' noses to find out whether they are aware that what they are seeing in the mirror is their own image. Such studies have revealed individual differences and age-related changes that go along with other changes in cognitive development.

Self-awareness is also related to an aspect of mother–infant relationship that is called attachment behavior. This has been studied using observations of young children and their mothers in a situation they had not before encountered. That "strange situation" consists of several episodes in which the mother leaves the child alone or with a stranger, later to reenter the room. Under these conditions children react in one of three distinct ways so that three forms of attachment can be identified. These are stable over time and are related to self-recognition in somewhat surprising ways.

Once language is available for studying the self-concept it becomes possible to investigate sex and gender differences. These differences can be attributed to an interaction of biological and social factors, but the relative contribution of these may be impossible to ascertain. Though the source of the differences is uncertain, it has been possible to establish that males and females differ in verbal and visual-spatial skills and mathematical abilities. The most striking difference between the sexes is in aggressive behavior, which males display far more than females.

The development of moral reasoning and moral judgment has been investigated by methods that elicit verbal solutions to moral dilemmas. It seems that these solutions become more sophisticated in the course of maturation, suggesting to some investigators that this development occurs in distinct stages. More relevant to actual behavior than these cognitive procedures are the observations investigators have made of children who are faced with the choice between a small, immediate reward and a larger reward for which they have to wait. The ability to delay gratification under these circumstances can be acquired by observing others who model such behavior, and it foretells good adaptations to later challenges.

Personality development continues through adolescence and into adulthood and old age. Each of these age levels entails potential crises. The adolescent must cope with independence strivings and establish an identity. Young adults encounter several periods of transition when they take stock of where they are and where they are likely to go with respect to occupation, family life, and general aspirations. Some find the midlife crisis a particularly stressful experience. Relatively little is known about personality changes in old age, but one important study has shown that assuming self-responsibility has many positive consequences.

Selected Readings

Baltes, P. B., and K. W. Schaie. 1973. *Life-Span Developmental Psychology: Personality and Socialization.* New York: Academic Press.

Levinson, D. J. 1978. *The Seasons of a Man's Life.* New York: Ballantine.

Lewis, M. 1986. *Origins of Self-Knowledge and Individual Differences in Early Self-Recognition.* In J. Suls and A. G. Greenwald (eds.). *Psychological Perspectives on the Self* (vol. 3). Hillsdale, NJ: Erlbaum. pp. 55–78.

Piaget, J. 1932. *The Moral Judgment of the Child.* New York: Harcourt Brace.

Ross, A. O. 1992. *The Sense of Self: Theory and Research.* New York: Springer Publishing.

Tannen, D. 1990. *You Just Don't Understand: Women and Men in Conversation.* New York: Morrow.

9

Anxiety and Stress

*A*t one time or another almost everyone has experienced anxiety. It is an unpleasant feeling of apprehension that is accompanied by one or more physiological reactions such as palpitations and perspiration. Some people are mildly anxious most of the time; that is called trait anxiety. When anxiety is experienced only in specific situations, it is called state anxiety. There is a variety of psychological and physiological tests that can be used to assess anxiety. Some of these have been used to predict how a person will react to conditioning experiments, learning tasks, or examinations.

Stress is very similar to anxiety. The concept of stress was used originally to describe the way the body reacts to illness, injury, or other trauma, but it was later extended to include experiences that a person considers to be threatening. In addition to the physiological reactions that accompany stress, there are several emotional reactions such as anger and sadness.

The constellation of high-intensity activities that has been identified as Type A behavior is particularly stressful. Those who manifest that behavior pattern are at risk to develop heart disease. They are likely to be rather dissatisfied people whose strong need to control everybody and everything antagonizes those with whom they come into contact.

ANXIETY

What Is Anxiety?

In the previous chapter we speculated that a young child might learn to label an emotion such as sadness by hearing a parent say something like "You are sad because dolly lost her arm." That way of learning a vocabulary for one's inner experiences is quite haphazard because it depends on who happens to be available to furnish an appropriate label and on that person's own vocabulary for emotions. It is therefore not surprising that different people use different words for their reactions to the same situation. This makes agreement on definitions of emotions difficult.

Anxiety is a prime example of this difficulty.

It is very likely that at one time or another everyone has experienced anxiety, although they may have called it something else. Such words as *terror, alarm, dread*, and *panic* are used when anxiety is severe. When it is mild, some call it *worry, distress, trepidation*, or *apprehension*. To make matters worse, even the physiological responses that accompany this condition vary from individual to individual. Some experience dryness and constriction in the throat, others tightness in the chest, sweaty palms, "butterflies" in the stomach, looseness of the bowels, weakness in the knees, or restlessness.

As mentioned in our review of the various theories of personality, each theorist had a different interpretation of anxiety. Freud saw it as a signal of threat to the ego. To Adler, anxiety was associated with feelings of inferiority. Horney attributed it to feeling isolated and helpless in a hostile world. Rogers viewed anxiety as resulting from the perception of a threat to the self-concept. In Kelly's theory anxiety is brought on by recognizing an inadequacy of one's construct system, and Rotter sees anxiety as reflecting a discrepancy between strong needs and low expectancies of having them met.

Given this confusing state of affairs, some clarification is in order. Let us begin by stating what anxiety is *not*.

ANXIETY, FEAR, STRESS, AND EAGER ANTICIPATION

Anxiety is not the same as fear. The physiological reactions to fear and anxiety are the same or very similar. The primary difference is cognitive in that fear has a specific object. The individual knows that he or she is afraid of *something*. This may be something that is present at the moment or something that is anticipated for the future. Anxiety, in contrast, does not have an object. It is a vague, generalized sense of discomfort or apprehension that the individual is usually unable to explain.

Although they have much in common, anxiety is not the same as stress. Stress is a reaction to events or conditions that the individual has experienced in the past or to which he or she is currently exposed. Anxiety, on the other hand, usually has to do with unspecified events that lie in the future. Anxiety is anticipatory; stress is reactive. Moreover, the source of stress can be identified, usually by the person experiencing it, but certainly by a trained professional person whose help is being sought. In contrast, the source of anxiety is usually difficult to identify.

Anxiety also is not the same as eager anticipation. When a friend tells you that her mother is coming for a visit and you say, "I am anxious to meet her," you probably don't mean that you are experiencing anxiety in anticipation of that encounter, but that you are looking forward to it. On the other hand, if you fear that your friend's mother won't approve of you, you should—in line with the definition here advocated—say, "I am afraid to meet her."

COMPONENTS OF ANXIETY

To summarize, anxiety is future-directed and lacks a specific object. It has two principal components. One is physiological, the other cognitive.

The *physiological component* is an arousal state of the nervous system. This identifies anxiety as an *emotion*. The arousal consists of physiological reactions that vary from individual to individual. The manifestations may be changes in heart rate, blood pressure, perspiration, salivation, skin color, or respiration, and nausea, stomach cramps, or diarrhea.

The *cognitive component* is a decidedly unpleasant experience of *vague future threat* with which, because it is undefined, the person feels unprepared to cope. There may be a sense of impending disaster, catastrophe, collapse, or even death, and, as we said, the experience may be given labels ranging from apprehension to terror.

ATTRIBUTION OF ANXIETY

The individual who experiences anxiety typically is unable to identify its source, but, in trying to understand why they feel that way, people often *attribute* their anxiety to something that may or may not be the source. Experiencing anxiety just before delivering a prepared talk before a group, for example, a woman may attribute her anxiety to the talk. However, if she is asked what about the talk is making her anxious she is likely to respond, "I don't know. I'm just anxious, that's all." This reaction is sometimes called "stage fright," but *public-speaking anxiety* is a more appropriate term for it.

CONSEQUENCES OF ANXIETY

How does anxiety affect a person's performance? Research has shown that the answer to this is "It depends." It depends on the intensity of the anxiety that the individual is experiencing. When anxiety is experienced before an impending task, such as an examination, low anxiety has little or no effect, whereas a high level of anxiety interferes with effective performance. A level of anxiety somewhere between too little and too much seems to enhance performance. In this respect anxiety has the property of motivation where an optimal amount is needed for performance to occur, whereas a lack of motivation prevents, and an excess of it disrupts, performance.

Two Kinds of Anxiety

As with almost everything else in the realm of personality, there are individual differences in anxiety. Some people are anxious only occasionally, whereas others are anxious most of the time. This observation has led psychologists to differentiate between two kinds of anxiety, *state anxiety* and *trait anxiety*.

STATE ANXIETY

A state is a temporary or momentary emotional reaction. Accordingly, *state anxiety*—sometimes called *A-state*—has been defined as a transitory condition that varies in intensity and fluctuates over time (Spielberger, 1975). In the example of the woman about to give a talk, the anxiety she experienced was state anxiety.

TRAIT ANXIETY

Like the traits we discussed in chapter 6, trait anxiety—sometimes called *A-trait*—is an enduring personal characteristic. Also like other traits, it varies from individual to individual. Some are low, others high, in trait anxiety. People high in trait anxiety are somewhat anxious most of the time. They are predisposed to perceive threat in many different, often harmless situations and to respond to these with *state anxiety*.

Anxiety-Arousing Situations

Although there are numerous situations that can elicit anxiety in people high in A-trait, some situations do so more readily than others. One of these is *social evaluation*. This is a situation in which the individual anticipates being judged by others, as in meeting a group of strangers, being interviewed for a job, or appearing before an audience.

Another condition under which high trait-anxiety people easily become anxious involves the *perception of physical danger*. The emphasis here is on the perception because the danger is usually unrealistic. Looking down from the observation deck of a high building, for example, may make high A-trait people anxious, although they are standing behind a firm steel railing that protects them from falling. When the *expectation of becoming anxious* prevents such a person from going to high places, the condition is a called a *phobia*, in this case *acrophobia*.

A third condition with high potential of being anxiety-arousing for high A-trait people is an *ambiguous situation*, one that is not clear-cut and fully known. When a man does not know what he is about to encounter, he is in an ambiguous situation, for it means that he does not know whether he will be able to cope with whatever lies ahead. Entering a cave, traveling to a foreign country, transferring to a different school, or eating an exotic food—all have such ambiguity in common. That is why many high-A-trait people prefer staying in familiar surroundings to venturing into the unknown.

Note that there is an overlap among the three anxiety-arousing conditions just listed. Meeting strangers not only has ambiguous qualities, it may also entail a certain amount of physical danger. Standing behind a railing of an observation deck could be considered ambiguous because one never knows whether the railing might not give way. Entering a cave might involve danger because one never knows what lurks inside. Note also that all of these conditions have to do with something that lies in the future. By definition, anxiety involves anticipation.

Measures of Anxiety

We have now spoken of too much and too little anxiety, of high anxiety and low anxiety, and of state anxiety and trait anxiety. It is obvious that some measure or measures are needed to quantify anxiety and to differentiate one kind of anxiety from another.

There are three ways for assessing anxiety. One is to record the *physiological changes* that occur when a person experiences anxiety, such as heart rate, respiration, and the electrical resistance of the skin, a measure that is related to the activity of the sweat glands. Another way for assessing anxiety is to observe the individual's *motor behavior* for such reactions as tremor or the rapid movements that we refer to as fidgeting. The third and most frequently used method is to obtain a subjective *self-report* from the individual—that is, to administer a paper-and-pencil questionnaire.

LOW CORRELATIONS

To the consternation of psychologists who have conducted research on measures such as these, the correlation among them is surprisingly low. As we pointed out before, different individuals have different physiological reactions when they are anxious. It is therefore not surprising that these measures correlate neither with one another nor with the two other approaches to assessment. We also know that a person may report that she or he feels very anxious without looking anxious—that is, without shaking, fidgeting, stuttering, or perspiring. That observation is reflected in statistics that show low correlations between self-report measures and records of motor responses.

Given this state of affairs, investigators who wish to study anxiety must decide somewhat arbitrarily which of the three assessment methods to employ. It turns out that self-report questionnaires are by far the most frequently chosen. This is so partly because, of the three methods, questionnaires are the most easily administered and most economical when large groups of subjects are to be examined, and partly because the way people feel is probably more relevant to the study of an inner experience like anxiety than how they look or how their sweat glands are responding.

Among the most frequently used paper-and-pencil measures of anxiety are the *State-Trait Anxiety Inventory (STAI)*, the *Manifest Anxiety Scale (MAS)*, and the *Test Anxiety Scale (TAS)*. We shall describe and discuss each of these.

STATE-TRAIT ANXIETY INVENTORY (STAI)

This instrument was developed by Spielberger, Gorsuch, and Lushene (1970), who wanted to differentiate between state anxiety and trait anxiety. The inventory consists of forty statements. Twenty of these make up the A-state scale and twenty the A-trait scale.

In line with the definition of the two kinds of anxiety, the A-trait scale measures how prone an individual is to experiencing anxiety whereas the A-state scale ascertains their level of anxiety when they experience it.

To assess *state anxiety* people responding to the inventory are therefore asked to indicate the *intensity* of their feeling *at the present moment.* To do this they are given a four-point scale, ranging from "Not at all" to "Very much so," with which to rate such statements as "I feel tense" and "I am worried."

On items that assess *trait anxiety* people are asked to rate—on a four-point scale ranging from "Almost never" to "Almost always"—the *frequency* with which they experience certain feelings. Examples are, "I feel like crying," "I lack self-confidence," and "I take disappointments so keenly that I can't put them out of my mind."

As the theory on which this inventory is based would predict, research has shown that trait anxiety is stable over time, whereas state anxiety varies as situational threats change. Moreover, individuals who differ in trait anxiety also differ in the intensity of the state anxiety with which they react to threat. For example, to a threat to their self-esteem such as a negative evaluation, those with high trait anxiety experience more intense state anxiety than those with low trait anxiety.

Cognitive Appraisal. Earlier, we stressed that whether a person reacts to physical danger with anxiety depends on whether a situation is *perceived* as dangerous. Perception is the cognitive process by which we assign meaning to the stimuli that reach our sense organs. Some call this process *cognitive appraisal.* Studies conducted with the STAI have shown that whether a person, even one who is high in trait anxiety, will respond to an event with state anxiety depends on her or his cognitive appraisal of that event.

Inasmuch as a person's cognitive appraisal of an event can be influenced by instructions, persuasion, modeling, and other manipulations, it is possible to reduce anxiety reactions even to situations that would ordinarily be threatening. Lazarus (1966) demonstrated this by showing a film of a bloody initiation ceremony to groups of college students who typically reacted with increases in anxiety, but when this film was shown to students whose cognitive appraisal had been modified by instructions to watch it from an anthropological point of view the increase in anxiety was far less.

MANIFEST ANXIETY SCALE (MAS)

The most frequently used of all anxiety measures is the *Manifest Anxiety Scale (MAS)*. This scale was originally developed by Janet Taylor Spence (Taylor, 1953) in the context of research on the drive-reduction theory of Clark Hull (1943) that was described in chapter 7. From there you will recall that Hull considered all behavior to be motivated by the need to reduce primary or secondary drives. Hull maintained that a response that leads to the reduction of a drive is reinforced and thus learned. To this we must now add a simplified version of another of Hull's postulates. It is that the intensity of a learned response can be calculated by multiplying its *habit strength*— that is, how well and how often that response had been reinforced in the past, by the drive level of the organism when the stimulus is presented.

A Hypothesis. One of Hull's former students, Kenneth Spence (1958), had defined anxiety as a drive and, based on the above postulate, he hypothesized that one could predict the outcome of eye-blink conditioning experiments from the level of the individual's anxiety. The habit strength of the eye-blink response can be assumed to be very high because we make that response hundreds of times a day. What was needed to test Spence's hypothesis was a measure of anxiety level. The MAS was developed to fill that need.

The Scale. To assemble the Manifest Anxiety Scale, Janet Spence selected 65 items (later reduced to 50) that five clinical psychologists deemed to reflect chronic, or what we would now call trait, anxiety. The items, which had been obtained from the *Minnesota Multiphasic Personality Inventory (MMPI)* (chapter 2), dealt with such issues as worry, low confidence, insomnia, and restlessness, and physical symptoms such as headaches and frequent diarrhea.

Three typical items are these:

"I find it hard to keep my mind on a task or job."

"I notice my heart pounding and I am often short of breath."

"I am easily embarrassed."

The Test of the Hypothesis. This new scale was then used to test Kenneth Spence's hypothesis. In the classical conditioning of the eye-blink response a puff of air directed at the eyelid is the unconditioned stimulus and the sound of a buzzer is the conditioned stimulus. Conditioning is demonstrated when the buzzer elicits the eye-blink in the absence of the puff of air.

The results of such conditioning sessions showed that subjects with high scores on the MAS acquired the conditioned eye-blink response more readily than subjects with low scores and that their conditioned response also extinguished more slowly. The hypothesis that the strength of the response is a function of drive level was thus confirmed—at least in the case of as simple a learning task as the eye-blink.

On more complex, cognitive tasks such as memorizing two lists of words in succession, high anxiety as measured by the MAS does not facilitate learning; in fact, it impedes it. On such tasks subjects with low MAS scores make fewer errors.

From the point of view of the theory that anxiety acts as a drive, these results can be explained in the following manner: High drive (in this case, high anxiety) strengthens stimulus-response connections indiscriminately. Consequently, when subjects have to learn complex tasks, they acquire not only correct responses, but also incorrect and irrelevant responses that then compete and interfere with the correct ones.

Regardless of whether one accepts this explanation and whether the formulation of anxiety as a drive is correct, it is now generally accepted that, as stated earlier, high anxiety disrupts performance, whereas moderate anxiety can enhance it.

TEST ANXIETY SCALE (TAS)

We turn now to a scale designed to assess anxiety that people experience in a specific situation—the taking of a test—where its disrupting influence can be particularly disconcerting and even damaging. The *Test Anxiety Scale (TAS)* was developed by Mandler and S. B. Sarason (1952), who theorized that when an individual perceives a test as a threat, anxiety is aroused and disrupts test performance.

Test Anxiety. I. G. Sarason (1980) later elaborated on this *cognitive-appraisal formulation* of test anxiety. He characterized test anxiety as having one or more of the following components:

> The situation is perceived as difficult, challenging, and threatening.
>
> The person sees himself or herself as incompetent or ineffective to handle the task.
>
> The person focuses on the undesirable consequences of being found inadequate.
>
> The person's self-deprecatory thoughts are so strong that they interfere or compete with the cognitive processes required for the task.
>
> The person expects failure and anticipates losing the regard of others.

Sarason also pointed out that once test anxiety is aroused it need not inevitably interfere with test performance. Whether it does depends on how the person reacts to the anxiety.

Those who try to reduce the anxiety by not thinking about the test and engaging in some distracting activity like going to the movies instead of studying are likely to anticipate failure and therefore be anxious while taking the test so that their performance will suffer.

More constructive responses would be to study more, consult the instructor, or practice on potential test questions or previously used tests. Feeling themselves well prepared, such students are less likely to approach the test with anxiety and may thus do well.

The Scale. The Test Anxiety Scale seeks to predict how a person will approach an evaluative task like a test. It consists of thirty-seven True or False items, similar to the following:

> I would worry a great deal before taking an intelligence test.
>
> Whenever I take a test I think about the consequences of failing it.
>
> When I take a test my emotions get in the way of my doing well.
>
> Examinations actually interfere with my ability to learn a subject.

Research with this scale has uncovered some of the ways in which anxiety interferes with test performance. Among these is that an anxious individual is likely not to pay attention to the appropriate cues the task presents. Moreover, the anxiety of an anxious person is likely to increase when he or she does not know the answers to some of the early questions on a test. Anxiety then mounts cumulatively and further impedes the performance.

Fear or Anxiety? Earlier, we defined anxiety as a reaction to an impending, ill-defined threat, whereas fear was said to be a reaction to a specific and known situation or object. Why, then, is the apprehensive anticipation of a specific examination called test anxiety and not test fear?

There are two answers to this question. One is that the items on the Test Anxiety Scale refer to tests in general—that is, to unknown and undefined tests, and not to a specific examination. High scores on the TAS therefore reflect a predisposition to react with anxiety to any test that might come along. They reflect a form of trait anxiety.

The other answer is that although the test a person approaches with apprehension is specific (it may be a calculus test, for example), the threat it represents is nonspecific and ill-defined. If asked why she is anxious about this test a student is likely to answer that she does not know what questions will be asked, whether the test will be easy or difficult, or whether she will be able to finish it in time. All of these are unknown aspects of an impending event, hence it is appropriate to speak of anxiety. However, if the student were to answer "I am afraid that I will fail," we ought not to call her condition anxiety; it should be called fear of failure.

Anxiety Reduction

High anxiety is not only very upsetting, it also interferes with studying, working, and other tasks of everyday life. For these reasons chronic high anxiety is classified as a psychological disorder for which treatment is indicated.

Anxiety, as we said, has two components; one is physiological, the other cognitive. The two components interact in such a way that if one administers a drug that increases heart rate the person will feel anxious. Conversely, if one makes a person feel anxious (as by showing a scary movie, for example), his or her heart rate will increase. A treatment that is aimed at reducing anxiety could thus proceed by influencing either the physiological or the cognitive component or by targeting both.

There are two ways of treating anxiety by aiming at the physiological component. One is to administer an anxiety-reducing medication, the other to teach the anxious individual *deep muscle relaxation*. Both of these approaches have the disadvantage that they reduce anxiety only as long as they are employed; when the individual stops taking the medication or ceases to practice relaxation the anxiety returns. What is needed is a method that will reduce anxiety to a tolerable, task-facilitating level that can be maintained after treatment has been terminated. There are several forms of therapy that seek to achieve that.

BEHAVIOR THERAPY

Behavior therapy as a treatment of anxiety takes the form of *systematic desensitization* (Wolpe, 1958, 1982). In it the client is taught muscle relaxation and then is gradually exposed to increasingly more anxiety-arousing mental imagery while in a relaxed state. The underlying principles of this approach are derived from classical conditioning in that the idea is to pair the anxiety-arousing stimulus with the anxiety-incompatible relaxation response. In effect, systematic desensitization seeks to reduce anxiety by targeting both the physiological and the cognitive component, although the latter is somewhat secondary.

COGNITIVE-BEHAVIORAL THERAPY

Behavior therapists eventually came to place more emphasis on the cognitive and less on the physiological aspects of anxiety by developing an approach called *cognitive-behavioral therapy* (Meichenbaum, 1977; Meichenbaum et al., 1989). Those who developed this form of treatment reasoned that if experiencing anxiety depends on a person's *cognitive appraisal* of a situation as threatening, one should be able to reduce or prevent anxiety by changing his or her cognitive appraisal so that the situation is not perceived as threatening.

There are several ways of doing this. One, called *cognitive restructuring*, teaches the client to replace negative self-statements ("I'll never find another husband") with positive ones ("I've done it before; I can do it again"). Another method, called *problem-solving therapy*, teaches the client the skills needed for coping with anxiety-arousing situations. A third method, *stress inoculation training*, prepares the client step by step to cope with increasingly more threatening situations. Yet another method, called *rational- emotive therapy*, seeks to replace such irrational notions as "I have to do things perfectly," which are bound to lead to disappointment, with more rational ideas such as "Nobody is perfect."

The effectiveness of these methods varies, depending on such variables as the skill of the therapist, the motivation, age, and history of the client, the severity of the client's disorder, and the match between client, therapist, and method. There is much that remains unknown about each of these variables and research on them continues.

STRESS

As was pointed out at the beginning of this chapter, anxiety and stress differ in that anxiety stems from the anticipation of an impending threat, whereas stress is the result of past and present experiences of a stressful nature. Furthermore, the anxiety-arousing, anticipated threat is often so vague that the person is unable to identify it, whereas the source of stress can usually be named.

Stress and Stressors

The notion of *stress* was originally introduced by the Canadian endocrinologist Hans Selye (1978), who saw it as a generalized physiological reaction that comes about when the body is exposed to any kind of extraordinary demand. The source of that demand, the *stressor*, can be physical illness or injury, exposure to extremes of heat or cold, or psychological strain such as that due to unemployment or marital conflict.

GENERAL ADAPTATION SYNDROME (GAS)

Selye maintained that the body reacts to stressors with a nonspecific sequence of processes that he called the *general adaptation syndrome (GAS)*. This consists of four stages. The immediate reaction to a stressor is a brief period of *shock* that is characterized by a decrease in the body's defensive processes. This is quickly followed by *countershock* as the body's defensive resources are activated by such physiological changes as increased rates of heartbeat and respiration, dilation of the pupils, a drop in body temperature, increased perspiration, and release of glucose into the bloodstream. Note that this physiological arousal is quite similar to the one we identified earlier as an aspect of anxiety.

If stress is maintained beyond this initial *alarm reaction* because the stressors persist, the next phase of GAS, *resistance*, sets in. Here, more intense, longer-acting defensive measures replace those that had their onset during countershock. In the case of physical injury or illness, resistance is manifested by inflammation of the affected tissue. If the stressor is psychological the individual may withdraw, become depressed, or go into mourning.

Whether the stressor is physical or psychological, the stage of resistance is one of coping, which should eventually help the individual to overcome whatever the insult to his or her system. Selye pointed out, however, that there is a limit to the individual's capacity for this adaptation. If the stressor is not overcome or removed in the stage of resistance or if an additional stressor is added, the system's ability to cope begins to fail. Such failure initiates the fourth stage of GAS, the stage of *exhaustion*, when the individual "gives up." In the case of physical stress caused by illness, exhaustion may lead to death. If the stress is psychological the person may commit suicide.

PSYCHOLOGICAL STRESS

People's ability to overcome such physical stressors as injury and illness depends on the state of their health at the time they encounter the stressor. Similarly, their ability to cope with psychological stressors depends on their personality characteristics when they experience a stressing event. This means that different people will react to stressors in different ways, and one source of this difference lies in how they appraise a situation.

Appraisal. Richard Lazarus (Lazarus and Folkman, 1984), one of the leading investigators of psychological stress, has identified two stages in the appraisal process. In the first, which he calls *primary appraisal*, the person evaluates the situation as either threatening or harmless. Depending on the individual's personality this appraisal may be realistic or unrealistic. A harmless situation may be appraised as threatening, a threatening situation as harmless.

In the second stage of the appraisal process, called *secondary appraisal*, a person who has judged a situation as potentially harmful considers the kind of action that is required to handle the threat. In this consideration the person takes into account the resources she or he has available, asking in effect, "What do I have to do, and am I able to do it?" (Note that the second part of this question deals with the *perception of self-efficacy* that we discussed in chapter 7.) How people answer that question depends not only on their personality and past experience, but also on the amount of information they have available and on whether they come upon the stressor unexpectedly or have time to prepare for it.

In general, available research indicates that information about what to expect helps one to cope better with stressors. People to whom a surgical procedure is explain beforehand are usually better able to cope with the experience than those who are kept in the dark. Similarly, being given time to make adequate preparations for a stressful experience is better than having to face it all of a sudden.

SOURCES OF STRESS

There are many sources of psychological stress. Some of them are such daily irritations and hassles as traffic jams, distracting noises, unwanted telephone solicitations, shoelaces that break when one is in a hurry to go out, and power outages while one is studying for an important test. Most people can put up with experiences when they occur once in a while, but when they increase in frequency or intensity they become a problem. It has been shown, for example, that living under crowded conditions or having to work in a hot and noisy environment is stressful for most people. There also are life events that are stressful to people even if they happen only once. Among these are the loss of a loved one, divorce, going to jail, one's house burning down, and a major illness or severe injury.

REACTION TO STRESS

Reaction to stress takes three forms: *emotional, behavioral,* and *physiological.* Generally, these occur together. Depending partly on the individual's personality characteristics and partly on the nature of the stressful event, the emotional reaction can be annoyance, anger, and rage; pensiveness, sadness, and grief, or apprehension, fear, and terror.

Behavioral responses to stress also depend on the individual's personality and the nature of the stressor. Some people react to stress with aggression, others by blaming themselves, and some by giving up. There are also those who attempt to reduce stress by numbing their sensibilities with alcohol or other drugs.

We have already mentioned the physiological reactions to stress in our discussion of the general adaptation syndrome. Recall that among these are changes in blood pressure and the rate of heartbeat, for this brings us to the final topic in this discussion.

TYPE A BEHAVIOR PATTERN

In 1974 Friedman and Rosenman described a pattern of behavior that seems to put people at risk for developing *heart disease* and having what the lay person calls a "heart attack." They named this behavior pattern *Type A,* and the absence of it *Type B.* We should keep in mind that "type" here refers to a cluster of behaviors and not to a personality type such as introversion, although informally people sometimes say, "He has a Type A personality" or "I am a Type A." In fact, because it is cumbersome to keep using the phrase "People who manifest the Type A behavior pattern," we shall occasionally abbreviate it by referring to such people as Type A's.

Type A Behavior

A person who manifests the Type A behavior pattern was originally characterized as "aggressively involved in a chronic, incessant struggle to achieve more and more in less and less time and, if required to do so, against the opposing efforts of other things or persons" (Friedman and Rosenman, 1974, p. 67). The behavior pattern also includes fast, explosive speech, a heightened pace of living, an impatience with slowness, and a pervasive, generalized hostility. People with this behavior pattern tend to concentrate on more than one activity at a time, have a sense of time urgency, are preoccupied with themselves, and feel dissatisfied with such aspects of life as their work, their marriage, and their achievement. In evaluating the worth of an activity they speak in quantitative terms, bragging about the number of deals they closed, the number of suits they own, and the number of dollars they spent for their late-model car. These people also have a tendency to challenge others to compete with them or to bet on an outcome even in situations that call neither for competition nor bets.

An element that most of these characteristics have in common is an overwhelming need to maintain *control,* control over others and control over the environment. Research with people who manifest the Type A behavior pattern suggests that they continually feel control slipping away from them, so that they are constantly engaged in attempts to regain it. That, of course, exposes them to considerable stress and it may be that this leads to their being prone to suffer from heart disease.

Type A and Health

A Risk Factor. In comparison to people who display the Type B behavior pattern, those with Type A report less fatigue and fewer physical symptoms, but they are at least twice as likely to develop heart disease before they are fifty years old. That is why the Type A pattern is considered a *risk factor* for that disease. In the field of public health a risk factor is a set of characteristics that, when present in a subgroup of a population, permits one to predict at better than chance that a certain percentage of that group will develop a given disease or disorder at some later time. Heavy smoking of cigarettes, for example, has been found to be a risk factor in developing lung cancer.

Assessment of Type A Behavior

To conduct research on Type A behavior one must have a procedure with which to identify it. Both an interview method and a questionnaire have been developed for that purpose, but although the interview is time-consuming and must be administered by a trained interviewer it is the more reliable of the two. Referred to as the *structured interview* (Rosenman, 1978), this method engages the individual who is being examined in an interaction that will elicit the coronary-prone behavior if it is present.

The interview consists of questions, but the interviewer is more interested in *how* the interviewee goes about answering them than in *what* he or she says. To elicit a Type A response style, the interviewer might ask in a hesitant and slow manner a question that has an obvious answer. For example, having just been told in what year the person being interviewed was born, the interviewer might repeat the year and then slowly say, "That would make you . . . let's see. . . ." At that point a Type A-prone man would impatiently interrupt and rapidly state his age before the interviewer would have a chance to finish the question. At another point the interviewer might express doubt about the accuracy of an answer and say, "Are you sure that's right?," thereby eliciting an angry response from a Type A, who does not like being doubted. Because the entire interview is tape-recorded it can later be analyzed and scored, taking into account the quality of the speech pattern, the style of responding, and the answers to such questions as "How do you react to having to wait in a long line?"

Physiological Correlates

When people whom the structured interview has identified as manifesting coronary-prone, Type A behavior are studied under laboratory conditions, several *physiological correlates* of that behavior can be identified. To frustrating, difficult, and moderately competitive situations, these people respond with the same loud, explosive, and rapid speech they exhibited in the interview. In addition, they exhibit physiological changes that indicate an activation of the sympathetic branch of the *autonomic nervous system* that is known instinctively to prepare the body for fight or flight.

These autonomic changes may include raised *systolic blood pressure*, increase in *heart rate*, and the discharge of *catecholamines* into the bloodstream. Catecholamines are *neurotransmitters*, the specialized chemical substances that facilitate the transmission of nerve impulses. When it occurs frequently and is maintained over long periods, that physiological arousal is thought capable of damaging the arteries and injuring the muscles of the heart. This could lead to irregularities in the heart's pumping action (called *cardiac arrhythmia*), which can turn out to be fatal.

Type A Behavior Is Counter-productive

Not only can Type A behavior kill you, it does not even pay while you are alive! One might think that a person who is highly competitive and apt to concentrate on two or more tasks simultaneously, who is impatient with delay and eager to achieve more and more in less and less time would be so successful in our competitive society that it might be worth risking a heart attack. But, as already mentioned, these people tend to be dissatisfied with their work, their marriage, and their achievements; they do not seem to be particularly happy with their lives. In addition we know from laboratory studies and surveys that under certain conditions their behavioral style can be self-defeating and disruptive of interpersonal relationships.

On various frustrating and competitive laboratory tasks, the performance of the driven, striving, high-pressure Type A people is neither better nor worse than that of people who display the calm, serene, and relaxed Type B behavior pattern. When it comes to difficult tasks that call for persistence or endurance, Type A's outperform Type B's, whereas Type B's do better than Type A's on tasks that require slow and careful responding. In highly stressful situations, Type A individuals prefer working alone to working with a partner. When they cannot avoid working with someone else they elicit competitiveness and anger regardless of whether the partner is Type A or Type B. When two Type A's must work together in a stressful situation, both engage in aggressive behavior.

We previously differentiated between angry and instrumental aggression (chapter 8). Because instrumental aggression is motivated by seeking external goals, it can work in one's favor by pushing obstacles aside and defeating competitors or antagonists who get in the way. Angry aggression, on the other hand, is an expression of hostility. It is motivated by the need to reduce feelings of anger and by the satisfaction derived from inflicting harm, injury, or damage to another person.

It turns out that the kind of aggression Type A individuals display, both in frustrating laboratory tasks and in daily life, tends to be the nonconstructive, angry variety that damages others without getting the aggressor ahead. In contrast, the kind of aggression Type B individuals display under these conditions tends to be the goal-directed, instrumental variety. All in all it would seem better to be Type B than Type A.

ANXIETY AND STRESS IN PERSPECTIVE

In certain situations the human body exhibits objectively measurable physiological changes in such vegetative functions as respiration, perspiration, elimination, and heartbeat. These changes are usually accompanied by subjective reports of an unpleasant feeling state. This much is well established, but beyond it much uncertainty prevails.

It is difficult to specify the situations that must be present for the physiological changes and psychological feeling state to occur. To some extent the situations differ for different individuals, depending on whether they are perceived as threatening. Moreover, the physiological changes and their combination are different for different individuals, and different people use different words to describe the feeling state they experience.

As a consequence of all this uncertainty, investigators have not been able to agree on what these reactions should be called. We have attempted to differentiate among fears, phobias, anxiety, and stress, but because this differentiation is not universally agreed upon, different writers use these terms in different fashion.

There also is no universal agreement on how the constructs discussed in this chapter should be defined and measured. There are different tests that are used to assess the different kinds of anxiety. It is not entirely clear when trait anxiety turns into state anxiety; and whether test anxiety should be called anxiety or fear is open to question. Moreover, there is a rather low correlation between psychological and physiological measures and among the various physiological manifestations themselves.

Aside from the semantic and conceptual confusions that beset this area of research, there is also a difficulty in conducting the research itself. This stems from the fact that for ethical reasons *genuine* fear, phobia, anxiety, stress, or whatever it might be called cannot be elicited in the laboratory so that it might be scrutinized under controlled conditions. The fear most people have when faced with an armed robber, the anxiety they experience during an earthquake, or the stress they are under when a loved one has a terminal illness simply cannot be intentionally produced for the sake of a scientific experiment.

As a result of this constraint, research in this area typically entails leading college students who are serving as subjects to believe that they are about to take an important test, or about to be given an injection, or about to experience an electric shock. Although most such subjects show psychological and physiological reactions to these manipulations, it is not known whether these reactions are the same as those people have in real-life situations. Another approach that is sometimes used when a group of people can be identified who have recently lived through a threatening experience, such as a bank robbery or a hurricane, is to take a survey of how they felt while in that situation. Such recollections can be informative, but their validity is impossible to establish, and measures of physiological reactions taken while these people were exposed to the threat are obviously not available.

*A*nxiety is an arousal state that has two components. One is physiological, the other cognitive. The physiological component consists of various changes in such functions as heart rate and respiration. These vary in their nature, combination, and magnitude from individual to individual. The cognitive component is a vague and uncomfortable feeling of impending threat. Depending on its intensity, anxiety can enhance or impede the performance of a task.

Two kinds of anxiety have been identified: state anxiety, which is a temporary reaction to a threat; and trait anxiety, which is an enduring personal characteristic. A person high in trait anxiety is more likely to experience state anxiety than one whose trait anxiety is low. A scale exists that measures both kinds of anxiety. A measure has also been constructed to assess test anxiety, the emotional reaction to taking a test. Scores from these measures can be used to predict a person's performance on learning tasks and in test-taking situations.

Anxiety can be reduced by influencing the physiological or the cognitive component. Various forms of psychological treatment have been developed. Some influence the physiological component by teaching relaxation, others change the cognitive component as by restructuring the client's self-statements.

Closely related to anxiety is the topic of stress. This is a generalized physiological reaction to illness or injury that can also be found under conditions of psychological threat. Cognitive appraisal plays a major role in determining which of many sources of potential stress is threatening to an individual.

When stress is sustained for a long period, it can impair a person's health. One such persistent stress has been identified as the Type A behavior pattern. A person who displays this pattern seeks to achieve more and more in less and less time, and this puts him or her at risk for heart disease. Not only is the Type A behavior pattern unhealthy and counterproductive; its driven, competitive, aggressive aspects also alienate others with whom the person who manifests that pattern comes in contact.

Putting the topics of anxiety and stress into perspective, we noted that there continues to exist a good deal of confusion in conceptualization, definition, and assessment. A part of this confusion is due to the fact that neither anxiety nor threat can be studied under laboratory conditions because human subjects must not be exposed to the realistic, powerful threat needed to create the kind of reactions people experience in their real lives. That constraint, however, is not unique to this topic. We encounter it again as we turn to aggression and love in the next chapter.

Selected Readings

Barlow, D. 1988. *Anxiety and Its Disorders: The Nature and Treatment of Anxiety and Panic*. New York: Guilford.

Lazarus, R. S., and S. Folkman. 1984. *Stress, Appraisal, and Coping*. New York: Springer Publishing.

Meichenbaum, D. 1977. *Cognitive-Behavior Modification*. New York: Plenum.

_____. 1985. *Stress Inoculation Training*. Elmsford, NY: Pergamon.

Sarason, I. G. 1980. *Introduction to the Study of Test Anxiety*. In I. G. Sarason, (ed.), *Test Anxiety: Theory, Research, and Applications*. Hillsdale, NJ: Erlbaum.

10

Social Interaction

Under the heading of social interaction we take up two of the many ways in which people can relate to one another. These two are direct opposites; one is negative and can ultimately bring about death; the other is positive and has the potential of creating life. They are aggression and love.

In discussing aggression we shall examine the relationship of the behavior we call aggression to the emotion we call anger. It is useful to differentiate between two kinds of aggression: instrumental aggression and angry aggression. We are going to explore the conditions that cause and maintain these. With these in mind, we are going to take a look at how aggression, with its many dangerous consequences, might be controlled and reduced.

Turning to the more pleasant topic of love, we trace its course from the point when two people first meet each other and become acquainted, through the formation of friendship, to the culmination of being in love. Asking "What is love?," we will explore its components as well as its varieties, all the way from infatuation to "the real thing"—consummate love.

AGGRESSION

The Problem of Definition

Aggression is a word in our common language and everybody knows what it means, but it is likely that few people will agree on what it is. To say, as some dictionaries do, that it is hostile, injurious, or destructive behavior is of little help. It simply brings one to look for definitions of hostile, injurious, and destructive. Is a verbal insult a form of aggression, is competition in the marketplace, is a mother spanking her child?

Psychologists, too, have trouble saying what aggression is, and different definitions of the word have been offered over the years. A widely cited version is one advanced by Baron (1977), who defined aggression as "any form of behavior directed toward the goal of harming or injuring another living being who is motivated to avoid such treatment."

INTENT

The requirement in Baron's definition that to be called aggression the behavior must be "directed toward the goal of harming or injuring" implies *intent* on the part of the person who engages in that behavior.

That phrase adds a cognitive component to the definition of aggression and requires one to ascertain what the person had in mind when she or he harmed or injured someone else. As usual, finding out what someone had in mind raises questions of veracity and validity. Asked what a man had in mind when he stepped on another's toes, is he telling us the truth when he says that it was an unintentional? Are we correct in inferring hurtful intent when we observe a girl pinching her brother's cheek while playing dentist and he cries "ouch"? It is a problem that has no solution.

OPERATIONAL DEFINITIONS

For the purpose of conducting research investigators typically conceptualize aggression rather narrowly and for their own particular purpose. In some studies, for example, aggression was defined as pushing a button that the subject had been led to believe would deliver an electric shock to another person. In other studies a particular score on a questionnaire identifies the respondent as aggressive. Proceeding in this fashion is known as making use of an *operational definition*. That is, the investigator states the procedure (the operation) she or he intends to employ to demonstrate aggression. Other investigators may use other operations to define aggression, but as long as everyone's definition is clearly and objectively stated so that others are enabled to reproduce the study, science can advance and help us to understand better and maybe even reduce all of the harmful, hurtful, and destructive forms of behavior that the word *aggression* brings to mind.

METHODS OF RESEARCH

Sitting as a volunteer subject in an investigator's laboratory with instructions to push a button that will result in someone else's receiving a painful electric shock may not strike one as particularly relevant to understanding what makes a person plunge a knife in another's chest. As in studies of anxiety and stress, it is impossible to bring real aggression into the laboratory for the purpose of studying it. Investigators are thus limited to conducting so-called *analogue studies* in which a harmless act is substituted for the real thing, asking subjects to answer *questionnaires*, holding *interviews* with people who committed or witnessed a violent crime, or doing statistical analyses of the results of *surveys* on the incidence of such crimes. Most of what we know about aggression stems from these sources.

Two Kinds of Aggression

INSTRUMENTAL AGGRESSION

In previous discussions (chapters 8 and 9) we spoke of two kinds of aggression, instrumental aggression and angry aggression. *Instrumental aggression*, you will recall, has as its goal the attainment of an external object; aggression here is the instrument through which that goal is reached. When a professional boxer hits his opponent in the face, his goal is winning a portion of the purse—money. That the opponent gets hurt in the process is incidental, a means to an end, and although the activity is called a sport, boxing is aggression—instrumental aggression, nonetheless. Note that instrumental aggression has a strong *cognitive component*; the offender knows what he is doing, is aware of his goal, and has a plan for reaching it.

ANGRY AGGRESSION

The other kind of aggression, *angry aggression*, is the more frequently encountered and the more troublesome of the two. Unlike instrumental aggression, in which the aggressor wants an object and uses aggression to get it, angry aggression is not preceded by a desire and it need not have a cognitive component. It tends to be impulsively emitted with little or no prior thought. Angry aggression is elicited by an emotion, *anger*, and the consequence of the aggressive act is the feeling of gratification, relief, or satisfaction that is experienced when that emotion subsides. Harm, injury, or damage to another person may or may not have been involved in bringing that satisfaction about. Angrily smashing a dinner plate on the floor is just as much aggression as is punching someone in the nose, although Baron's definition cited earlier does not cover that behavior.

Incidentally, there are instances when angry aggression and instrumental aggression are combined, and that usually results in more violent behavior than when only one of them is involved. When a boxer is angry in addition to wanting to win, he tends to fight harder. Trainers and seconds take advantage of this by "psyching up" their man, hoping to make him more effective by getting him angry.

Aggression and Emotion

Instrumental aggression, as we said, has a strong cognitive component. The strong *emotional component* of *anger* gives angry aggression its name. Anger entails physiological arousal that the person experiences as an unpleasant state of tension. After the aggressive act, that tension is reduced and this makes the person feel better. In the terms of learning theory (chapter 7), it is possible to construe angry aggression as learned behavior that is made more likely later to be repeated in similar circumstances because it had led to relief from the unpleasant tension—negative reinforcement. What are the circumstances that arouse anger, and what is the relationship between anger and aggression?

ANTECEDENTS OF ANGER

It appears that there are two major classes of events that elicit the physiological arousal state that we call anger. They are *physical assault* or *verbal attack*, and the *interruption of goal-directed behavior*.

Physical assault does not necessarily require an assailant such as another person or an animal. It can also be a can of beans that falls on your head as you reach for the ketchup in the kitchen cabinet, or threats to your physical well-being, such as excessive heat or unbearable noise. Verbal attack, of course, requires another person, but it can be a direct insult, a negative evaluation, sexual harassment, or similar provocations delivered face to face or by means of a letter or anonymous telephone call.

The interruption of goal-directed behavior can also take several forms. It can involve another person who is blocking your way as you try to get somewhere or who fails to give you something that you expected to receive, such as a paycheck or a timely meal. Impersonal sources of goal blocking can be doors that are stuck, vending machines that are broken, telephones that don't work, or elevator doors that close just as you get to them.

Crowded conditions can also result in the blocking of goal-directed behavior in that people are less likely to reach their goals when many others get in their way or compete for limited resources. Goals are also blocked when personal choice is greatly reduced or taken away, as when one is imprisoned or under the control of an arbitrary authority. The source of goal blocking need not be external, however. People's own conditions, such as lack of competence or physical inadequacy, can also have the effect of keeping them from goals they set out to reach.

All of these instances of interrupted goal-directed behavior—blocked access, crowding, shortages, loss of freedom, or lack of competence—arouse anger that may lead to aggression. In view of the frequency with which people encounter such experiences, the frequency of aggression is not surprising, but since many of the frustrating conditions are not inevitable, the possibility of reducing that frequency is not beyond our scope. We shall return to this point a little later.

FRUSTRATION, ANGER, AND AGGRESSION

Definition. As used in the ordinary language, the word *frustration* has several meanings. It is used to refer to an internal state ("I am frustrated"), an emotion ("I feel frustrated"), an action ("It frustrates me"), and a motivation ("I did it out of frustration"). That is confusing. Let us therefore agree that in the present context frustration has only one meaning, the one psychologists have in mind when they use that term. Frustration is the *situation* that exists when goal-directed behavior is interrupted. What one feels when this happens is appropriately referred to as anger, not frustration.

At one time it was thought that frustration inevitably led to aggression and, conversely, that all aggressive acts were the result of frustration. This view, expressed in the *frustration–aggression hypothesis*, had been advanced by Dollard, Doob, Miller, Mowrer, and Sears, in 1939. Research conducted since that time has shown that there is nothing inevitable about the link between frustration and aggression, and that encountering frustration can lead to a variety of behaviors that have nothing to do with aggression.

The widely accepted, contemporary view is that the interruption of a goal-directed behavior elicits anger, a physiological (emotional) arousal that has the effect of increasing the magnitude or intensity of whatever response the individual makes at that point. The most likely response, of course, is the one the person was in the process of making when the interruption was encountered. When that response is resumed it is emitted with increased vigor. The door we tried to open and found to be stuck will be pulled harder; the lever of the vending machine that failed to deliver will be pulled several more times with increasing intensity. An observer watching this *high-magnitude behavior* may well call it aggression. It has, in fact, been suggested that high magnitude is one of the characteristics of what we call aggression.

Door banging and machine rattling, however, are not the only responses available to a person who encounters frustration. The physiological arousal can also energize alternative responses such as thinking about how the problem might be solved, seeking help, or finding a detour around the obstacle. When another person is the source of the goal blocking, the alternative to aggression might be discussion, persuasion, compromise, or other peaceful forms of conflict resolution.

Whether a person resorts to constructive alternative responses to aggression depends, in part, on his or her prior experiences, beginning in childhood. If physical aggression has been rewarded in the past, physical aggression is the most likely response, but if physical aggression has not been rewarded or has actually been punished while constructive alternatives were rewarded, it will be one of these that becomes the most likely response to frustration.

Aggressive behavior, in other words, can be construed as learned behavior. But learning, as we found in chapter 7, does not require direct reinforcement; it can also come about through the observation of models. In a classical study Bandura, Ross, and Ross (1961) demonstrated that children who observed an adult engage in aggressive behavior later displayed such behavior themselves. These findings, which subsequent studies supported, have far-reaching implications for child-rearing and the models to whom children are exposed, including those who appear on television (Eron, 1982). But prior experiences are only one part of what makes people engage in aggressive behavior. The other part has to do with their present circumstances and living conditions.

Circumstances Conducive to Aggression

WEAPONS

Laboratory studies have shown that the presence of *aggressive cues*, such as weapons in the room, increases the likelihood of subjects behaving aggressively when they encounter frustration. In these studies aggression took the form of (presumably) delivering an electric shock to another person; it did not involve the weapons. It stands to reason, however, that in real life the ready availability of a handgun is likely to lead to its use when frustration arouses a person's anger.

ALCOHOL

The consumption of *alcohol* has also been shown to increase the likelihood of aggression, but only in combination with frustration or other aggression-instigating stimuli. As we said earlier, stimuli that instigate aggression include heat, crowding, noise, insults, and physical attack. When one of these is present, alcohol seems to favor aggressive behavior by lowering the individual's impulse control and by impairing his or her judgment and attention to cues that might diminish anger.

LIVING AND WORKING CONDITIONS

Even without alcohol, *heat, crowding*, and *noise* lead to an increased rate of aggressive behavior. This fact is well established by laboratory experiments as well as by population statistics that show the incidence of the ultimate form of aggression—homicide.

Control of Aggression

Before leaving this unsavory topic and turning to the more pleasant one of love, it is worth considering whether aggression can be controlled, reduced, or even eliminated. Few would deny that aggression is undesirable. It disrupts social harmony, destroys property, damages and hurts people, and far too often results in someone's death.

Although it is difficult to study aggression because of necessary ethical constraints on laboratory research, we know enough to permit some speculations. Here are a few. If children learn aggression by observing it, we should stop exposing them to aggressive models. That includes not only the aggression modeled on television, but also the angry father who beats his child, thereby modeling that when one is angry the thing to do is to beat a person who is smaller than you. If heat, crowding, noise, and limited resources increase the rate of aggression, a concerned and responsible society must find ways to alleviate these conditions. If the presence of guns makes violence more likely, the solution is obvious; all that is needed is to implement it. Aggression is a problem for society; society will have to muster the will to control it.

FRIENDSHIP AND LOVE

The Investigator's Predicament

We already touched on the ethical constraints on the laboratory study of anxiety, stress, and aggression. At the end of the previous chapter we mentioned that similar constraints pose a dilemma for the investigator who wants to conduct controlled research on love.

SCENARIO

Imagine having volunteered to participate in a study on a topic advertised as dealing with "interpersonal attraction." When you arrive at the appropriate room at the appointed time, you find that it is dimly lit by candlelight and that soft music is playing in the background. A white-coated experimenter greets you, asks you to take a seat on a soft sofa, which, except for a small table which holds a bottle of wine and two glasses, is the only furniture in the room. Before leaving the room the experimenter explains that another student, your partner for this study, will join you in a moment. There now enters a very attractive, well-dressed person who looks about your age. What happens next I leave to your fantasy, but the outcome of whatever transpires between you and your partner is that you fall in love. The partner now leaves the room and the experimenter returns and says, "Okay, that is all. Thank you very much for helping us with our study. I'd now like to take your blood pressure and have you fill out a questionnaire. Then you can go. Please do not attempt to contact the trained actor who was your partner and who followed our experimental protocol by pretending to be attracted to you."

It is obvious that this could never happen. No experimenter would manipulate the emotions of research participants in this callous fashion. That is why almost all theoretical formulations and scientific knowledge about friendship and love are based on interviews, questionnaires, or paper-and-pencil tests and not on laboratory research.

Interpersonal Attraction

We precede the discussion of love with a look at the conditions under which *friendship* develops because most of the time the same conditions are the antecedents of love. Neither friendship nor love can occur unless two people meet and respond positively to each other. That is what social scientists call by the prosaic term *interpersonal attraction.*

In examining the sequence of steps that lead from the point where two people meet for the first time to when they become friends, it is helpful to follow a conceptualization proposed by Levinger and Snoek (1972). According to this view the formation of friendship has three major phases: *awareness*, *surface contact*, and *mutuality*. We shall examine these in turn.

AWARENESS

It would seems obvious that if two people are to end up as friends they must first become aware of each other. But what is it that makes them take special notice of each other when both encounter lots of people every day in all kinds of situations?

Proximity and Frequency. It seems that becoming aware of a particular person is greatly influenced by *physical proximity* and *frequency of contact.* Research has shown that the likelihood of two people becoming acquainted is increased if they live near each other or occupy adjoining seats in a classroom. That, in turn, is influenced by their economic circumstances, social status, age, and, to some extent, gender. Economic circumstances and social status influence where one lives and where one goes to school. Age determines whether one is in school, and, if so, whether it is high school, college, or graduate school. If one is in school, gender may have something to do with which courses one is taking, which means which class one is in. Taken together, these factors influence the frequency with which a particular person is likely to occupy an adjoining seat so that one becomes aware of her or him.

SURFACE CONTACT

Once physical proximity and repeated encounters have led two people to become aware of each other, they may interact in a casual fashion, enabling each to form an impression of the other. These *first impressions* are crucial because they determine whether the contact ends there or serves as a step to further interactions. There are three factors that enter into the formation of first impressions and determine whether they will be favorable or unfavorable. These factors are *physical appearance, patterns of behavior*, and *cognitive attributes.* Keep in mind that all of the following statements are generalizations based on studies conducted on groups and their average results. There are individuals to whom these conclusions do not apply and who became friends by exchanging letters or fell in love at first sight.

Physical Appearance. A person with good looks is more likely to be found attractive than one who is not so endowed. What is it about good looks that attracts other people? Research suggests that both men and women assume that a physically attractive person of either sex has more of such socially desirable attributes as altruism, dependability, sensitivity, and warmth than an unattractive person. Moreover, in comparison with unattractive people, attractive ones are judged as more likely to be successful, to have happier marriages, and to be more competent as marriage partners. This suggests that good looks are not only attractive in themselves, but that they also lead others to infer additional positive attributes.

Patterns of Behavior. What one says and how one says it serve as another basis on which people form first impressions. By and large, people prefer those who speak the way they do. That includes not only dialect, grammar, and pronunciation, but also the content of what is said. Those who use what society considers "proper" speech are not likely to be attracted to people who sprinkle their sentences with profanities. The converse is also true, for the profane speaker is likely to view the proper one as haughty.

Another verbal communication that has been shown to play a role in interpersonal attraction during the phase of surface contacts is *self-disclosure*. This consists of revealing intimate information about oneself. Here, however, it depends on whether the speaker is male or female. Members of either sex find a woman who readily self-discloses to be more attractive and better adjusted than one who is reticent about herself. Conversely, both men and women view a man who reveals such intimate information as less well adjusted and less attractive than one who keeps such personal information to himself.

In addition to these verbal behaviors that enter into first impressions there are nonverbal behaviors by which we judge others. Among these are eating habits and table manners, helpful gestures such as picking up something the other has dropped, and handshakes that accompany greetings.

Cognitive Attributes. The third factor that enters into the formation of first impressions overlaps with the other two. It has to do with such cognitive attributes as a person's thoughts and feelings, attitudes, interests, opinions, and values. Information about these attributes comes to us from how people look and act and, of course, from how they speak and what they say.

How people are dressed and groomed communicates their views about social norms, shows whether they care about themselves, and indicates whether they are concerned about the impressions they make on others. Manner of dress also often announces whether a person is formal or informal, sporty or reserved, tight or relaxed. From the books they carry or the newspaper they read we draw conclusions about their interests, their politics, their education, and their intelligence. From how they speak one can usually tell about other people's social, cultural, or ethnic background, and from what they say one can discern their political opinions, values, and attitudes. Often these confirm the inferences one has already drawn from purely visual information.

Given a choice, we prefer to associate with people who hold attitudes that are similar to our own. Moreover, when we believe that someone else shares our attitudes, we tend to find that person to be more likable, more intelligent, better informed, more moral, and better adjusted than someone who holds attitudes that differ from our own.

SIMILARITY

What is it about physical appearance, behavior patterns, and cognitive attributes that determines whether one finds the other person attractive or unattractive? The answer is *similarity*. Although there is an exception that we shall examine in a moment, the proverb "Birds of a feather flock together" holds true for interpersonal attraction. The more similar we judge the other person to be to ourselves, the more likely we are to find that person attractive. Which is to say that we find ourselves attracted to her or him.

We mentioned already that we are attracted to people who are good-looking and that we attribute to them all sorts of desirable characteristics. To this we can now add that we are also likely to judge good-looking strangers to hold attitudes that are similar to our own. It may in fact be that we tend to be attracted to good-looking people not only because we infer that they have desirable personal characteristics but also because we assume that they are like ourselves.

The Reciprocity Rule. One reason we are attracted to people who are similar to us in important respects seems to be that we expect them to accept and like us. That is known as the *reciprocity rule*. Being liked and accepted is reinforcing and so we seek out people who are likely to reinforce our approaching them. Added to this is the expectation that people who have similar attitudes will endorse and confirm our own. This enhances our self-esteem and serves as further reinforcement for seeking out those who are like us. One might (apologetically) venture to say, "If they are like us they are likely to like us and we will like that."

COMPLEMENTARITY

We mentioned that there is an exception to the mutual attraction of similar people. For that, too, there is a proverb. It is "Opposites attract each other." That holds true when an important characteristic of one person complements that of the other; when, for example, a submissive woman finds a domineering man attractive and vice versa. In that situation the *principle of complementarity* is said to govern the relationship.

The rule of mutual attraction of similar people also has an exception in the realm of physical attractiveness. Good looks do not always lead to interpersonal attraction, particularly when the two people are of the same sex. A highly attractive person may refrain from associating with an equally attractive one, preferring a less-attractive partner so as to benefit from the contrast. Conversely, a less-attractive person may seek out a more attractive one, apparently on the assumption that this association will enhance his or her own status in the eyes of peers.

MUTUALITY

All of what we said thus far dealt with the initial stages of interpersonal attraction, with the conditions that promote awareness and the factors that determine the outcome of surface contacts. Research on these topics is relatively easy because it can be done by showing photographs to subjects and asking them to rate their attractiveness or by asking them to indicate their preferences among people with various characteristics that are described in written statements.

The next and final phase in the development of friendship is *mutuality*. Now two people who met and were attracted to each other have established an ongoing relationship. As we pointed out at the beginning of this discussion, such a relationship cannot be created in a laboratory, and neither photographs nor written descriptions contained in questionnaires can be used as substitutes. What is known about mutuality is therefore limited and rather banal.

Friends. It does not come as a surprise to learn from published studies that friends are generally of the same age, sex, and race and that they share interests, experiences, and activities. Friends feel comfortable talking to each other and they see each other as dependable, supportive, understanding, and accepting. Friends are people one can count on. Men, it has been found, tend to emphasize the sharing of activities and interests, whereas women tend to place more emphasis on the supportive aspects of their friendship.

There is a game in which two players can share optimal rewards if they trust each other and cooperate, but if they do not trust each other and compete, one of them gains and the other loses. In one study (Morgan and Sawyer, 1979) that game was used to compare people who were friends to people who did not know each other. The results showed that the friends were more likely than the strangers to trust that their partner would not be guided by self-interest to take advantage of them.

Having now traced the formation of friendship, we can turn to the state in which interpersonal attraction occasionally culminates—love.

Love

WHAT IS LOVE?

Friends like each other, lovers love each other. What is the difference between liking and loving? To answer that question Rubin (1970) developed a self-report questionnaire that consists of two scales, a Liking Scale and a Love Scale. On the Liking Scale are items that touch on respect for the partner's judgment, maturity, similarity, and likability. On the Love

Scale are items that have to do with communication, sharing, support, feelings, and concern. Each scale yields a score and these scores are moderately correlated, which shows that liking is not the same as love. But what is love?

On the basis of a study that used Rubin's Love Scale, Sternberg and Grajek (1984) concluded that love comprises affect, cognition, and motivation and that these find expression in *communication, sharing,* and *mutual support*. These investigators report that people who love each other:

> have a profound mutual understanding;
>
> share ideas and information;
>
> can talk to each other about personal feelings;
>
> give each other emotional support;
>
> experience personal growth in the relationship;
>
> further each other's personal growth;
>
> help each other;
>
> make the other feel needed and need each other;
>
> show each other affection.

THE TRIANGULAR THEORY OF LOVE

Sternberg (1986) developed what he called a *triangular theory of love*. According to this theory love has three components: intimacy, passion, and decision/commitment. We shall define each of these and then take a look at the theory.

Intimacy. Intimacy entails mutual communication and understanding, concern for the other's welfare, sharing, emotional support, the conviction of being able to count on the other when needed, and happiness in each other's company.

Passion. This has to do with the romance and excitement of a love relationship that includes, but is not limited to, sexual needs and their satisfaction. Other needs such as affiliation, dominance, and self-esteem may also contribute to passion.

Decision/Commitment. The cognitive component of this three-dimensional model of love is decision/commitment. It concerns the initial recognition that one is in love and the long-term commitment to behave in such a way as to keep that love alive.

Each of these components can blend with the others in various combinations. This permits one to differentiate among liking, relationships that seem like love, and true love, as follows:

> *Liking* = intimacy without passion or commitment. This state is exemplified by friendship.

Infatuation = passion without intimacy or commitment. This is the relationship that is primarily based on the satisfaction of the partners' sexual needs.

Empty love = decision/commitment without intimacy or passion. This relationship is not only "empty," it also is not love. It is found in couples whose marriage has deteriorated and who decided to stay together only for reasons of convenience or "for the sake of the children."

Romantic love = passion and intimacy without commitment. This is a relationship to which neither partner wishes or is able to make a permanent commitment. Both are aware that the relationship may suddenly end, but while it lasts they find it rewarding.

Companionate love = intimacy and commitment without passion. We shall have more to say about this love in a moment. It is typified by a couple who have been happily married for many years.

Consummate love = intimacy and passion and commitment. This is the relationship our culture idealizes and celebrates in song and literature. When found it is highly rewarding and if maintained it eventually leads to the life-long satisfaction of companionate love.

Cultural Relativity. Sternberg's three-dimensional model appears to encompass all of the varieties of close relationships with which people *in our culture* are familiar, either through personal experience or indirectly from literature, films, and similar sources. It is noteworthy that whereas we consider consummate love to be a prerequisite for marriage, there are other societies whose culture is not obsessed with the notion of love, where marriages are arranged by parents, where young people do not expect to "fall in love," and where they do not think that they have missed something if they fail to do so. The notion that consummate love is a product of our culture is also supported by historians who report that this kind of love was unknown before the days of chivalry in medieval Western Europe.

SUSTAINED RELATIONSHIPS

We have now traced interpersonal attraction from the moment of first awareness through forming impressions, the discovery of similarities, and the establishment of mutuality, to the development of love in its different varieties. The next step in this sequence is the forming of sustained, long-term relationships such as marriage. What are the conditions that lead to such relationships?

Similarity. In a longitudinal study 231 dating couples were followed for two years. At the end of that period only 128 of these couples were still together (Hill, Rubin, and Peplau, 1976). When the couples who had maintained their relationship were compared to those who had parted, similarity was found to have been a major factor.

The couples who had stayed together were more alike in age, career plans, intelligence, and physical attractiveness than those who had broken up. Those who had not stayed together gave as reasons for their breakup differences in interests, conflicting sexual expectations, unlike backgrounds, contrasting ideas of marriage, and unequal intelligence. The explanation most frequently given for the breakup was boredom with the relationship. That is probably another way of saying that the couple had little in common that would keep them interested in each other.

Lasting Marriage. As previously suggested, consummate love with its three components is (in our culture) the ideal basis for a marriage, whereas companionate love is found in marriages that have lasted a long time. This is probably the case because the excitement of passion, one of the ingredients of consummate love, is too exhausting to be maintained for any length of time. That is not to say that sexual activity is absent in long-lasting marriages. It is well established that healthy men and women can remain sexually active and interested well into old age.

Because companionate love contributes to lasting marriages and similar long-term relationships, we will take another look at what type of love it contains. Recall that it is composed of commitment and intimacy. Commitment is self-evident when two people decide to live together for many years. Intimacy, we said, entails mutual communication, trust and understanding, concern for the other's needs and welfare, sharing of experiences, emotional support for each other, and happiness in each other's company. All of these might be summed up in the word *caring*.

The impersonal phrase, social interaction, that serves as the heading for this chapter covers the most profound forms that human relationships can take, aggression and love. Both, we discovered, are difficult to study, partly because they are hard to define and partly because they do not lend themselves to experimental study, for researchers cannot produce and control them in the laboratory.

There are two kinds of aggression. Instrumental aggression has a strong cognitive component; it is intentional and aimed at a desired goal. Angry aggression has a strong emotional component; it is elicited by external circumstances. Among these are attack and assault and the interruption of goal-directed behavior, which is often called frustration.

Frustration does not inevitably lead to aggression. It is likely that aggression is one of many possible responses that people can learn to emit when they are thwarted in something they are trying to do. Because society is capable of changing many of the conditions that lead to aggression, such as crowding, excessive noise, heat, limited resources, and the presentation of aggressive models, the incidence of aggression could be reduced.

The attraction of two people to each other that may lead to friendship and potentially to love begins when they become aware of each other. The likelihood of this is a function of the frequency with which the two people come into contact, and that depends, in part, on their age, their socio-economic status, and their gender. First impressions have a lot to do with such external characteristics as physical appearance and behavior patterns from which cognitive attributes are inferred.

Similarity is a major condition on which the mutual attraction of two people depends, although when differences complement each other these can also lead to the mutuality of friendship. Friends are often of the same age, sex, and ethnic background. They share interests and activities and see each other as dependable and understanding.

Love can be construed as having three components. They are intimacy, passion, and commitment. Different combinations of these components lead to different kinds of relationships. They range from purely passionate infatuation, through romantic love that lacks commitment, companionate love in which passion plays a minor role, to consummate love that encompasses all three components.

A study that investigated the conditions necessary for sustaining a long-term relationship found that similarity, so important in two people becoming attracted to each other, continues to be important in whether they stay with each other over time. Differences in intelligence, background, and interests often lead to the termination of a relationship.

The chapter ended with a look at the components of good and lasting marriage and similar long-term relationships. We found that these are based on companionate love that entails not only a mutual commitment but also such essentials as mutual trust and understanding, concern for the other's needs, a sharing of experiences, and the happiness that comes from being with each other.

Selected Readings

Averill, J. R. 1982. *Anger and Aggression: An Essay on Emotion*. New York: Springer Verlag.

Evans, P. 1989. *Motivation and Emotion*. New York: Rutledge.

Hatfield, E., and G.W. Walster. 1981. *A New Look at Love*. Reading, MA: Addison-Wesley.

Novaco, R. W. 1975. *Anger Control: The Development and Evaluation of an Experimental Treatment*. Lexington, MS: Lexington Books.

Sternberg, R. J., and M. L. Baram (eds.). 1988. *The Psychology of Love*. New Haven, CT: Yale University Press.

Glossary

A-state *see* State anxiety.

A-trait *see* Trait anxiety.

Acrophobia Disabling fear of high places.

Adaptability Ability to adapt to new situations.

Affective disorder Mental illness manifested by manic behavior and/or depression.

Aggression Behavior intended to inflict harm.

Alienation Separation or detachment from other people.

Alpha press Physical aspects of the environment that influence a person's behavior (Murray).

Ambivalence Simultaneously experienced positive and negative attitudes or feelings.

Anal character Neat, clean, orderly, perfectionistic personality type (Freud).

Anal stage Developmental stage during second year of life marked by toilet training (Freud).

Analogue study Research design in which behavior that cannot be brought into the laboratory is replaced by a similar activity.

Analytic psychology Jung's personality theory.

Angry aggression Aggression elicited by the emotion of anger.

Anima The feminine, passive element in the male's unconscious (Jung).

Animus The masculine, assertive element in the female's unconscious (Jung).

Anthropo-morphism   Attributing human qualities to objects or nonhuman animals.

Anxiety   Physiological arousal state, similar to fear, that has no immediate object.

Apperception   Perception that reveals a person's inner experience (Murray).

Approach-approach conflict   Conflict between two positive goals.

Approach-avoidance conflict   Conflict with respect to a goal that has both positive and negative aspects.

Archetype   Primeval content of the collective unconscious (Jung).

Assessment   Testing or evaluating aspects of an individual's personality.

Asthenic   Tall and slender body type (Kretschmer).

Autia   Imaginative personality trait (Cattell).

Autonomic nervous system   Part of the nervous system that controls the internal organs.

Avoidance-avoidance conflict   Conflict between two negative goals.

Axiom   Statement regarded as self-evident and not in need of proof.

Basic anxiety   Primary motivation that stems from the child's inherent helplessness (Horney).

Behavior genetics   Study of the contribution that hereditary factors make to behavior.

Behavior potential   Strength of a response (Hull).

Behavior therapy   Psychotherapy based on principles of conditioning and learning.

Behaviorism   Orientation to psychology that focuses studies on observable, objectively measurable actions.

Beta press   Psychological aspects that influence a person's behavior (Murray).

Biofeedback   Method enabling a person to monitor his or her own physiologic responses, such as muscle tension.

Cardiac arrhythmia   Irregular heartbeat.

Cardinal trait   Primary motive that rules much of a person's behavior (Allport).

Case study   Detailed observation and description of a person's behavior in his or her own environment.

Castration anxiety Extreme fear of physical injury (Freud).

Catecholamine Group of substances, such as dopamine, that transmit nerve impulses.

Cerebrotonia Restrained, somewhat withdrawn temperament associated with ectomorphic body type (Sheldon).

Choleric Irritable temperament (Hippocrates).

Classical conditioning *see* Respondent conditioning.

Client-centered therapy Psychotherapy that focuses on patient's perceptions and experiences (Rogers).

Cognition Mental processes, including thinking, perceiving, and remembering.

Cognitive appraisal Decision process evaluating potential threat that some believe to precede the experience of fear.

Cognitive restructuring Method of treating psychological problems by changing a person's way of thinking.

Cognitive-behavioral therapy Method of treating psychological problems based on combining behavior therapy and cognitive restructuring.

Collective unconscious Inherited memory of ancestral past (Jung).

Common trait Trait that many people have in common (Allport and Cattell).

Complementarity principle Mutual attraction of two people whose principles, unlike physical characteristics, meet each other's needs.

Complex A configuration of problematic traits.

Concurrent validity Validity of a test based on its correlation with existing tests.

Conditioned response A response to a previously neutral stimulus, established by pairings with an unconditioned stimulus (Pavlov).

Conditioned stimulus A stimulus that comes to elicit a new response by pairings with an unconditioned stimulus.

Conditions of worth Conditions under which a child receives love, approval, and attention (Rogers).

Confederate A researcher's assistant who deceives the subject by pretending to be another subject.

Confounding Invalidating the results of an experiment by unwittingly introducing an uncontrolled variable.

Construct A concept.

Construct validity	Validity of a test in terms of how it fits into the theoretical framework on which it was based.
Constructive alternativism	Variety of different concepts individuals use to cope with their environment (Kelly).
Content validity	Validity based on the relevance of the test items for what the tester seeks to measure.
Control group	Subjects in an experiment who are exposed to the same treatment as the experimental group except for the key variable under study.
Conversion disorder	Physical symptoms that have no physical basis and are thought to be due to psychological factors such as anxiety. Once called *conversion hysteria*.
Corollary	Inference that logically follows from a proved proposition.
Correlation coefficient	Statistic expressing the relationship between two measures.
Correlation matrix	Rectangular array of the correlation coefficients for a large number of measures.
Co-twin method	Research method in behavior genetics that compares identical and fraternal twins to isolate relative contributions of heredity and environment.
Creative self	Ability to choose consciously one's actions and goals (Adler).
Criterion group	Subjects with a characteristic who are used in the development of a test of that characteristic.
Criterion-keyed test	Test that is scored with reference to the performance of a criterion group.
Criterion validity	Validity based on a test's ability to identify a known characteristic.
Cross-sectional research	Developmental research method that compares various age groups (e.g., two-, four-, and six-year-olds).
Cue	*see* Stimulus.
Cue-producing response	Response, such as a thought, that serves as stimulus for another response (Dollard and Miller).
Data	Information gathered in the course of research (singular = datum).
Deductive reasoning	Drawing conclusions from general laws to specific instances.
Defense mechanism	Unconscious strategies that allow a person to reduce or avoid anxiety (Freud).
Delusion	Organized set of beliefs unrelated to reality.
Demographic variables	Variables such as age, sex, social variable status, and place of residence that describe a group of subjects.

Denial Defense mechanism by which a person denies the existence of a threatening impulse or event (Freud).

Dependent variable Variable in an experiment that changes as a result of the experimenter's manipulations of the independent variable.

Depression State of profound sadness and hopelessness often accompanied by reduced activity and feelings of worthlessness.

Developmental crises Periods in the life span when specific developmental tasks must be resolved (Erikson).

Dichotomy Division into two, often mutually exclusive or contradictory, parts.

Discrimination Ability to tell two or more things apart.

Discriminative stimulus Stimulus that controls when, where, and how a response is to be emitted.

Displacement Defense mechanism by which a person redirects an impulse to a less dangerous target (Freud).

Disposition *see* Trait.

Dizygotic twins Fraternal twins, developed from two eggs and two sperm cells; genetically not identical.

Dysplastic Body build manifesting features of several body types (Kretschmer).

Ectomorphy Body type characterized by delicate, fragile features and light musculature (Sheldon).

Ego Conscious part of personality that mediates between id and reality (Freud).

Ego defense *see* Defense mechanism.

Ego ideal Part of superego that represents the person's standards of perfection (Freud).

Ego integrity Condition achieved late in life marked by peace and contentment (Erikson).

Ego psychology Revision of Freudian psychoanalysis that places greater emphasis on conscious processes.

Electra conflict Counterpart in girls of the Oedipus conflict in boys (Freud).

Emotion Feeling state with cognitive, physiological, and behavioral components.

Empathy Participation in another's emotion.

Empirical method Gathering knowledge by observations, as opposed to theorizing or speculating.

Endomorphy Body type characterized by soft, round features and well-developed visceral structure (Sheldon).

Epigenetic principle Personality develops according to an innate framework that guides it toward ever wider social interactions (Erikson).

Erogenous zones Highly sensitive parts of the body which, when manipulated, produce pleasurable sensations.

Ethical principles Code that guides members of a profession in their activities.

Expectancy Expectation, anticipation.

Experimental method Scientific procedure in which the experimenter manipulates the experimental variable to observe the effect of this manipulation on the dependent variable.

Explanatory label Circularity in which the label given to an observation is used to explain it ("He achieves a lot because he has a need for achievement").

Extinction Decline in the frequency or intensity of a conditioned response after repeated omission of reinforcement.

Extraversion Orientation toward other people, often marked by friendliness and sociability.

Factor analysis Statistical method that reduces a large number of correlation coefficients to relatively few, presumably more basic dimensions.

Field studies Research done away from the laboratory.

Fixation Failure to progress to age-appropriate levels of personality development (Freud).

Fixed-role therapy Psychotherapy in which patients follow a prescribed role for a specified period (Kelly).

Focus of convenience Situations or events for which a person's personal constructs are best suited (Kelly).

Free association Key feature of psychoanalysis in which the patient says without censoring whatever comes to mind (Freud).

Free operant Response emitted before it is brought under the control of a discriminative stimulus (Skinner).

Frustration Situation in which a goal cannot be reached. Incorrectly used to describe the reaction of the person in this situation.

Frustration-aggression hypothesis Formulation according to which frustration inevitably leads to aggression, and all aggression is the consequence of frustration (Dollard et al.).

Functional analysis Method used to identify the environmental conditions that control a behavior.

Functional autonomy Formulation that adult motives are independent of their innate origins (Allport).

Gene Unit of hereditary transmission.

General adaptation syndrome	Sequential physiological reactions to stress (Selye).
Generalization	Responding in the same way to stimuli that are similar to the one to which that response had been learned originally.
Generativity	Developing the next generation or being otherwise productive (Erikson).
Genital stage	Normal adult level of personality development (Freud).
Genotype	Genetic makeup of an individual that may or may not be manifested in appearance and behavior.
Habit strength	Strength of a response based on how well and how often it has been reinforced in the past (Hull).
Habitual response	Numerous frequently performed responses that comprise a trait (Eysenck).
Hallucination	Perception of stimuli that are not present in the environment.
Halo effect	Assumption that a person with one positive quality will have other positive qualities as well.
Harria	Tough-minded personality trait (Cattell).
Hedonism	View that behavior is fundamentally motivated by seeking pleasure and avoiding pain.
Heritability	Measure of relative importance of genetic and environmental contributions to a trait.
Heritability ratio	Symbolized by *H*. Proportion of population variance attributable to genetic factors.
Hierarchy	Vertically ranked series of factors, each subordinate to the one above.
Homeostasis	Tendency to maintain present condition by means of self-regulation.
Homunculus	Imaginary, internal "little person" who controls the individual's behavior.
Humanism	View that emphasizes the essential goodness of human beings and belief in their potential for growth.
Humors	Body fluids thought to control life (Hippocrates).
Hypothesis	Assumption to be tested.
Id	Repository of primitive needs and impulses (Freud).
Ideal object	Internalized gratifying mother (Fairbairn).
Identification	Process through which child assumes attributes of a role model, such as a same-sex parent.
Identity crisis	Period when the adolescent seeks to establish whom he or she is.

Idiographic research   Intensive study of individual cases.

Independent variable   Variable in an experiment that the experimenter manipulates to observe the effect on the dependent variable.

Individual psychology   Adler's revision of Freudian theory.

Inductive reasoning   Reasoning from the study of individual cases to a general principle.

Inquiry   Stage in administration of Rorschach inkblot test during which examiner seeks to establish the determinants of subjects' responses.

Insight   Intellectual and emotional understanding of the psychological basis of one's behavior (Freud).

Instinct   Innate behavior pattern.

Instrumental aggression   Aggression that has an objective goal.

Internalization   Process through which a person makes another's characteristics or values his or her own.

Interpretation   Procedure through which therapist seeks to help patient make connections among diverse events (Freud).

Interval schedule   Conditioning method in which delivery of reinforcements is governed by time elapsed since last reinforcement (Skinner).

Introspection   Thinking about one's own thought processes.

Introversion   Orientation toward one's own thoughts and feelings.

L-data   Data gathered by examining life records (Cattell).

Latency period   Quiescent developmental phase that follows resolution of Oedipus conflict (Freud).

Law of Parsimony   Principle that the best explanation is the one requiring the least number of assumptions.

Libido   Life energy, usually sexual in nature (Freud).

Locus of control   Expectation as to whether reinforcement is due to one's own efforts or outside sources (Rotter).

Longitudinal study   Research method in which the same individuals are studied over time.

Manic-depressive disorder   Mental illness marked by alternating periods of excited happiness and deep depression.

Manifest Anxiety Scale   Measure of anxiety level (MAS).

Masochism Pleasure in being abused and hurt.

Maturation Natural growth process.

Mean Statistical average.

Mediated response Overt behavior brought about by an unobservable, internal event that connected stimulus and response.

Melancholic Depressive temperament (Hippocrates).

Mesomorphy Body build characterized by well-developed musculature.

Midlife crisis Period in adult development during which individuals assess the course of their lives (Levinson).

Mirror studies Research method to assess infants' self-recognition.

Model Person whose behavior is observed by another who is expected to imitate it (Bandura).

Modeling Acquisition of new behavior through observing another person's performance.

Monozygotic twins Identical twins, developed from a single fertilized egg and sharing identical genes.

Moral realism Stage in moral development during which children are absolute in their moral judgments (Piaget).

Mucous membrane Sensitive, moist lining of body passages that communicate with the exterior.

Mutuality Final stage in the formation of friendship.

Need hierarchy Organization of needs from most basic to most sophisticated (Maslow).

Negative reinforcement Strengthening a response by following it with relief from unpleasant stimulation. Not the same as punishment!

Neurosis Broad term for anxiety-based psychological disorders.

Neurotransmitter Chemical substance that facilitates transmission of nerve impulses.

Nomothetic research Research method using groups of subjects in search for general laws.

Norms Standards.

Object permanence Developmental phase reached when infants recognize that objects continue to exist even when out of sight (Piaget).

Object relations Personality theory emphasizing importance of mother–child relationship (Fairbairn).

Observational learning Acquisition of new behavior by observing another who engages in it (Bandura).

Oedipus complex Condition that persists when Oedipus conflict has not been satisfactorily resolved (Freud).

Oedipus conflict Developmental phase during which jealous boy fantasizes killing his father so he can possess his mother (Freud).

One-way mirror Mirror that permits covert observations of person on other side.

Operational definition Definition that specifies procedures to be followed for demonstration of a given phenomenon.

Operant conditioning Procedure for teaching a response by providing reinforcement only after the response has occurred (Skinner).

Oral character Personality type characterized by obtaining pleasure by using and stimulating the mouth.

Oral stage First developmental stage during which stimulation of the mouth is central to mother–infant interaction (Freud).

Organ inferiority Congenital bodily weakness that arouses feelings of inferiority (Adler).

Paranoid schizophrenia Mental illness marked by systematized delusions of persecution or grandeur.

Parmia Venturesome personality trait (Cattell).

Peak experience Naturally achieved moment of awe or ecstasy (Maslow).

Peer nominations Research method based on asking classmates to rate one another on specified dimensions.

Perception Process of attributing meaning to sensory input.

Permeability Quality of personal constructs that permits them to encompass novel experiences (Kelly).

Persona Public face put on in response to social demands (Jung).

Personal construct Individual's interpretation and categorization of experiences and events (Kelly).

Personologist Psychologist who studies personality; personality psychologist.

Phallic stage Developmental phase during which Oedipus conflict is experienced (Freud).

Phenomenology View that subjective experiences are the basis of a person's thoughts, emotions, and behavior (Rogers).

Phenomenon An observable fact or event (plural = phenomena).

Phenotype Constellation of a person's observable characteristics produced by the interaction of genetic and environmental influences.

Phlegmatic Slow, lethargic temperament (Hippocrates).

Phobia Disabling fear of specific object or situation.

Phrenology	System of assessing personality by examining the shape of the person's skull (Gall).
Physique	Form or structure of a person's body.
Pleasure principle	Demand for immediate gratification of impulses attributed to id (Freud).
Polygenic characteristic	Inherited aspect based on the interaction of more than one gene.
Postulate	Essential premise of a line of reasoning.
Praxernia	Practical, realistic trait (Cattell).
Preconscious	Almost conscious level lying between the conscious and the unconscious levels of awareness (Freud).
Predictive validity	Validity based on a test's ability to predict behavior.
Premsia	Tender-minded personality trait (Cattell).
Press	Environmental factors that facilitate or impede goal attainment (Murray).
Primary drive	Innate, biological need that motivates behavior.
Primary process	Tension reduction by the formation of the mental image of a need-satisfying object (Freud).
Projection	Defense mechanisms by which unacceptable impulses are attributed to another person (Freud).
Projective technique	Personality assessment based on the assumption that people reveal unconscious material when asked to interpret vague, ambiguous stimuli.
Propriate strivings	Realistic planning of long-term goals (Allport).
Proprium	Sense of self, self-concept (Allport).
Psychoanalysis	Method of investigation and of therapy (Freud).
Psychoanalytic theory	Freud's personality theory.
Psychodynamic theory	View of personality as resulting from an interplay of conscious and unconscious pressures and counterpressures (Freud).
Psychological determinism	View that all behavior is caused by psychological forces and that nothing happens by chance or accident (Freud).
Psychopathology	Psychological disorders; mental illness.
Psychosis	Profound psychological disorders such as schizophrenia and manic-depressive disorder.
Psychotherapy	Any of a variety of psychological treatments.

Puberty   Developmental stage marked by the maturation of the sex organs and other sexual characteristics.

Punishment   In learning theory, anything that follows a response and makes it less likely to recur.

Pyknic   Round, stocky, heavy body type (Kretschmer).

Q-data   Date gathered by means of self-report questionnaires or interviews (Cattell).

Range of convenience   Limit of the category of events to which a construct is applicable (Kelly).

Ratio schedule   Conditioning method in which reinforcement is given to conform to a predetermined proportion of responses and reinforcements.

Rational-emotive therapy   Psychotherapy aimed at changing the client's irrational thoughts.

Rationalization   Defense mechanism that seeks to justify unacceptable impulses (Freud).

Reaction formation   Defense mechanism that gives unacceptable impulses expression through their logical opposite (Freud).

Reality principle   Basis of ego's activities (Freud).

Reciprocal determinism   Interaction of person, behavior, and environment in causing action (Bandura).

Reciprocity rule   Expectation: "If he likes me, he'll agree with me."

Regression   Defensive mechanism of returning to a less mature level of behavior (Freud).

Reinforcing stimulus   Reinforcer (Skinner).

Reliability   Consistency with which a test measures what it is supposed to measure.

Repression   Holding an impulse or memory at the unconscious level of awareness (Freud).

Resistance   Unconscious refusal to accept psychoanalyst's interpretation (Freud).

Respondent conditioning   Pavlovian or classical conditioning in which a conditioned stimulus is repeatedly paired with an unconditioned stimulus.

Response cost   Means to reduce strength of a response by taking a positive reinforcer away from the subject (a fine) (Skinner).

Risk factor   Hereditary, behavioral, or demographic features that raise the probability that the individual will develop a specific disease.

Role Construct Repertory Test   Self-report instrument designed to reveal an individual's construction system (REP test) (Kelly).

Rorschach inkblots   Projective technique for assessing personality.

Sanguine   Cheerful, optimistic temperament (Hippocrates).

Schizophrenia	Group of severe disorders marked by withdrawal, thought disorder, delusions, and hallucinations.
Secondary drive	Learned drive acquired on the basis of an innate, primary drive.
Secondary process	Conscious mental activity (Freud).
Self-actualization	Process of realizing one's potential.
Self-concept	An individual's own perception of his or her personality.
Self-disclosure	Revelation of intimate information about oneself.
Self-efficacy	A person's estimate of his or her capacity to accomplish a given task (Bandura).
Self-image	Ideas people have about themselves, particularly with respect to hopes, aspirations, and achievements.
Sensations	Stimuli that impinge on a sense organ before they are given a meaning through the process of perception.
Sex typing	Expectations of behavior based solely on the individual's sex.
Shadow	Archetype representing the evil, animalistic side of human nature (Jung).
Shaping	Gradual building of a complex behavior by reinforcing successive approximations of it (Skinner).
Significance	Statistical statement of the probability that a given result was due to something other than chance.
Somatotonia	Active, assertive, vigorous temperament (Sheldon).
Somatotype	Theory linking body type to personality (Sheldon).
Source traits	Basic characteristics of personality structure that determine surface traits and behavior (Cattell).
Spontaneous recovery	Intermittent return of responses that had undergone extinction.
State anxiety	Temporary anxiety related to a specific situation.
Stimulus	Any event that occasions a response.
Stimulus control	Linking a response to a stimulus as the result of operant conditioning (Skinner).
Stimulus generalization	Emitting a response to stimuli that are similar to the stimulus to which that response was originally learned.
Stress	Internal condition resulting from person's efforts to cope with environmental demands.
Stressor	Environmental conditions that cause stress.

Sublimation Defense mechanism that gives unacceptable impulses a socially acceptable outlet (Freud).

Superego Part of personality that represents conscience, values, and ego ideal (Freud).

Surface contacts First stage in formation of friendship during which first impressions are formed.

Surface traits Related clusters of trait elements, responses, or behaviors (Cattell).

Symbiosis Infant's inability to differentiate between self and mother (Mahler).

Sympathetic nervous system Part of autonomic nervous system that mobilizes the body's energies for emergencies.

Systematic desensitization Method of behavior therapy that gradually exposes the relaxed client to anxiety-arousing stimuli.

Systolic blood pressure Blood pressure during contraction of heart muscle.

T-data Data based on objective measures.

Temperament Behavioral characteristics that are present at an early age and are thought to have a hereditary basis.

Testosterone Principal male sex hormone.

Thema Combination of need and press that determines a given outcome (Murray).

Threctia Shyness (Cattell).

Trait Relatively stable and enduring response disposition.

Trait anxiety Generalized tendency to experience anxiety in a wide variety of situations.

Transference Patient's tendency to attribute to the psychoanalyst characteristics of significant persons encountered in the past (Freud).

Type A Driven, competitive, ambitious behavior identified as a risk factor for heart disease.

Type B Relaxed, easygoing, sociable behavior that contrasts with Type A behavior.

Unconditional regard Positive acceptance of a person regardless of his or her behavior (Rogers).

Unconditioned response Innate response to a particular stimulus (Pavlov).

Unconditioned stimulus Event that elicits an innate response from the organism (Pavlov).

Unconscious Part of personality inaccessible to awareness (Freud).

Unconscious motivation Motivation of which the person is not aware (Freud).

Validity Extent to which a test measures what it is supposed to measure.

Variable	Any measurable entity that can have different values.
Vicarious reinforcement	Reinforcing effect of having observed another person being reinforced (Bandura).
Viscerotonia	Relaxed, comfort-loving, sociable temperament (Sheldon).
Word association	Assessment method in which subjects verbalize the first word that comes to mind upon hearing the stimulus word.
Working through	Stage in psychoanalysis in which patient applies insights gained to cope adaptively with former problems (Freud).

References

Ainsworth, M. D. S., M. C. Blehar, E. Waters, and S. Wall. 1978. *Patterns of Attachment*. Hillsdale, NJ: Erlbaum.

Allport, G. W. 1961. *Patterns and Growth in Personality*. New York: Holt, Rinehart & Winston.

Allport, G. W., and H. S. Odbert. 1936. "Trait Names: A Psycholexical Study." *Psychological Monographs, 47* (No. 211), 1-171.

American Psychological Association. 1990. "Ethical Principles of Psychologists" (amended June 2, 1990). *American Psychologist, 45*, 390-395.

Averill, J. R. 1982. *Anger and Aggression: An Essay on Emotion*. New York: Springer Verlag.

Baars, B. J. 1986. *The Cognitive Revolution in Psychology*. New York: Guilford.

Baltes, P. B., and K. W. Schaie. 1973. *Life–Span Developmental Psychology: Personality and Socialization*. New York: Academic Press.

Bandura, A. 1986. *Social Foundations of Thought and Action: A Social Cognitive Theory*. Englewood Cliffs, NJ: Prentice-Hall.

Bandura, A., D. Ross, and S. Ross. 1961. "Transmission of Aggression Through Imitation of Aggressive Models." *Journal of Abnormal and Social Psychology, 63*, 575-582.

Bandura, A., and R. Walters. 1959. *Adolescent Aggression*. New York: Ronald.

Barlow, D. 1988. *Anxiety and Its Disorders: The Nature and Treatment of Anxiety and Panic*. New York: Guilford.

Baron, R. A. 1977. *Human Aggression*. New York: Plenum.

Cattell, R. B. 1957. *Personality and Motivation, Structure, and Measurement*. Yonkers, NY: World Books.

Dollard, J., L., W. Doob, N. E. Miller, O. H. Mowrer, and R. R. Sears. 1939. *Frustration and Aggression*. New Haven, CT: Yale University Press.

Dollard, J., and N. E. Miller. 1950. *Personality and Psychotherapy: An Analysis in Terms of Learning, Thinking, and Culture*. New York: McGraw-Hill.

Erikson, E. H. 1963. *Childhood and Society.* 2nd rev. ed. New York: Norton. (Original work published 1950.)

Eron, L. D. 1982. "Parent-Child Interaction, Television Violence, and Aggression in Children." *American Psychologist, 37,* 197-211.

Evans, P. 1989. *Motivation and Emotion.* New York: Rutledge.

Eysenck, H. J. 1953. *The Structure of Human Personality.* New York: Wiley.

Eysenck, H. J., and S. B. G. Eysenck. 1963. *Eysenck Personality Inventory.* San Diego, CA: Educational and Industrial Testing Service.

Eysenck, H. J., and S. Rachman. 1965. *The Causes and Cures of Neurosis.* San Diego, CA: EDITS/Robert R. Knapp.

Fairbairn, W. R. D. 1952. *Psycho-Analytic Studies of Personality.* New York: Basic Books.

Feshbach, S., and B. Weiner. 1991. *Personality.* 3rd ed. Lexington, MA: Heath.

Freud, A. 1966. *The Ego and the Mechanisms of Defense.* Rev. ed. New York: International Universities Press.

Freud, S. 1953. *The Interpretation of Dreams.* In *The Standard Edition of the Complete Psychological Works of Sigmund Freud.* Vols. 4 & 5. London: Hogarth Press. (Original publication in 1900.)

Friedman, M., and R. Rosenman. 1974. *Type A Behavior and Your Heart.* New York: Knopf.

Graham, J. R. 1990. *MMPI-2: Assessing Personality and Psychopathology.* New York: Oxford University Press.

Guilford, J. P. 1959. *Personality.* New York: McGraw-Hill.

Hall, C. S., and G. Lindzey. 1978. *Theories of Personality.* 3rd ed. New York: Wiley.

Hartmann, H. 1958. *Ego Psychology and the Problem of Adaptation.* New York: International Universities Press.

Hatfield, E., and G. W. Walster. 1981. *A New Look at Love.* Reading, MA: Addison-Wesley.

Hill, C. T., Z. Rubin, and L. A. Peplau. 1976. "Breaking Up Before Marriage: The End of 103 Affairs." *Journal of Social Issues, 32,* 147-168.

Horney, K. 1967. *Feminine Psychology.* New York: Norton. (Original work published between 1923 and 1937.)

Hull, C. L. 1943. *Principles of Behavior.* New York: Appleton-Century-Crofts.

Jung, C. G. 1923. *Psychological Types.* New York: Harper.

_____. 1928. *Contributions to Analytical Psychology.* New York: Harcourt Brace.

Kohlberg, L. 1969. *Stages in the Development of Moral Thought and Action.* New York: Holt.

Kretschmer, E. 1925. *Physique and Character.* New York: Harcourt Brace.

Lazarus, R. S. 1966. *Psychological Stress and the Coping Process.* New York: McGraw-Hill.

Lazarus, R. S., and S. Folkman. 1984. *Stress, Appraisal, and Coping.* New York: Springer Publishing.

Levinger, G., and J. D. Snoek. 1972. *Attraction in Relationship: A New Look at Interpersonal Attraction.* Morristown, NJ: General Learning Press.

Levinson, D. J. 1978. *The Seasons of a Man's Life.* New York: Ballantine.

Lewis, M. 1986. "Origins of Self-Knowledge and Individual Differences in Early Self-Recognition." In J. Suls and A. G. Greenwald, eds. *Psychological Perspective on the Self*. Vol. 3. Hillsdale, NJ: Erlbaum. pp. 55–78.

Lewis, M., J. Brooks-Gunn, and J. Jaskir. 1985. "Individual Differences in Visual Self-Recognition as a Function of Mother–Infant Attachment Relationship." *Developmental Psychology, 21*, 1181-1187.

Liebert, R. M., and M. D. Spiegler. 1987. *Personality: Strategy and Issues*. 5th ed. Chicago, IL: Dorsey.

Mandler, G., and S. B. Sarason. 1952. "A Study of Anxiety and Learning." *Journal of Abnormal and Social Psychology, 47*, 166-173.

McClelland, D. C. 1975. *Search for Power*. New York: Irvington Publishers.

McClelland, D. C., J. W. Atkinson, R. A. Clark, and E. L. Lowell. 1953. *The Achievement Motive*. New York: Appleton-Century-Crofts.

Megardee, E. I. 1972. *The California Psychological Inventory Handbook*. San Francisco: Jossey-Bass.

Meichenbaum, D. 1977. *Cognitive-Behavior Modification*. New York: Plenum.

_____. 1985. *Stress Inoculation Training*. Elmsford, NY: Pergamon.

Meichenbaum, D., R. Price, E. J. Phares, N. McCormick, and J. Hyde. 1989. *Exploring Choices: The Psychology of Adjustment*. Glenview, IL: Scott, Foresman.

Miller, N. E., and J. Dollard. 1941. *Social Learning and Imitation*. New Haven, CT: Yale University Press.

Mischel, W. 1968. *Personality and Assessment*. New York: Wiley.

_____. 1974. "Processes in Delay of Gratification." In L. Berkowitz (ed.), *Advances in Experimental Social Psychology, vol. 7*. New York: Academic Press.

Morgan, W. R., and J. Sawyer. 1979. "Equality, Equity, and Procedural Justice in Social Exchange." *Social Psychology Quarterly, 42*, 71-75.

Murray, H. A. (and collaborators). 1938. *Explorations in Personality*. New York: Oxford University Press.

Novaco, R. W. 1975. *Anger Control: The Development and Evaluation of an Experimental Treatment*. Lexington, MA: Lexington Books.

Phares, E. J. 1991. *Introduction to Personality*. 3rd ed. New York: HarperCollins.

Piaget, J. 1932. *The Moral Judgment of the Child*. New York: Harcourt Brace.

Rodin, J., and E. J. Langer. 1977. "Long-Term Effects of a Control-Relevant Intervention with the Institutionalized Aged." *Journal of Personality and Social Psychology, 35*, 897-902.

Rosenman, R. H. 1978. "The Interview Method of Assessment of the Coronary-Prone Behavior Pattern." In T. M. Dembroski, S. M. Weiss, J. L. Shields, S. G. Haynes, and M. Feinlieb, eds. *Coronary-Prone Behavior*. New York: Springer Publishing.

Ross, A. O. 1987. *Personality: The Scientific Study of Complex Human Behavior*. New York: Holt, Rinehart & Winston.

_____. 1992. *The Sense of Self: Theory and Research*. New York: Springer Publishing.

Rotter, J. B. 1954. *Social Learning and Clinical Psychology*. Englewood Cliffs, NJ: Prentice-Hall.

Sarason, I. G. 1978. "The Test Anxiety Scale: Concept and Research." In C. D. Spielberger and I. G. Sarason (eds.). *Stress and Anxiety*. Vol. 5. Washington, DC: Hemisphere.

_____. 1980. "Introduction to the Study of Test Anxiety." In I. G. Sarason (ed.). *Test Anxiety: Theory, Research, and Applications*. Hillsdale, NJ: Erlbaum.

Selye, H. 1978. *The Stress of Life*. rev. ed. New York: McGraw-Hill.

Sheldon, W. H., and S. S. Stevens. 1942. *The Varieties of Temperament: A Psychology of Constitutional Differences*. New York: Harper.

Skinner, B. F. 1938. *The Behavior of Organisms: An Experimental Analysis*. New York: Appleton-Century-Crofts.

_____. 1948. *Walden Two*. New York: Macmillan.

_____. 1953. *Science and Human Behavior*. New York: Macmillan.

_____. 1971. *Beyond Freedom and Dignity*. New York: Knopf.

Spence, K. W. 1958. "A Theory of Emotionally Based Drive (D) and Its Relation to Performance in Simple Learning Situations." *American Psychologist, 31,* 131-141.

Spielberger, C. D. 1975. "Anxiety: State-Trait Process." In C. D. Spielberger and I. G. Sarason (eds.). *Stress and Anxiety*. Vol. 1, pp. 115–143. New York: Wiley.

Spielberger, C. D., R. L. Gorsuch, and R. E. Lushene. 1970. *The State-Trait Anxiety Inventory (STAI) Test Manual for Form X*. Palo Alto, CA: Consulting Psychologists Press.

Sternberg, R. J. 1986. "A Triangular Theory of Love." *Psychological Review, 93,* 119-135.

Sternberg, R. J., and M. L. Baram, eds. 1988. *The Psychology of Love*. New Haven, CT: Yale University Press.

Sternberg, R. J., and S. Grajek. 1984. "The Nature of Love." *Journal of Personality and Social Psychology, 47,* 312-329.

Sullivan, H. S. 1953. *The Interpersonal Theory of Psychiatry*. New York: Norton.

Tannen, D. 1990. *You Just Don't Understand: Women and Men in Conversation*. New York: Morrow.

Taylor, J. A. 1953. "A Personality Scale of Manifest Anxiety." *Journal of Abnormal and Social Psychology, 48,* 285-290.

Watson, J. B. 1913. "Psychology as the Behaviorist Sees It." *Psychological Review, 20,* 158-177.

Wolpe, J. 1958. *Psychotherapy by Reciprocal Inhibition*. Stanford, CA: Stanford University Press.

_____. 1982. *The Practice of Behavior Therapy*. 3rd ed. New York: Pergamon.

Zubin, R. 1970. "Measurement of Romantic Love." *Journal of Personality and Social Psychology, 16,* 265-273.

Index